SPORT PEDAGOGY
Content and Methodology

International Series on Sport Sciences

Series Editors: **Richard C. Nelson and Chauncey A. Morehouse**

The principal focus of this series is on reference works primarily from international congress and symposium proceedings. These should be of particular interest to researchers, clinicians, students, physical educators, and coaches involved in the growing field of sport sciences. The Series Editors are Professors Richard C. Nelson and Chauncey A. Morehouse of The Pennsylvania State University.

Since the series includes the eight major divisions of sport science, a Board of Associate Editors, comprised of internationally recognized authors acts in an advisory capacity to the Series Editors. The Associate Editors, with their institutional affiliations and designated areas of responsibility, are as follows:

Biomechanics	Dr. Mitsumasa Miyashita	University of Tokyo (Japan)
History	Dr. John A. Lucas	The Pennsylvania State University (USA)
Medicine	Dr. Hans Howald	Sporthochschule, Magglingen (Switzerland)
Pedagogy	Dr. Herbert Haag	Christian Albrechts Universität, Kiel (West Germany)
Philosophy	Dr. Robert G. Osterhoudt	Arizona State University (USA)
Physiology	Dr. James S. Skinner	University of Montreal (Canada)
Psychology	Dr. John E. Kane	West London Institute of Higher Education (England)
Sociology	Dr. Kalevi Heinila	University of Jyväskylä (Finland)

Each volume in the series is published in English but is written by authors of several countries. The series, therefore, is truly international in scope and because many of the authors normally publish their work in languages other than English, the series volumes are a resource for information often difficult if not impossible to obtain elsewhere. Organizers of international congresses in the sport sciences desiring detailed information concerning the use of this series for publication and distribution of official proceedings are requested to contact either the Series Editors or the appropriate Associate Editor. Manuscripts prepared by several authors from various countries consisting of information of international interest will also be considered for publication.

The *International Series on Sport Sciences* serves not only as a valuable source of authoritative up-to-date information but also helps to foster better understanding among sports scientists on an international level. It provides an effective medium through which researchers, teachers, and coaches may develop better communications with individuals in countries throughout the world who have similar professional interests.

Volume 1
    Nelson and Morehouse. **BIOMECHANICS IV** (Fourth International Seminar on Biomechanics)

Volume 2
    Lewillie and Clarys. **SWIMMING II** (Second International Seminar on Biomechanics of Swimming)

Volume 3
    Albinson and Andrew. **CHILD IN SPORT AND PHYSICAL ACTIVITY** (First International Symposium on the Participation of Children in Sport)

Volume 4
    Haag. **SPORT PEDAGOGY: Content and Methodology** (First International Symposium on Sport Pedagogy)

Volume 5
    Figueras. **SKIING SAFETY II** (Second International Conference on Ski Trauma and Skiing Safety)

Volume 6
    Eriksson and Furberg. **SWIMMING MEDICINE IV** (Fourth International Congress on Swimming Medicine)

International Series
on Sport Sciences, Volume 4

SPORT PEDAGOGY Content and Methodology

Selected publications and reports given at the First International Symposium on Sport Pedagogy, Karlsruhe, Federal Republic of Germany

Edited by: **Professor Dr. Herbert Haag**
Institut für Sport und Sportwissenschaften der Christian Albrechts Universität, Kiel, Federal Republic of Germany

Series Editors: **Richard C. Nelson, Ph.D.**
and
Chauncey A. Morehouse, Ph.D.
The Pennsylvania State University

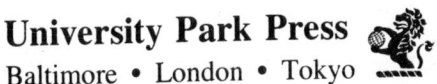

University Park Press
Baltimore • London • Tokyo

UNIVERSITY PARK PRESS
International Publishers in Science and Medicine
233 East Redwood Street
Baltimore, Maryland 21202

Copyright © 1978 by University Park Press

Typeset by The Composing Room of Michigan, Inc.
Manufactured in the United States of America by Universal Lithographers, Inc., and
The Optic Bindery Incorporated

All rights, including that of translation into other languages, reserved. Photomechanical reproduction (photocopy, microcopy) of this book or parts thereof without special permission of the publisher is prohibited.

Selected publications and reports given at the First International Symposium on Sport Pedagogy [organized by the Ausschuss Deutscher Leibeserzieher (ADL)], held September 29 to October 3, 1975, Karlsruhe, Federal Republic of Germany.

Library of Congress Cataloging in Publication Data

International Symposium on Sport Pedagogy, 1st, Karlsruhe, Ger., 1975.
Sport pedagogy.

(International series on sport sciences; v. 4)
Organized by the Ausschuss Deutscher Leibeserzieher.
1. Physical education and training—Methodology—Congresses. 2. Physical education and training—Curricula—Congresses. I. Haag, Herbert, 1937– II. Ausschuss Deutscher Leibeserzieher. III. Title. IV. Series.
GV205.I64   1975a   613'.7   77-25144
ISBN 0-891-1201-7

Contents

Contributors		vii
Foreword	*H. Haag*	ix

SCIENTIFIC NATURE OF SPORT PEDAGOGY

Introduction

Introduction	*H. Haag*	5

Sport Pedagogy as Part of Education

The Problem of the Science of Physical Activity (or Physical Education) as a Pedagogical Discipline	*O. Grupe*	11
The Correlation Between Physical Education and the Science of Education	*L. Mester*	15

Sport Pedagogy as a Part of Sport Science

The Body of Knowledge, Sport Studies	*R. G. Osterhoudt*	29
Introduction to *Sport Science*	*O. Grupe*	35

The Content of Sport Pedagogy

Tones of Theory—A Theoretical Structure for Physical Education—A Tentative Perspective	*C. Ulrich and J. E. Nixon*	45
The Content of Sport Pedagogy as a Theoretical Field of Sport Science	*H. Haag*	59

Scientific Research Methods in Sport Pedagogy

The Methodological Problem of Physical Education as Theory	*K. Widmer*	71
Considerations of the Scientific Character of Sport Pedagogy	*St. Grössing*	83

Research Concepts for Sport Pedagogy

Typology of Research Tasks Concerning School Physical Education and Definition of Priorities of Research in School Physical Education	*H. Nupponen*	95
The Sport Pedagogy Research Program of the Federal Institute of Sport Science	*A. Kirsch*	111

INTERNATIONAL SYMPOSIUM ON SPORT PEDAGOGY

Introduction

Introduction   E. Beyer   119

The Relationship Between Teacher and Pupil in Sport Instruction

The Problem of the Teacher-Pupil Relationship in Sport Instruction (*main address*)   K. Widmer   123

The Teacher-Pupil Relationship in Sport Instruction G. Landau   151

Research on the Teacher-Pupil Relationship in Sport Instruction (*summary*)   M. Piéron   161

Sport in the Institution Called School

The School as the Organizational and Structural Framework for Physical Education (*main address*)   J. E. Nixon   165

Sport in School—Physical Education in the School Z. Zukowska   177

Models for School Sport in Austria (*summary*)   H. Ertl   189

Aims and Objectives of Physical Education

The Aims of Sport Instruction (*main address*)   C. Menze   193

Aims and Objectives of Physical Education: Subject Matter and Research Methods of Sport Pedagogy as a Behavioral Science A. E. Jewett   213

Aims and Objectives of Sport Instruction (*summary*) D. Brodtmann and A. H. Trebels   225

APPENDIX

Scientific Terminology for Sport Pedagogy

The Development of a "Thesaurus" for the Scientific Terminology of Sport Pedagogy as Part of Sport Science   H. Haag and W. Weichert   231

Structure of the Terminology for Sport Pedagogy   241

Selected Publications on the Concept and Nature of Sport Pedagogy

German Language Publications   255

English Language Publications   257

General Information Related to Sport Pedagogy

Journals and Organizations   261

Contributors

E. Beyer, Ph.D., Professor of Sport Pedagogy, Institut für Sport und Sportwissenschaft, Universität Karlsruhe, Karlsruhe, Federal Republic of Germany

D. Brodtmann, M.A., Professor of Sport Pedagogy, Pädagogische Hochschule Hannover, Hannover, Federal Republic of Germany

H. Ertl, Ph.D., Professor, Österreichisches Dokumentations—und Informations—Zentrum für Sportwissenschaften, Universitäts C-Sportzentrum Schmelz 1150, Vienna, Austria

St. Grössing, Ph.D., Professor of Sport Pedagogy, Zentralinstitut für Sportwissenschaften, der Technischen Universität München, Munich, Federal Republic of Germany

O. Grupe, Ph.D., Professor of Sport Pedagogy, Institut für Sportwissenschaft, Universität Tubingen, Tubingen, Federal Republic of Germany

H. Haag, Ph.D., Professor of Sport Pedagogy, Abteilung Sportpädagogik, Institut für Sport und Sportwissenschaften, der Christian Albrechts Universität, Olshausenstrasse 40-60, D-2300, Kiel, Federal Republic of Germany

A. E. Jewett, Ph.D., Professor of Physical Education, Division of Health, Physical Education and Recreation, University of Georgia, Athens, Georgia, USA

A. Kirsch, Ph.D., Professor, Bundesinstitut für Sportwissenschaft, Cologne, Federal Republic of Germany

G. Landau, M.A., Pädagogischer Mitarbeiter, Institut für Sport und Sportwissenschaften, Universität Frankfurt, Frankfurt, Federal Republic of Germany

Cl. Menze, Ph.D., Professor of Education, Pädagogisches Seminar, Universität Köln, Cologne, Federal Republic of Germany

L. Mester*, Ph.D., Professor of Sport Didactics, Betriebseinheit Sportwissenschaft, Universität Giessen, Giessen, Federal Republic of Germany

J. E. Nixon, Ph.D., Professor of Physical Education, School of Education, Stanford University, Stanford, California, USA

H. Nupponen, M.Sc.P.E., Lecturer, Liikunnan ja Kansanterveyden tutkimuslaitos, Jyväskylä, Finland

R. G. Osterhoudt, Ph.D., Professor of Physical Education, Department of Health, Physical Education and Recreation, Arizona State University, Tempe, Arizona, USA

M. Piéron, Ph.D., Suppléant Professeur, Institut Supérieur d'Education Physique, Université de Liège au Sort Tilman, B4000 Liege, Belgium

---

*Deceased, 1975.

A. Trebels, Ph.D., Professor of Sport Pedagogy, Institut für Leibeserziehung, Wissenschaftliche Hochschule Hannover, Hannover, Federal Republic of Germany

C. Ulrich, Ph.D., Professor of Physical Education, Department of Physical Education, University of North Carolina-Greensboro, Greensboro, North Carolina, USA

W. Weichert, Ph.D., Assistant Professor of Sport Pedagogy, Abteilung Sportpädagogik, Institut für Sport und Sportwissenschaften, der Christian Albrechts Universität Kiel, Kiel, Federal Republic of Germany

K. Widmer, Ph.D., Professor of Education Psychology, Pädagogisches Institut, Universität Zurich, Zurich, Switzerland

Z. Zukowska, Ph.D., Zaklad Pedagogiki, Akademie Wychowania Fizycznego, Warsaw, Poland

Foreword

The field of sport science has undergone a tremendous development during the last few years. The following aspects help to verify this development:
1. There are an increasing number of scientific journals devoted specifically to sport.
2. There has been an enlargement of the number of book series related to topics in sport science.
3. The number of single books dealing with sport science has increased.
4. An increasing number of meetings, symposia, and congresses dealing with sport science are being held.
5. Associations and organizations devoted to different aspects of sport science are being established.
6. In graduate schools, new programs of study leading to master's and doctoral degrees in sport science are being offered.
7. Separate organizational units for sport science are being organized at institutions of higher learning.

These developments are noticeable on both a national and an international level. This means that the development of sport science can be observed all around the world, which is indicative of the increasing importance of science in our lives in general. Within the realm of science, an interesting development has been seen during recent years. In addition to the so-called traditional sciences, such as philosophy, law, medicine, history, etc., a new category of sciences is forming. These new sciences could be characterized as theme or problem-oriented sciences. They come into existence when urgent problems within our social life call for answers through scientific investigations. Examples of such areas of social concern today are: nutrition, information, environment, and also sport. This new category of sciences is also interdisciplinary, because it depends upon many of the various traditional sciences.

The construct of this new science—sport science or sport sciences—is an example of this relationship.

In this regard, the *International Series on Sport Sciences* is playing an important role in publicizing this new area of applied science. The various subsections of this series, which express the nature of sport science(s) and indicate at the same time the position of sport pedagogy within this new concept of science, are: physiology, biomechanics, medicine, psychology, sociology, history, philosophy, and education.

These subfields of sport science can be presented in a more structured way, as is exemplified in the following pattern:

1. Anatomical-physiological and biomechanical foundations
   1.1. Sport medicine
   1.2. Sport biomechanics
2. Social-behavioral foundations
   2.1. Sport psychology
   2.2. Sport pedagogy
   2.3. Sport sociology
3. Historical-philosophical foundations
   3.1. Sport history
   3.2. Sport philosophy

These various subfields of sport science show different degrees of conceptualization and development. Sport pedagogy as one major theoretical field of sport science is in urgent need of clarification of its nature. This is especially true because the majority of students are studying sport science in order to become prepared as physical education teachers. Therefore, sport pedagogy is a major area of study within the sport curriculum. Because it has such a relatively high importance, it may be more difficult to get a clear concept of the nature of sport pedagogy.

This volume is an attempt to contribute to this needed clarification and conceptualization of sport pedagogy as a theoretical field of sport science. The articles are organized into two sections:

In the first section, "Scientific Nature of Sport Pedagogy," key articles are collected that have been published in various journals and books. They were chosen from the international literature under the criterion of contributing to the scientific nature of sport pedagogy.

In the second section, "International Symposium on Sport Pedagogy," internationally known experts discuss the dimensions of content, scientific understanding, and research methodology by dealing with selected topics from the theoretical field of sport pedagogy. This international exchange of ideas and concepts was intended to further enlarge and deepen the foundations of sport pedagogy.

The Appendix provides valuable information about the following aspects of sport pedagogy: scientific terminology, selected publications, and general information. These three parts of the Appendix should help to a great extent in additional study of the nature of sport pedagogy and in further development of this aspect of sport science.

At this point it should be acknowledged that the editors of the *International Series on Sport Sciences*, Drs. R. C. Nelson and C. A. Morehouse (The Pennsylvania State University), have agreed to establish a subsection on education within the series and that they have included this volume on sport pedagogy within the series shortly after the initiation of this international series.

The ADL ("Ausschuss Deutscher Leibeserzieher") and the Hofmann Company (Schorndorf, FRG) should also be acknowledged for making available the papers from the Karlsruhe Symposium.[1]

To the authors and respective book companies thanks are extended for their permission to reprint important materials that have contributed to further clarifying the foundations of sport pedagogy.

---

[1]The reports given at the symposium in Karlsruhe have also been published in the German language in: E. Beyer and P. Röthing (Red.), Beiträge zur Gegenstandsbestimmung der Sportpädagogik, Verlag Karl Hofmann, Schorndorf, 1976.

University Park Press (Baltimore, USA) was very cooperative in helping to realize a publication with material from many different countries, especially with respect to the problems associated with translation.

Last but not least, the members of the Department of Sport Pedagogy at the Institute for Sport and Sport Science at the Christian Albrechts University in Kiel, FRG, assisted to a great extent in preparing this volume through fruitful professional discussion and technical assistance.

H. Haag

SPORT PEDAGOGY
Content and Methodology

Scientific Nature of Sport Pedagogy

Introduction

Introduction

H. Haag

Sport pedagogy can be defined as a theoretical field of sport science that deals with the possibilities and boundaries of education through sport. It includes a wide variety of factors that are important for the teaching-learning processes in sport.

Besides the necessity to define content and methods for sport science as a whole, every theoretical field of sport science must gain a proper understanding of itself. The process of acquiring such an understanding has been realized differently within the separate fields of sport science.

Sport pedagogy had to overcome three primary difficulties in undergoing this process. First, the number of theories not scientifically proven was relatively large, since aspects of sport pedagogy, sport medicine, and sport history for a long time constituted the body of knowledge of what earlier was called "theory of physical education." Second, there was hardly any distinction between sport pedagogy, or physical education, as an art of teaching and as a scientific field. Finally, for a long time sport pedagogy was not recognized as a theoretical field of sport science like sport psychology or sport history, especially within the English-speaking countries. Physical education was mainly seen as a process within education that had to be explained by the other theoretical fields of sport science.

With the development and recognition of sport science as a scientific field, the educational aspects of sport science (or sport pedagogy/physical education) can be seen in a proper perspective.

The articles published within this first section have been selected according to the following criteria:

1. That they are contributions that clarify the nature of sport pedagogy.
2. That they are key articles within the sport science literature.
3. That they give recognition to developments on the international level.

Five basic concepts have been defined that are considered basic to understanding the scientific nature of sport pedagogy:

SPORT PEDAGOGY AS PART OF EDUCATION

One basic sign of the theoretical fields of sport science is their close relationship to the respective "mother sciences," such as education, medicine, psychology, etc. O. Grupe and L. Mester describe the close relationship of sport pedagogy (or physical education) to general education and to the science of education.

SPORT PEDAGOGY AS PART OF SPORT SCIENCE

The nature of the various theoretical fields can only be understood in close relationship to the total field of sport science. Therefore, it is necessary to observe different facets of sport science, for example, as they are developed by R. G. Osterhoudt and O. Grupe, because being familiar with sport science as a whole enables one to define the position and role of sport pedagogy within it.

THE CONTENT OF SPORT PEDAGOGY

One of the basic questions within a scientific theory of a certain discipline is about the content dimension. There are many answers to this question. J. E. Nixon and C. Ulrich in their chapter and H. Haag in his contribution attempt to answer this question from their own points of view. The main point, however, is that there is a clearly defined body of knowledge for sport pedagogy, and this is one fundamental requirement for being acknowledged as a scientific field.

SCIENTIFIC RESEARCH METHODS IN SPORT PEDAGOGY

Besides the content dimension, research methodology is very important in the characterization of a scientific field. K. Widmer and St. Grössing provide a discussion of this aspect of scientific work. The development of a scientific terminology belongs in this context, too, because it facilitates the carrying out of investigations and research projects in a proper way. The article by H. Haag and W. Weichert (see Appendix, p. 231) summarizes a report of a large research project that dealt with the development of a so-called "thesaurus" for sport pedagogy. (This "thesaurus" is also included as a structured compilation of terms used in sport pedagogy.)

RESEARCH CONCEPTS FOR SPORT PEDAGOGY

In the last part of the first section of this text, some examples are given of possible research concepts for sport pedagogy. Research concepts are very important for expressing the nature of a scientific discipline. This section contains articles that relate to proposals made in Finland (article by H. Napponen) and in the Federal Republic of Germany (article by A. Kirsch), where the research concepts for sport science in general and sport pedagogy specifically are coordinated by the Federal Institute of Sport Science.

In summary, there are five dimensions that seem to be constitutive elements of the search for a scientific structure of sport pedagogy, namely: its relationship to education; its relationship to sport science; its content; the research methodology it employs; and its research concepts.

The contributions in the second section of this publication further clarify the position of sport pedagogy as a theoretical field of sport science.

In the Appendix valuable information is given on the following aspects, which are important for the understanding of sport pedagogy as one theoretical field of sport science: terminology, selected publications (German and English), journals, and organizations.

Sport Pedagogy as Part of Education

The Problem of the Science of Physical Activity (or Physical Education) as a Pedagogical Discipline

O. Grupe

"PHYSICAL EDUCATION" AS DISCIPLINE OF EDUCATIONAL SCIENCE

The scientific theory of physical education can first of all be treated as a subject or a term that is one part of educational sciences. This is justifiable for two specific reasons: first, a human being exists basically as a "physically in-the-world being"; second, play (some activity other than work) is one of the original (but so far not fully acknowledged) modes of human existence. Physical education investigates within education the consequences and results that can be derived from these two preconditions for education in a broad sense. It deals with that particular part of education in which the world and life can be specifically experienced through movement and play. The following issues belong to this field: the reality of education, gymnastics, play, and sport in general; the attitude of individuals and groups toward the physical, and their actual dealings with it; and, finally, the educational environment of children and young people, along with its normative, sociological, and other factors.

Dealing with this field requires the application of the usual questions and methods of pedagogy; the intention is systematic, historical (problem-oriented), comparative, phenomenological, and hermeneutic, as well as didactic. All basic terms of pedagogy appear in this field, even if the specific subject area has to be observed and analyzed in a particular way, because

---

Reprinted by permission from: Grupe, O. 1964. Über das Problem einer Wissenschaft der Leibesübungen (oder Leibeserziehung) als pädogogischer Disziplin. Pädogogische Rundschau 847–868 (pp. 864–868 reprinted here). This article is also published in: Grupe, O. 1965. *Studien zur pädagogischen Theorie der Leibeserziehung,* pp. 5–34, Karl Hofmann Druckerei und Verlag, Schorndorf (pp. 30–34 reprinted here).

there is no complete agreement within the subject field of pedagogy in general. This ensures that the field has a certain independence within educational science without being isolated.

Physical education, therefore, is a further (and one might also say, a necessary) differentiation of education science. It has developed as a special or single science; pedagogy is its basic science, and in a preliminary way it can be termed "theory of physical education." It is comparable to areas like economic education, social education, or education in regard to the "gymnasium" as a type of secondary school in Germany, all of which are also fields of educational science, dealing with basic educational problems in a specific way. These are only some of the fields that are emphasized to a greater extent, others may not have been mentioned or others are developing even if they have not yet become recognized. In addition to sport pedagogy, sport medicine, sport psychology, and sport sociology are not only possible but also necessary subfields of sport science. These subfields are related in that physical education could initiate the common dealing with an intensification of problems, and by this lead to a fruitful cooperation of sciences, as pedagogy has done for the field of anthropology. In much the same way that pedagogy must include, interpret, and deal with medical, psychological, or sociological investigations, physical education must deal with these sciences in a similar way within its own area of questions. Physical education also needs the aid of medicine, sociology, psychology, and anthropology in order to be complete; however, this does not constitute the whole of physical activity or physical education as a science. If one only sees these subfields, a false picture results. Something must be added that is a focus, and that constitutes the specific area of questioning. Thus, physical education is that portion of educational science that deals almost exclusively with questions of the physical and of play, and with all their consequences with regard to room and organization. These questions are somewhat broader than the traditional forms of gymnastics, play, and sport; one has to think only of the problem of a "healthy" school and of a "healthy" school day to understand this. The proposed broad term of physical education not only allows this thought but also requires it, because the entire spectrum of education is being investigated from a particular point of view.

POSSIBLE PARTS OF A
PEDAGOGICAL THEORY OF PHYSICAL EDUCATION

Pedagogy serves as a unifying aspect for physical education and its questions and problems, thereby preventing dispersion within the field and supporting its scientific nature, making possible scientific procedures. The resulting field of work and research can be divided into several parts, in which the problems of this field appear in various ways. Thus, physical education concentrates in a systematic way, first, on the question of the reality of the human being's physical existence. Within this area one deals with the relationship of man to his body. Theories concerning the body-soul problem are discussed. Furthermore, one deals with the "unity" of man, with play as a mode of existence, as one "primary life-category" (Huizinga), with play theories, and with the muse, the aesthetics, and the *agon*. One will have to draw educational conclusions derived from these considerations, conclusions related to the following question:

> What are the meanings of the words *agon, muse,* and *play,* and also of *physical* in its different forms of expression (in sexuality, in health and sickness, and in movement and posture), for education, for development, for world and life experience, and for the realization of men?

This might seem to be a self-interpretation of physical education with regard to its educational possibilities and its related or necessary areas, aspects, and preconditions. The question that must be dealt with is whether gymnastics, play, sport, calisthenics, and hiking are relevant to education. Therefore, the question of the relationship of physical education to total education should also be included. The meaning of elementary experiences of success and of experiences of a personal and social type would have to be investigated. Research results of other disciplines would have to be analyzed, dealt with, and, if necessary, integrated. For example, relevant results could be taken from sociology (the role of sport in modern society, of free time, of recreation behavior, of youth groups, and of the social position of youngsters, etc.), from psychology, and from medicine (health, performance, and training). Single problems would also be included, such as aesthetic education, education outside of school, youth work, and hiking, etc. Furthermore, consideration would be given to the history of physical education (distinctly a legitimate consideration). In this regard, the following questions could be posed:

> What is the relationship between the interpretation of what it means to be a human being (e.g. Rousseau, new humanism, philanthropists, romanticism, Pestalozzi, Jahn, or, in the time of national socialism, the youth movement) and physical education?
>
> What is the position, evaluation, and inclusion of physical education within total education?

Another principal part might be the didactic field of physical education, characterized by the following questions:

> What is the relationship of the specific didactics of physical education to general didactics?
>
> What is the relationship between the aims and objectives and the content of education? (This includes questions about the individual situation and about the development of young people with regard to their bodies and minds, including questions about acceleration, grading, and curricula. In this regard, physical education could be characterized as an applied field or as art, in the sense of technology).

These main parts, which could be expressed in more detail, and which are not at all complete, should explain physical education in its teaching and research dimensions, and confirm it as part of the educational science. At the same time, education science is represented in a certain way. If physical education can develop sufficient scientific foundations within its own field, the scientific acknowledgment will only be a question of time.

Should physical education become partly independent or should it become the center of sport sciences by modifying or giving up its basic educational structure? Diem and others have indicated that this question can only be answered after physical education and the other "sport sciences" have further consolidated themselves. As long as physical education as scientific theory is not quite certain of its scientific nature, it would be very unwise to take this second step, because one does not yet know whether or not physical education has a secure stand. This development depends not only on good will, but also on convincing performances.

On the other hand, in the light of the dangerous situation within physical education and the attitude of society toward the questions of physical life, an attitude broadly reflected in universities, philosophical faculties, and the field of pedagogy, the question should be asked whether or not more should be done to support scientific innovations in physical education, to encourage these developments, and to assist them with institutional, personal, and organizational improvements. These considerations could also serve to initiate discussion of the position of physical education with respect to teaching and research.

As long as this does not happen, physical education will be stifled by barriers that it cannot remove by itself, even if there are convincing arguments available. Recognition of the scientific status of physical education from outside the discipline is necessary; even the beginning of a scientific discussion would be something, because it would show that the question is at least being taken seriously.

The Correlation Between Physical Education and the Science of Education

L. Mester

The contemporary situation in sport science is a unique one, in that departments and professorships in this field have been set up for the first time in a large number of universities and teacher training colleges. In order to better understand one aspect of this situation, the correlation between the study of physical education and education science, two problem areas should be discussed here:

1. the interaction of the theories of physical education and the science of education in reform pedagogy in the 1920's and in its renaissance in the 1950's and 1960's.
2. the correlation between the study of physical education and the science of education in the contemporary institutional structuring of sport science in universities and teacher training colleges.

1. THEORIES OF PHYSICAL EDUCATION—SCIENCE OF EDUCATION

After the first World War all areas of life were so affected by a basic change in orientation, that schools and the subjects taught in schools came under the dynamic influence of a large scale "reform pedagogy." In the course of the renewal efforts in education since approximately 1900, along with socially critical efforts in the youth movement, the art education movement, and the women's movement, all hitherto existing physical exercises were radically questioned in terms of educational goals. In a mesh of pedagogical contradictions the traditional powers in gymnastics and sports tried to assert their will by using modernistic phraseology. A new "rhythmical gymnastics" was

---

Reprinted by permission from: Mester, L. 1973. The correlation between physical education and the science of education. *International Journal of Physical Education* 1: 10-14, 20.

rampant in many different forms in many ideological sects based on spiritual literature from Nietzche to Klages and Steiner. Because demands were being made on education and schools from many areas of life, including politics, economics, and art with a splintering effect, it is only logical that education science and the theory of school subjects should have defended their authority against this onslaught and should have called for an "autonomy" of pedagogy and school. At first human needs were questioned in a sort of "pedagogical province." The educators involved believed that they could satisfy these needs with certain principles regarding developmental laws. The right of children to a place where their potentialities are carefully encouraged to develop leads to certain consequences. The nature of these consequences in terms of physical exercises was particularly clearly demonstrated in theory and practice by the Austrian school reformers Karl Gaulhofer and Margarete Streicher in their "natural gymnastics" (1). The name for the school pedagogy of physical exercises was "school gymnastics" both in Austria and Germany (2). The basic spiritual powers and the pedagogical dynamics here may be transferred without interruption to the renaissance of the education movement after 1945.

1. Reform pedagogy considered school gymnastics "as a strictly pedagogically structured exercise of the body, in which the body itself may be the starting point, but the whole man is the goal" (3).

2. In the "Handbook for Pedagogy" from Nohl-Pallat (4) the regulating principle for pedagogy in the school was not the "school subject" but the basic spiritual orientations of education and instruction. The following orientations may be named: a. education of the body, b. sex education, c. games, d. aesthetic education, e. religious education, f. state and nationalistic education, g. speech education, h. scientific education, i. arts and crafts education, j. education for the role of housewife and mother, k. education for particular jobs, l. therapeutic pedagogy.

The fact that school gymnastics was worked out by Margarete Streicher points to a personally and objectively based correlation between education science (Nohl) and the theory of "natural gymnastics" in Austria. This basis was the clear point of departure for the renaissance of reform pedagogy after 1945, when the correlation between a theory of "political physical education" and education science of Alfred Bäumler had come to an abrupt end.

3. In the renaissance of reform pedagogy after 1945, physical education achieved its theoretical self-conception through studies of the organic relationships in the household of human life. The model—Soul—Spirit was raised from formal superficiality to the level of phenomenological-scientific reasoning. Educational functions in the various kinds of sport activities can only find fulfillment in the adequate recognition of the body as part of a whole personal entity (5).

4. The autonomy of physical education in the school as opposed to other subjects was captured in the formula "physical education as principle." As a result of this position the teacher who taught several subjects in one class in grade school for decades was afforded more status than the teacher of only one subject. This is because opportunities for playing on the playground, hikes, one and two week long field trips, and parties were seen as areas of "school life" in which physical exercises could be practiced in a recreational setting. These activities were under the jurisdiction of that teacher who had several subjects with the class. In a school with classes all day, physical exercises are more likely to become a life-long habit than in a school that has only half-day sessions.

From the theory of physical education Grupe formulated in this direction a "physical education in a changed school" (6) and in education science Heise called for an "unscholastic school" (7).

5. The sport movement was observed critically by the public because of concern about a hypertrophy of performance demands in schools. As a result, a "musical gymnastic" training was planned.

6. The theory of physical education was logically developed and representatives of the theory offered many kinds of answers (8). The main problem was still a clarification of the structure of physical education as a pedagogical area in the school. Categories such as games, competition, performance, social structure, kinds of activities, basic forms of behavior, elements of sport activities, etc., were described as pedagogical fields for the strategy of instruction in physical education, in many answers. An unprecedented number of education scientists supported and expanded the features in the theory of physical education—not only factually, but also in the setting of dissertation themes in physical education [Nohl, Hammelsbeck, Fischer (9), Keilhacker, Petzelt, Dolch, etc.]. Nohl (10) should be briefly interpreted here: In his contributions to the anthropological basis of education, he referred to Plato's structuring of the soul, and pointed out that, in the stratum of the thymos, gymnastics, games, and sport could develop into an activity that is delightful to men. Nohl formulated the most valuable impulses for school didactics—not only for physical education—in his articles "The Polarity in Didactics" and "Competition in the School." As no other pedagogue had done, he substantiated the possibility not only that competition might lead to a separation between the winner and the loser, but also that with proper guidance in attitude and goals, it might contribute to community and friendship. In the Education Department at Göttingen University he set up an experimental school according to a principle of group competition based on the model of competition in sports.

In all his contributions to the self conception of physical education, it is important to recognize that Nohl considered the various contents to be interchangeable with one another. "In sports, in the physical exercise of games, and in gymnastics all those great joyful experiences develop, which, when combined, bring about a spiritual feeling of freedom." An example of this, that in the theory of physical education preference was given to abilities, behavior, and capacities before the mastery of certain content, may be found in a formulation from Schmitz (11): "The specific educational task of physical education cannot be developed from the details of its content. On the contrary, it remains relatively insignificant in what form the structural principles are realized." In contrast to other subjects, the educational task here is overlapping; the structural principles referred to by Schmitz are determined by "the phenomena of movement, games, competition, and their respective arrangements."

2. THE STUDY OF PHYSICAL EDUCATION—EDUCATION SCIENCE

The junction of these considerations of the problematic history of the correlation between the study of physical education and education science has been characterized by three processes in recent years:

1. The concepts *sport* and *physical education,* as well as *physical education* and *sport instruction,* have come to be used with equal significance beside one another; the concepts *sport* and *sport instruction* have gained acceptance as the proper name for the subject both in general colloquial speech and among teachers and pupils. A logical decision must be made here.

2. In universities and teacher training colleges the didactics of school subjects are being increasingly fitted into the non-didactic scientific departments of these subjects. With this, the term *sport science* is being increasingly urged as the contemporarily preferable self conception, if the field is not to lose its connection to the realization of a new theoretical model. In this way, considerations about teaching methods are no longer afforded their previously preeminent status, but are placed within the scope of didactic questions and their relations to practical instruction.

3. In the area of our social lives, the contradictions among physical training, sport, and gymnastics have been so completely removed that there are no limits to the freedom of decision available to every individual interested in sport participation. The way leads from the pedagogical province of physical education to socially relevant sport instruction.

All the results of decade-long considerations of anthropological and social components should not be lost in sport or in the future study of physical education. The progress of curriculum research to date shows that such a loss may in no way be discussed. Of course, the entire context must be seen according to another theoretical model.

Sport instruction is only possible, in terms of factual and material interpretation, in the same sense as instruction in other school subjects such as mathematics, physics, chemistry—German, English, French—music and art. In all subjects the structure of the material is considered and the choice of contents for various classes is determined by its cultural and educational relevance.

The *study of physical education* as a science is structured according to two basic references—first, to education science, and, second, to the disciplines of a departmentalized sport science, including sport sociology, sport psychology, movement research and theory, and sport medicine. The Physical Education Board of the German Sport Federation (DSB) in their consideration of research plans, did not derive their criteria for subsidies so much from the above-named scientific disciplines as from the effectiveness of the problem formulation in connection with four areas of research: social research, behavioral research, movement research, and instructional research. Research in sport medicine represents its own field of inquiry that is still extremely relevant to the study of physical education. The discussion themes at the congress of the Organization of German Physical Educators (Ausschuß Deutscher Leibeserzieher) point out very clearly the fields of reference of the different directions of research: games / competition / performance—organization / motivation / socialization. In universities and teacher training colleges these basic problems are offered as themes for seminars, lectures, and colloquia. etc., as well as many themes to which no limits may be set by imagination, but which must find their limitation in very clear problem formulations. The following problems may serve as examples: the functions of sport in various social systems and their reflection in the study of physical education: large events like the Olympic Games according to concept and realization, also their relevance to instruction; group research, group pedagogy, group instruction in their interdependence and as individual questions; questions in behavioral research under the aspects of learning psychology, behavioral psychology, and developmental psychology; teaching and learning in relation to learning psychology and to motor learning; performance, competition, games, and social order as basic questions of the study of physical education and their relation to didactics and to instruction.

Many themes of contemporary significance have resulted from instructional research, particularly in the aspect of curriculum problems—for instruction, teaching plans, and methods, etc. Without doubt, it will be problematic to place methodology and its questions in the right position within the context of didactics as educational science.

At present we can name three tendencies in didactics that may be particularly informative for the study of physical education.

1. W. Himmerich (12) calls for the direct educational effectiveness of instruction in his conception of "didactics as science." Instruction becomes

educationally relevant by means of a) its content, b) its method of encouraging pupil activity and spontaneity, which may be used for the acquisition, mastery, and representation of subject matter, and c) the conditions of the situation under which the processes of dealing with the subject matter are completed.

2. W. Klafki (13) conceives of didactics within an educational theory which, as categorical educational theory derived from older functional and formal educational theories, promises to provide a direct educational effectiveness.

Particularly significant for physical education is Klafki's formulation of a two-sided development between the factual regularities of the subject matter on the one hand and the abilities of the person on the other hand. K. Dietrich (14) gives an example of this. Didactic models with various consequences for methodology can be developed according to the interpretation of the idea of a game and the importance of technique and tactics for success and victory, on the one hand, and according to the interaction between the two teams, on the other hand.

3. The "Berlin School," as represented by P. Heimann, G. Otto, and W. Schulz (15) has acquired a very strong influence on the conceptualization of didactics for individual subjects. Their conception is an excellent instructional theory with enlightening and practical criteria. Decision fields and condition fields are distinguished from one another. Intention, theme, methodological structures, and media structures belong to the decision fields of instructional planning. Anthropogenic presuppostions (determination of the information and opinion status of the learning group) and socio-cultural presuppositions about the learning group belong to the condition fields. This theory of didactics that is based on practical instruction can be helpful for the conceptualization of physical education.

The way to sport science as an interdisciplinary science is opened with the problems which are to be solved by the study of physical education as a science in correlation with education science (16). As long as teacher training has preeminence in the study in universities, the connections between the study of physical education (including didactics) and the disciplines of sport sociology, sport psychology, biomechanics (the study of the sensory motor system, kinematics, kinesiology), sport medicine, and sport philosophy will strongly determine the nature of the scientific problem formulation. It is possible that, in the future, educational emphases in the individual disciplines could lead to other professions in recreation, administration and journalism.

In the following diagram the concepts that have been interpreted up to this point can be made clearer in their mutual connections.

Sport science as a recognized independent science

Disciplines:

physical education (including didactics and methodology) ⟷	education science (17) (including didactics as education science)
	Fields:
	school pedagogy
sport sociology	preschool education
sport psychology	special education
the study of the sensory motor system (kinesiology)	social education
	adult education
sport medicine	job training
sport philosophy	business education
	economics, planning, and politics of education

Sport history is understood here as a history of problems in reference to individual disciplines and is seen in the general context without being individually added to the list. Similarly, coaching theory has not been named because its problems are considered from interdisciplinary points of departure.

Two questions concerning this educational model should still be answered.

1. How is physical education in school to be substantiated and supported by education science in an educational strategy?
2. What research process from a scientific study of physical education can be named as a typical example for instructional research?

An answer from Theodor Wilhelm (18) should be given to the first question. He describes the school in relation to the teaching plan as a "landscape of imagination" and organizes it according to various "horizons." These "horizons" include faith, rights, structures, interpretations, continuity, and hygiene. To the horizon of hygiene belong sport training, psycho-hygiene or mental health, and recreational aids. With reference to sport he maintains the following. It is important for the school to remember that class time is too precious to fill it with activities that the pupils can do just as well or even better outside the school. Therefore school is a programmer and not a trainer. The learning program should also be valid for recreation and for the future. Spiritually productive activity is always keyed both to work and to leisure. The main role of the school is the clarification of the world of imagination and although sport does not have any controllable effectiveness in such a context, it does serve the intention "to equip the world of imagination of the pupil with a program for maintaining physical health."

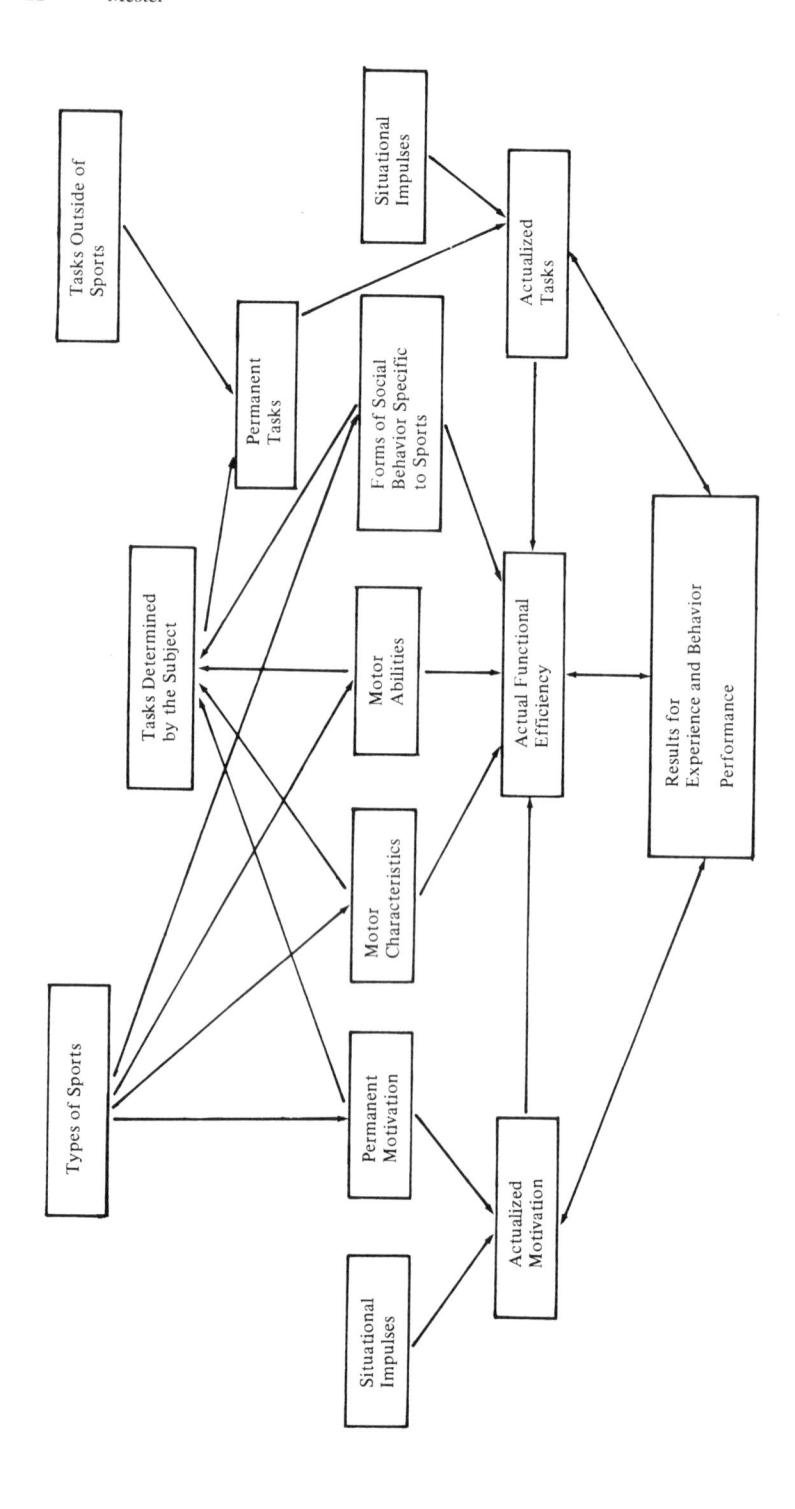

In curriculum research, questions about the legitimacy of sport and physical education still play a decisive role. This complex has not yet been considered in the present article, because it is somewhat beyond its scope. The "stimulating" piece from H. von Hentig about "Learning Opportunities for Sports" (19) exhausts this theme of the basic motive of every science, "to question something," with thorough radicalness. It applies both to sport in general and sport in the school. However, this very article with its positive negations proves all the more that a sport science is necessary from the perspective that the realities of sport, including its educational and instructional dimensions, are so "importunate" that we may not leave the children and young people in our schools without equipping them with their own experiences and standards.

By way of further discussion of the necessity of sports as a school subject and as a substantiation of that necessity, this example of instructional research should be provided here: O. G. Hecker's study, "The development of performance in sport, a contribution to curriculum development for physical education in elementary school" (20). The work is named as an example for instructional research, because very clear methods are discussed and used in it. These methods especially deal with the quantitative consideration of the results of observation in instructional research. The first part brings, with hermeneutical methods, a clarification of concepts and categories (performance, development, motivation, etc.) and leads to the model of a "system of interlocking effects" that serves as a basis for the second, empirical part of the experiment. This system seems so decisive to me in its formulation of didactically relevant concepts and in its explanation of their connections to one another, that I have included it at the end of my remarks about the correlation between the study of physical education and education science (21). The above-mentioned question concerning physical education has been scientifically answered only after consideration of education science and motivational psychology and this answer has lost nothing in worth, but, on the contrary, has gained in originality and independence. The work of teachers in 40 schools in Hessen who participated in the main experiment is exemplary and should be recognized. With this example from instructional research, I have attempted to answer the second question asked at the beginning of this analysis of the "correlation between the study of physical education and education science."

REFERENCES

1. Gaulhofer, K., and Streicher, M. 1962. Das neue Schulturen—Abdruck aus den Bänden "Natürliches Turnen". (The New School Gymnastics—reprint from the volumes "natural gymnastics.") Klein Pädagogische Texte. Julius Belz OHG., Weinheim.

2. Neuendorf, E. 1930. Methodik des Schulturnens. (Methods of School Gymnastics.) Limpert, Leipzig.
3. See No. 1.
4. Nohl, H. 1930. Die Didaktik der geistigen Grundrichtungen. (Didactics of intellectual basic points of view.) In: Nohl-Pallat (ed.), Handbuch der Pädagogik. (Handbook of Pedagogy.) Vol. 3. Julius Belzohg, Weinheim, (Langensalza). (G. Dresel, Die Körpererziehung, p. 155–172; M. Streicher, Das Schulturnen. p. 173–190.)
5. O. Grupe collected many anthropological investigations and combined for the first time the term "physical education" and "sport pedagogy"; Grupe, O. 1969. Grundlagen der Sportpädagogik. (Fundamentals of Sport Pedagogy.) Johann Ambrosius Barth, München.
6. Grupe, O. 1967. Leibliche Erziehung in einer gewandelten Schule. (Physical Education in a Changed School.) Aloys Henn-Verlag, Ratingen.
7. Heise, H. 1960. Die entscholastisierte Schule. (The School Without Scholastics.) Metzler, Stuttgart.
8. Examples: Bernett, H. 1965. Grundformen der Leibeserziehung. (Basic Forms of Physical Education.) Karl Hofmann, Druckerei und Verlag, Schorndorf; Hanebuth, O. 1961. Grundschulung zur sportlichen Leistung. (Basic Training of Sport Performance.) Limpert, Frankfurt; Mester, L. 1969. Grundfragen der Leibeserziehung. (Basic Questions of Physical Education.) Westermann, Braunschweig; Paschen, K. 1966. Didaktik der Leibeserziehung. (Didactics of Physical Education.) 2nd Ed. Limpert, Frankfurt; Schmitz, J.N. 1966–1972. Studien zur Didaktik der Leibeserziehung. (Studies Concerning Didactics of Physical Education.) Karl Hofmann, Druckerei und Verlag, Schorndorf; Stöcker, G. 1970. Grundlagen der Leibeserziehung. (Foundations of Physical Education.) Schwann, Düsseldorf.
9. Schmitz, J.N. (ed.) 1966. Aloys Fischer und die Leibesübungen. Beiträge zum Selbstverständnis der Leibeserziehung. (Aloys Fischer and the Physical Exercises. Contributions Concerning the Nature of Physical Education.) Karl Hofmann, Druckerei und Verlag, Schorndorf.
10. Mester, L. (ed.) 1962. Schuld und Aufgabe der Pädagogik. (Guilt and Task of Pedagogy.) Karl Hofmann, Druckerei und Verlag, Schorndorf.
11. Schmitz, J.N. 1967. Das Grundproblem einer Didaktik der Leibeserziehung. (The basic problem of didactics of physical education.) In: H. Plessner, H.-E. Bock, and O. Grupe (eds.), Sport und Leibeserziehung, pp. 91–102, R. Piper & Co. KG., München.
12. Himmerich, W. 1970. Didaktik als Erziehungswissenschaft. (Didactic as Educational Science.) Moritz Diesterweg, Frankfurt.
13. Klafki, W. 1964. Studien zur Bildungstheorie und Didaktik. (Studies Concerning Educational Theory and Didactics.) p. 44 ff., Julius Belz OHG., Weinheim.
14. Dietrich, K. 1972. Die Kontroverse über die Lehrweise der Sportspiele. (The discussion on the teaching of sport games.) In: J. Recla, K. Koch, and D. Ungerer (eds.), Beiträge zur Didaktik und Methodik der Leibesübungen. Karl Hofmann, Druckerei und Verlag, Schorndorf.
15. Heimann, P., Otto, G., and Schulz, W. 1965. Unterricht, Analyse, und Planung. (Instruction, Analysis and Planning.) Hermann Schroedel Verlag KG., Hannover.
16. Himmerich, W., and Ricker, G. 1972. Uber Beziehungen zwischen dem Gießener Didaktischen Modell und Mesters Sportdidaktik. (Concerning the relationships of the Giessen didactic model and the sport didactic of Mester.)

In: H. Haag, (ed.), Didaktische und curriculare Aspekte des Sports. Karl Hofmann, Druckerei und Verlag, Schorndorf.
17. The sections of educational science in the system are listed in: W. Klafki (ed.) 1972. Funk-Kolleg "Erziehungswissenschaft". (Radio-college "Educational Science.") Vol. 3. Julius Belz, OHG., Weinheim; Röhrs, H. 1970. Allgemeine Erziehungswissenschaft. (General Educational Science.) 2nd. Ed. Julius Belz, OHG., Weinheim. (Röhrs includes in the general educational science "pedagogy of physical education and sport pedagogy" as a systematic part. Klafki refuses this solution. In view of our theoretical model, this solution cannot be justified, even if one recognizes the high level of the content.)
18. Wilhelm, Th. 1969. Theorie der Schule. Hauptschule und Gymnasium im Zeitalter der Wissenschaften. (Theory of School. "Hauptschule" and "Gymnasium" During the Scientific Century.") 2nd. Ed. Metzler, Stuttgart.
19. Hentig, H. v. 1972. Lerngelegenheiten für den Sport. (Learning Possibilities for Sport.) Sportwissenschaft 3:239.
20. Hecker, G. 1971. Leistungsentwicklung im Sportunterricht. Ein Beitrag zur Curriculumentwicklung für den Sportunterricht in der Grundschule. (The Development of Performance in Sport Instruction. Contribution to Curriculum Development for Sport Instruction in Primary School.) Julius Belz OHG., Weinheim.
21. Hecker, (1971) p. 105.

Sport Pedagogy as a Part of Sport Science

The Body of Knowledge, Sport Studies

R. G. Osterhoudt

It is the intent of this chapter to develop a discussion of sport as a legitimate object of liberal study, and thereby to demonstrate the general organization of liberal knowledge with respect to sport. That is, the attempt here is to establish sport as an object of liberal inquiry by showing the central core of liberal understandings concerning it. This central core of such understanding poses itself in two stems: the *disciplinary stem,* in which sport is treated as a generic category of human activity and is understood by reference to archetypal bodies of knowledge (such as biology, psychology, sociology, and the like); and the *psychomotor stem,* in which particular sports are distinguished, and are understood largely by self-reference. These particular sports, of course, provide involvement in the actual substance of sport, as well as the primitive data for disciplinary treatments of sport generally.

DISCIPLINARY STEM

The constituents of the disciplinary stem treat the most fundamental orders of understanding with respect to sport. That is to say, they treat the integral, or archetypal, orders of such understanding—orders of understanding that exhaust the pure forms of knowledge with respect to sport—namely, the biological, psychological, sociological, historical, and philosophical orders. (The ordering here is from most specific to most general.) These bodies of knowledge (or academic disciplines) are taken to be integral by virtue of their each being necessary for a fully complete, and therefore satisfactory, account of the nature and significance of sport. That is, the absence of any one leaves an irreplaceable chasm in our knowledge of sport—there are no pure and unified alternatives to them. They examine dimensions of sport that cannot be otherwise examined; in effect, they show up the most distinctive, and therefore the determinate, features of sport. They neither reduce themselves to other orders of ideas nor are they forthcoming as combinations (or composites) of such others. They are the absolutely primary forms of understanding with respect to sport, and they are the only such forms. Only they can prosecute a rigorous, systematic, and comprehensive account of sport.

This view is not, of course, to be confused with the claim that these are the only ways in which sport may be studied and understood. It is merely to assert that they are the most fundamental of such ways. That is, it is both common and proper for us to study subdisciplines of these integral bodies of knowledge, composites of them, and derived applications of them. Most notable among understandings of the first sort are, for example, the geography of sport and the economics of sport—conceived as subdisciplines of the sociology of sport. Most significant among those of the second type are the social psychology of sport and the anthropology of sport—a composite of the psychology of sport and the sociology of sport in the case of the former, and one of the sociology of sport and the history of sport in the case of the latter. Most important among those of the third form are the study of tests and measurements (to include a treatment of research methods and statistics), organization and administration (to include treatments of curriculum and intramural athletics), therapeutic exercise, athletic training (or, prevention and care of athletic injuries), and coaching, teaching, and officiating methods.

While the subdisciplinary and composite disciplinary forms of sport studies contribute centrally to the substantive forms of knowledge discussed here, albeit in a secondary way, the applied forms of understanding make more reference to procedural, or methodological, than to substantive concerns. That is to say, they are principally devoted to securing a comprehension of the means or manner by which substantial bodies of knowledge may be applied or used in the conduct of sport or in a secondary study of sport. As such, they do not so much inform with respect to the distinctive, the fundamental, nature and significance of sport (they do not so much inform with respect to the liberal understanding of sport at principal issue here) as they instruct with respect to the manner of employing such understandings in the actual conduct or secondary study of sporting activity. They are, then, not primary but derivative, not central but largely incidental to the body of knowledge, sport studies.

A more specific treatment of each of the pure orders of understanding sport (i.e., the biological, psychological, sociological, historical, and philosophical dimensions of sport studies) may now serve to demonstrate further the merits of the view thus far presented. That is, such treatment may serve to reveal more precisely the terms of the body of knowledge, sport studies.

Biology

Biology may be generally conceived as the science concerned with explaining the physical (structuro-mechanical) and chemical (functional) characteristics of plants and animals. As such, the biological dimension of sport studies gives rise to two derivative forms: kinesiology-biomechanics (or, applied anatomy—to include sport cinematography and electromyography) and applied physiology. The former treats the structuro-mechanical bases of sporting activity, considering such issues as the laws of simple machines, action of forces, and the types and laws of motion and equilibrium as they serve to reveal the nature of sport. The latter examines the functional bases of sport in the form of considering the effects of sporting activity on biological variables of a functional order (such as heart rate, stroke volume, blood pressure, oxygen consumption, metabolic rate, blood chemistry, and the like), as well as the influences of physiological characteristics upon sporting achievement (i.e., strength, speed, endurance, flexibility, agility, and balance) under various environmental conditions.

Psychology

Psychology may be generally characterized as the science concerned with explaining individual animal behavior, most commonly by reference to mental phenomena. Like the biological dimension of sport studies, the psychological aspect divides itself into two forms: motor learning and the psychology of sport. Motor learning concerns itself with a study of the terms in which sporting skills, knowledge, and attitudes are acquired and retained, i.e., learned. Yet, more specifically, it considers neurological conceptions of this process, developmental perceptual-motor behavior (kinesthetics and motor performance), general methods of instruction, and laws and principles of learning appropriate to psychomotor skills. The psychology of sport examines the psychological variables of personality, motivation, intelligence, and emotional states as they affect, or are affected by, sporting activity. That is, it considers the relationship of such variables to participation and success patterns in sport.

Sociology

Sociology as it is generally thought of qualifies as the science concerned with explaining animal group (interpersonal, or inter-individual) behavior: it is principally the study of groups of persons, or institutions. The sociology of sport examines sociological variables as they affect, or are affected by, sporting activity. It considers the relationship of such variables to participation and success patterns in sport. Principal among these variables are: social status, social mobility, the socialization process, sex and age groups, political institutions, economic institutions, religious institutions, race (race relations, segregation, integration, and discrimination), social deviancy, social change, social conflict, and collective behavior, as well as ethnic cross-cultural studies (comparative, sociological studies) of sport.

History

History may be generally characterized as the science concerned with explaining or describing the narrative of past events, actualities, and occurrences. It is a recounting and an interpretation of past events. The history of sport entails an examination of such events as they are located in sporting activity, as larger socio-cultural orders of affairs have influenced such activity, and as such activity has influenced larger, socio-cultural orders of occurrence. It reveals the place that sport has enjoyed throughout the historico-cultural experience of man; that is, in ancient primitive, ancient River (Egypt and Mesopotamia), ancient Oriental (China, India, and Persia), ancient Hebrew, ancient Greek, ancient Roman, medieval, Renaissance, and seventeenth-, eighteenth-, nineteenth-, and twentieth-century culture.

Philosophy

Philosophy may be generally characterized as the humanistic discipline concerned with achieving a reflective apprehension of reality in its most general, accessible perspective. The philosophy of sport examines issues peculiar to sport (which is not, as implied more persuasively by subsequent argument, itself inherently philosophical) until those issues are unveiled as matters of a uniquely philosophical sort. It assesses the status of sport with respect to reality (nature, man, and God), knowledge, and value (ethical, aesthetic, and socio-political) generally; that is to say, it reveals the metaphysical (concerning reality), epistemic (concerning knowledge), and axiologic (concerning value) status of sport. With this, then, the body of knowledge, sport studies, is taken to have exhausted its pure forms—to have completed itself.

The view thus far adduced allows for both the discrete status of sport [as, together with dance, exhausting the whole of the movement arts; and being an instance of that form of distinctly human activity conceived of as game, which primarily involves skill (as opposed to chance) of a physical sort, which enjoys a wide following that has achieved a certain historico-culturally determined measure of institutional stability, and which is conducted at play (in the spirit of intrinsicality; that is, in and for itself) and under competitive conditions], as well as its study being comprised of academic disciplines that are themselves subdisciplines of integral bodies of knowledge. That is, with respect to the first allowance, sport is conceived as itself an integral form of human activity, neither reducible to other forms nor a part of other forms—not an applied discipline in the fashionably thought and obsequious sense (in the sense of its being nothing but the collectivity of biological, psychological, sociological, historical, and philosophical explanations of it), but, like the arts (most particularly, like dance), distinguished absolutely by reference to its own fundamentally substantial features alone. In fact, it is held here, albeit somewhat dogmatically, given the limited scope and alternate intent of the present effort, that this distinctiveness of sport resides in, is indeed determined by, and is at one with, its artistic dimension. Which is to say that this dimension qualifies as a sixth pure form of understanding sport; in fact, that of sport as such, that of sport proper, sport itself. It is the next and the last pure frontier of sport studies, in which sport comes to know itself as sport. Concerning the second allowance, the study of sport is, despite its inviolate integrity, nonetheless fundamentally comprised of a study of kinesiology-biomechanics, applied physiology, motor learning, psychology of sport, sociology of sport, history of sport, and philosophy of sport—themselves subdisciplines of biology, psychology, sociology, history, and philosophy proper. As in the case of a study of the arts generally, the study of sport (which has been numbered here among the arts) is constituted as an apprehension of it by the more particular disciplines of integral stature. The entire sweep of this position squares with what we understand of sport itself at its best, as well as with what we have here held to be the case with respect to its serious, scholarly study.

The view concerning the study of sport thus far defended also presupposes some prior insight into the organization of knowledge generally. That is, the study of sport as here outlined requires prior association with the pure disciplines, of which kinesiology-biomechanics, applied physiology, motor learning, and the like are subdisciplines. This places their study with respect to sport in full relief; it allows for a necessary understanding of general perspectives prior to turning those perspectives onto a more particular examination of sport. This body of pure liberal understandings includes:

1. The methodological disciplines: language, logic, and mathematics, which suggest the means or manner by which all orders of ideas relate one to the other(s), and which are therefore pertinent to, but not in themselves a part of, all disciplines.
2. The natural scientific disciplines: physics, chemistry, and biology (as the explanation of physical and chemical phenomena as they appear in living entities—to include most importantly a study of human anatomy and physiology).
3. The social scientific disciplines: psychology, sociology (to include a study of political science, economics, and religion), and history.
4. The humanistic disciplines: philosophy and the arts (to include a study of the plastic arts, literary arts, theater arts, movement arts, and music).

PSYCHOMOTOR STEM

The constituents of the psychomotor stem of sport studies treat the particular sports, which provide involvement in the actual substance of sport, as well as the primitive data for disciplinary treatments of sport generally. In order to obtain a systematic and comprehensive understanding of sport, these constituents must provide kinesthetic experiences of particular sports, as well as treatments of teaching-learning progressions and structuro-mechanical, physiological, and historical concerns peculiar to the particular sports, and not taken up in the more general disciplinary accounting of such matters. Although the composition of, or relative emphasis upon, the activities included in this category may well be revised according to alternative cultural and sexual preferences, a reasonably systematic and comprehensive understanding of this aspect of sport studies seems assured with an examination of:

1. track and field athletics (to include cross country)
2. gymnastics (to include both tumbling and apparatus)
3. swimming and diving
4. wrestling
5. boxing
6. soccer (association football)
7. basketball
8. racquet and court sports: tennis, badminton, squash, handball
9. other individual sports: modern pentathlon, cycling, rowing, canoeing, weightlifting, fencing, judo, equitation, yachting, shooting, golf, bowling, curling
10. other team sports: baseball, football, ice hockey, field hockey, water polo, lacrosse, rugby, volleyball, cricket
11. classic winter sports: skiing (to include both alpine and cross country), ski jumping, speed skating, figure skating, bobsledding, luge

SUMMARY AND CONCLUSION

This chapter develops a discussion of sport as a legitimate object of liberal study by showing the general organization of liberal knowledge with respect to it. This organization is then further distinguished in terms of its disciplinary and psychomotor components. Moreover, recognizing the limited scope of the chapter, it ought to be considered more a provocation to further reflection than a final concluding statement.

Introduction to *Sport Science*

O. Grupe

THE VARIETY OF SPORT AND NECESSITY TO MEET IT

Without doubt, sport as it is presently known belongs to that class of phenomena that have not yet been investigated with regard to their consequences and structures, and on which no general information, but only partial information, is available. One's first impressions of sport are that it is not complicated, that it is without problems, that it has a clear structure, and that it is understandable in its obvious relationships. Such seeming transparency is responsible for its archaic intensity and unbroken attractiveness. However, it should not be overlooked that there is not much research available about the position of sport with respect to the individual, with respect to social life, and with respect to its social relevancy. This may explain why sport has not been free of misunderstanding, wrong interpretation, and ideology. The systematic interest of serious research has barely reached the field of sport. Medicine can provide some information on the healthful aspects of sport, i.e., its prophylactic, rehabilitative, and therapeutic dimensions, but there is not very much empirical research available on the many relationships between social relevancy and sport, or on its possibilities in education. The available scientific results are not at all in agreement with the obvious public importance, and the usage, of sport.

Apologetic statements are mixed with undifferentiated evaluations, expectations not to be fulfilled, and unreasonable hopes, along with critical statements at every level and from different sides. This extends from criticism within sport and society to a total criticism of sport, including the system to which it belongs. The following aspects are criticized: exaggerations of sport, commercialization, political and economical ideology, and crowd phenomena started or favored by sport. These are often seen as symptoms of stressing the importance of the body and of intellectual decay, and include criticism of

---

Reprinted by permission from: Grupe, O. 1971. Einleitung in die Sportwissenschaft. *Sportwissenschaft* 1:7–18 (pp. 9–17 reprinted here).

sport in general as a means by which the upper class may hide its true intentions and indoctrinate the sport participants in civic behavior patterns. Civic resentment and old traditions are changing only gradually, as are the total defense and romantic self-interpretation of sport as part of a world which is still without conflicts. Therefore, a solid judgment of sport or of its different parts is not available.

Judgment, critical distance, and willingness to thoroughly investigate a phenomenon are missing; the mass character and the proletarian origin of this phenomenon (if one does not deal with the upper class sports and the International Olympic Committee) are still barriers to the development of a science. Therefore, it is important for sport science to differentiate sport according to its aspects. This means a precise differentation and distinction of content according to the functions that are valid for certain groups or systems, instead of speaking in a global way of the nature of sport and of simply imposing general aims to sport. Such a differentiation, however, is quite difficult.

PROBLEMS OF DEVELOPING A SYSTEM

Sport science cannot yet be accepted as a unique discipline. Developing a system for sport science is a problem chiefly because of the complexity of the research subject and the differences in methods and techniques of observation that can be applied to sport. However, this is not the main methodological problem for which there are patterns for solution in other scientific disciplines. The main problem of sport science is the following: the challenge of its system, its questions, and its methods can only be met by interdisciplinary research. Certainly there are many problems of sport that also can be solved by questions and methods of other scientific disciplines. However, this is normally limited to certain problem aspects of the respective science, without reaching sport as a problem of a number of different scientific disciplines. Sport science, as it is often practiced, should assume as its basis a conventional division according to scientific disciplines, which would mean a division according to educational, psychological, sociological, medical, and other questions. Then, through the word *sport* one could see a unique research subject. Only by doing this would an integrative procedure be possible. This is also true for another traditional possibility for division, namely the development of the organizational aspects of sport in which it is mainly presented. Such aspects are:

Physical education, school sport and/or sport for youth as forms of physical activity and sport that are chosen, stressed, and realized according to educational criteria (preschool education; primary level; secondary I and secondary II; higher education; education outside of school; youth associations; actions in regard to social, special, and remedial education; education in boarding schools; resocialization)

Mass sport/recreational sport/sport for all as forms of sport and physical activity that comprise play and movement of children, youth, adults, and older people (club; community activities, sport groups in the working area, extension courses; unorganized sport activity; sport activity on weekends and during vacation)

Performance and competitive sport as sport of individuals and groups that undertake regular planned training and competition

Top performance sport/sport of top athletes as a field of sport with a different structure that can be clearly distinguished from sport for all because of its aims and application, principally its political and economic dimensions. This kind of sport is much more dependent on spectators and public interest than are sport for all and competitive sport. The transfer from top performance sport to professional sport (professionalism) is very easy as soon as there is a market and the interest of the public is increased. This is part of the modern amusement and recreation offerings.

No matter how these divisions are made and how detailed sport is divided into its various aspects, such a system remains within a conventional understanding of sport and a traditional meaning of science. On the basis of an integrated approach it would be logical to search for criteria that cross over scientific questions and divisions to form the basis for organization. Thus, a multidimensional classification would be possible. Multidimensionality means in this regard that, within the realm of sport, the questions within a given classification are especially stressed. However, this would not mean that the organizational differences between certain aspects of sport would be eliminated and that methods and techniques of certain scientific disciplines would be used in an undifferentiated way. Such questions could be, for example, the problems of performance, consumption, spectators, requirements and stress, political and economic use of sport, group dynamics, and motivation. With the help of these topics, a differentiated pattern could be developed by which it would be possible to define the contents, structure, functions, and possibilities of sport (and its different aspects) more precisely. The main reason for classifications in an attempt to develop a system can only be greater exactness.

The journal *Sportwissenschaft (Sport Science)* will attempt to use as a guideline for its content and planning such a differentiated and even more precisely categorized content, *sport*. Attempts will be made to gear questions of theoretical and empirical nature towards this aspect. Furthermore, a special effort will be made to reflect constantly the questions that cut across certain areas and therefore define those criteria that are the bases for research programs. This will especially involve topics from anthropology and philosophy and from social and cultural anthropology, as well as questions from social and behavioral sciences, and from general medicine. It should be noted that these problem areas are so many-sided in themselves that they cannot be part of only one aspect of sport science but normally they require differentiated and at the same time integrated methods. Such a classification system needs to be diversified according to the interest of the participating people. From the perspective of the athlete, sport looks different than it does from the perspective of the spectator. Other perspectives are important for the scientist as compared to the politician; for officials there are other solid perspectives different from those of people who are professionals in sport. There is some question whether or not there is a common basis independent of time for such different interests and for the needs reflecting these interests. One can suppose that the different aspects of sport can only be defined with respect to the different expectations, interests, wishes, and needs of the participating individuals, groups, and institutions. Therefore, for sport science the question that has to be urgently answered is whether or not an unhistorical analysis of sport based on a fixed interpretation of physical activity has to be eliminated in favor of an analysis oriented on other presuppositions.

SOME PRESUPPOSITIONS OF THE ANALYSIS WITHIN SPORT THEORY

If the basis for *Sportwissenschaft* is the fact that there is nothing like one "sport," two presuppositions are assumed that should at least be stated. These relate to the following points:

> Social areas like sport and physical education cannot be defined once and for all, independently of their social cultural context. This means that, within categories such as anthropology, sport could not be changed (as such only the game could be accepted). It should be noted that sport and physical education depend on the possibilities, interpretations, norms, and functions of the respective social cultural and social economic situation. Sport and physical education are dependent on historical development. They don't have timeless values that remain the same forever. Values, meanings, and structures are changed within the historical relationship, thereby stressing the importance of historical questions.

If these presuppositions are correct, sport is not independent of the basic structures of society, with its contradictions and conflicts that also are found within the field of sport. It means that sport is dependent for its products and results (if one interprets health, performance ability, or top-level sport performance and records as products) on the same criteria of usage and application that science and industry use.

For the journal *Sportwissenschaft* this has many consequences: the more it can be seen that certain presuppositions are expressed openly, that they are either accepted without discussion or ignored, the more it is necessary to analyze these assumptions. As far as possible, the journal *Sportwissenschaft* will support this process through publication of articles. Only through the analysis of all presuppositions and decisions of different kinds, which form the basis of theoretical and empirical questions, is it possible to overcome the uncertain level of casual judgments and experiences and of guessing and over-interpretation, in favor of reliable results and statements. The most important consequence, however, is that analysis and reflection should not (as the presuppositions have shown already) be restricted to sport and its different aspects. They should also include the social system in which sport is carried out, organized, and administered.

This consequence is valid for the journal *Sportwissenschaft* in two ways. On the one hand, how the functions of sport are defined within social relationships and groups is important. On the other hand, how sport science analyzes its own social relationships and to what extent sport science can reflect the usage and application of the results, which are not completely free and without relevance for the research process, is also important. This question leads beyond reflecting on the problem of how sport science can constitute itself as a science through its questions, methods, techniques, and performances. The important question is: How can sport science meet those conditions that allow sport science to be seen as a science? Furthermore, this means that the definition of its function within social developments and reforms, with their conditions and aims, must be stated. At the present time this problem is discussed under the headline *emancipative* understanding of science. Within this discussion the term *emancipative* has degenerated to a term that is used too much, which means that this term can be used for each interpretation. From a content point of view it can be learned from this discussion that sciences have to face the question: To what extent are the results useful for mankind, and what can these results contribute to the happiness of people?

Such a concept requires an open discussion of the scientific point of view. Such a discussion should be void of irrationalism, dogmatic judgment, polysyllabic words, knowledge of the *best* way, disqualifying unpopular arguments, and the suppression of contradiction. The journal *Sportwissenschaft* will try to develop in this way and to become a national and international forum that is undogmatic, free, open, and inclined to criticism and conflicts.

Sportwissenschaft will have to assume for quite some time that there is no theory of sport or theory of sport science available. Neither euphoria, inadequate expectations combined with empirical research, nor philosophical thinking disregarding empirical verification can help to develop such a discipline. Instead of this, serious empirical research in all aspects is necessary to form a sound, socially oriented philosophy of the individual and social implications of sport. In the face of increasing faith in science and of high expectations put forth by scientists it is necessary to develop doubts about both aspects.

INTERDISCIPLINARY TRIALS

Whatever results such a discussion may lead to, it remains only a formality, because such a discussion does not provide any insight into content-problems of sport science. Questions of the scientific foundations of the fields of sport science theory—especially in physical education—have been discussed for several years. These discussions have been held on different levels of competency and with different results. However, important questions have not been answered. For example, Where does sport science belong? It cannot be categorized in connection with one science; it is something like an interdisciplinary integration science that arises from its content. How can sport science be developed with regard to methods and questions, and how can this be expressed in a publication with the name *Sportwissenschaft?* For sport pedagogy, however, with its close relationship to educational science, as well as for sport medicine, the problem cannot be expressed in the same way.

With the assertion of sport science as an interdisciplinary science, only a common object is required, not a community of methods and theory development. However, the common basis in terms of research objectives is not quite clear. Sport is an area that is many-sided, and can be divided into several sub-areas that are judged quite differently. Sport is constantly changing, depending on the conditions of the social, political, and economical situation, which are all too often assumed and only seldom analyzed.

With the claim of being an integrated science, a science that involves somewhat different questions and divergent results, the interdisciplinary nature of the research concept is provided. This is a format that is discussed within methodological questions for sport science to a great extent. "Interdisciplinary" means that problems of the science evolve from sport and not from the specific methods and techniques that would lead immediately to problems related to a single science. This stress on integration for the development of sport science and that on the necessity of interdisciplinary research, therefore, have a close relationship.

Interdisciplinary views within sport science, however, still have to be developed, because appropriate methods, techniques, and questions have not yet been developed. These cannot be derived from sport science itself; corresponding behavior patterns of the researchers themselves are necessary that can be described by the terms, *teamwork* or *ability for cooperative work,* in a very general way. He who states that the time of *research at the desk* is over must create research behavior patterns for sport scientists, because most of the researchers in sport science today, except the people engaged in medical research, do not have research methods.

SPORT SCIENCE OR SPORT SCIENCES—PLAY ON WORDS?

The editorial committee discussed for a very long time the most appropriate name for the publication. This name had to be precise and susceptible to the expected scientific contributions, but also adequate for the given content and the possibilities for interdisciplinary research. There was an option between the terms, *Sport Sciences* and *Sport Science*. Until about two years ago there was a strong inclination for the term, *Sport Sciences*. It seemed to have a greater affinity for different disciplines; it seemed to be more adequate for the variety of possible research methods within sport; and it seemed to be free of ideology and adequate for the present status of sport science research without requiring something else, but there were problems. First of all, this term did not express that there is a *unique* sport science. The plural term would have drawn attention to the scientific variety of *Sportwissenschaft*, which shows not only a variety of subjects but also a great differentiation of questions and methods.

During the last few years, the term *sport science* has been used to a great extent (e.g., Federal Institute of Sport Science, Professorships for Sport Science, Diplomas, Dissertations in Sport Science, etc.), even in the German Democratic Republic. During this time the arguments in favor of the term *sport sciences* have been put forth; however, the influence of this argument has decreased and the arguments for use of the singular term have been accepted to a much greater extent. These arguments stress the projective character of the term *sport science,* even if they admit that until now there has been a certain skepticism about the results of sport science. This indicates that the treatment of sport has one research area that is being investigated under the aspects of different sciences. In a similar way, this is also true in education science, which is interpreted more and more as a social and behavioral science including the cooperation of related scientific disciplines. There is a tendency to construct sciences starting from the subject area, which also determines the scientific questions and the treatment of the questions. Especially within the field of sport, one sees that there is no science by itself in which only subject-specific methods without cooperation with other scientific disciplines can be utilized. An accidental addition would lead to vagueness. Instead of this, it is necessary to have a differentiation within integration (subject fields of sport science).

Autonomy, uniqueness, and uniformity of sport science are not implied by such an argument. Also, the use of the term *sport science* is not intended to compensate for a yet undeveloped scientific prestige and scientific misrepresentation. The time of prescientific work, or resentments, of people who are scientifically underprivileged, and the time of hidden ideological presuppositions seem to be over. The beginning of serious sport science research can be envisioned and therefore the title should indicate the development and not so much the status quo. Therefore, the decision had to be made for *Sport Science (Sportwissenschaft)*, in the sense of an integrated science that regards relevant results of other scientific disciplines by summing up the results and integrating them under its specific questions, in order to achieve a unity that cannot be without contradiction. Furthermore, the field of sport science must develop sufficient substance for its own scientific performance.

With skepticism about its own arguments, the editorial committee has decided to help sport research on its way. Therefore, the decision was made for the term *Sportwissenschaft,* a program and a challenge that have to be met.

The Content of Sport Pedagogy

Tones of Theory—A Theoretical Structure for Physical Education—A Tentative Perspective

C. Ulrich and J. E. Nixon

This chapter presents a tentative theoretical structure of physical education—a tentative perspective. It begins with a brief discussion of the nature of theory followed by a specific description of conceptual theory as it is related to physical education. Then follows a clarification of the relationship between physical education as a discipline and the body of knowledge of physical education. Next, the life-education relationship is described, followed by the process-media-result relationship. Then physical education knowledge, as a conceptual entity, is analyzed. Finally, the chapter concludes with a synthesis of these major aspects and suggestions of important implications for the future.

THE NATURE OF THEORY

Definition. It is necessary to define the key terms *theory, facts, hypotheses,* and *laws* which constitute the foundational elements of this account of the AAHPER Project on the Theoretical Structure of Physical Education.

Theory. Theories are general assertions about various aspects or elements of the world. A theory is a conceptual structure based on a set of interrelated concepts which has for its purposes: (a) the tentative *description* of an event, object, or idea; (b) the tentative *description of relationship* between two or more variables (events, objects, ideas, or phenomena); (c) the tentative *explanation* of the cause and effect relationship between two or more variables (events, objects, ideas, or phenomena); and (d) the tentative *predic-*

Reprinted by permission from: Ulrich, C. and Nixon, J. E. (eds.) 1972. *Tones of theory.* A Theoretical Structure for Physical Education—A Tentative Perspective. AAHPER, Washington D.C. (pp. 6–23 reprinted here).

tion of the occurrence of an event or activity based upon the acquisition of warranted evidence.

A *theoretical structure* is a broadly conceived set of descriptive, explanatory, and predictive statements. The purpose of these statements is to explicate and clarify the *key organizing concepts,* basic beliefs, explicit and implicit assumptions, and the specific theories, hypotheses, and facts which constitute the inventory of the symbolic expressions and records of the accumulated human experience concerning the phenomena under consideration.

Facts. Facts constitute the basic building blocks with which hypotheses, theories, and laws are constructed. A fact is a specific piece of information; it is the recognition and observation of a single event. Facts, as well as hypotheses, theories, and laws are intellectual constructions. Hypotheses and theories are abstracted from observable facts. Laws are deduced from hypotheses and theories and are verified by comparing their assertions with the world of observable facts.

Hypotheses. An hypothesis is more specific than a theory. It is not a broad proposition. It is a particular statement which can be used with theories and laws to provide an explanation of certain events. Hypotheses are constructed and confirmed by empirical (experimental) evidence. The 'truth' or acceptance of an hypothesis rests upon its ability to be confirmed through experience. Evidence used to test hypotheses can be in the form of either (1) statements based on natural law, or (2) sense-datum statements (facts).

Laws. On the other hand, laws are statements of confirmed invariant relationships in nature. Laws provide the most accurate method for explaining events and phenomena. Ultimate laws, those most rigorously validated, are explained by other laws and theories, and, often, these in turn are further explained by still other laws and theories.

Summary. Thus, *theories, facts, hypotheses,* and *laws* are inevitably intertwined and interdependent. Together they enable man to express conceptually his current understanding of occurrences and events. They are essential elements in man's scientific enterprise. Their major contribution is that of *explanation.*

Varieties of Theory. Gowin (1) indicates that there are five different meanings which commonly are accorded the term theory in various specialized segments of the academic world:

1. a set of spectacles (glasses) for viewing things—which suggests that theory is speculative;
2. scientific theory—a set of logically related verified hypotheses;
3. philosophical theory—as a general assertion of value;
4. a set of prescriptions or rules to govern some activity (e.g., teaching);
5. a conceptual framework, a logically related set of ideas.

The person proposing a specific theory, or a broad theoretical structure, should state explicitly the definitional context he selects to use for his theory formulation. In developing a theoretical structure an essential early step is to arrive at a set of operational definitions about the phenomena which are deemed to constitute the central, significant concerns (foci) of the domain being studied.

APPROACHES TO THEORY DEVELOPMENT IN PHYSICAL EDUCATION

Fraleigh (2) identifies three different approaches to theory development as applied to physical education.

1. The application approach. Data and concepts from related fields of knowledge are selected and applied to the activities, operations, and practices of another field (e.g., physical education).

2. The implication approach. This approach is similar to the application approach but derives its elements mainly from philosophical study and inquiry. It involves the utilization of conceptual structure and content of philosophical systems (e.g., realism, idealism, pragmatism). Educational principles are deduced from these philosophical systems to form an educational philosophy. Likewise, principles are deduced as a basis for physical education theory. Physical education practices and decision making evolve from these principles.

3. The translation approach. This approach involves the acceptance of a given model as having the faculty to adapt, and to accept into it, some segment of physical education theory. The model, in turn, is expanded and modified by an inflow of content from specific types of investigation and analyses of human movement activities.

Concluding Statement. Theory may be concerned with any or all of the processes of description, interrelationship, and prediction about events, objects, ideas, and phenomena identified by the scholars and researchers in the area of study. From key theoretical assertions a more operational level of theorizing and hypothesis formulation may be constructed. The results provide guidance for the practical application of the main theory and its conceptual components, to the selection and employment of promising practices and effective decision making in realms of human activities (e.g., education, physical education).

Theory has one more major role. Not only is it based on the *known* (facts), on warranted concepts, and on logically consistent philosophical tenets, but it also proposes tentative projections into the unknown and the unexplored. Comprehensive theory assists us to realize that which we do not know, or what we know or believe only imperfectly. Thus, it points the way, and encourages further exploration, research, and rational thought on significant phenomena that, in turn, result in modification, revision, expansion, and clarification of the phenomena under scrutiny.

There is no one permanent theory. Theory is ever changeable as new data, enlarged and novel empirical evidence, rational thought, verified and rejected theories, intuitive leaps, and creative insights combine with philosophical viewpoints to spawn new and revised theories at all levels of conceptualization and articulation.

As new theories of physical education are generated and existing ones refined and modified, research specialists can more clearly identify significant phenomena to investigate. New evidence, in turn, will modify theories and result in warranted statements about regularities in man's scientific and philosophical thought systems which can attain the status of accepted generalizations or, ultimately, of laws.

Practitioners are guided by theories they hold either implicitly or explicitly as bases for decisions and judgments they make as they perform their assigned roles. In reality, teachers are *hypothesis makers,* because each plan they make, each action they take to effect desirable pupil behavior, is based on some understanding of what they, as teachers, believe and predict will happen to the pupil under planned conditions. Theory and practice are inseparable.

As theories of physical education are developed, clarified, tested, revised, and extended through this continuous process, the understanding of the nature and purpose of this area of study will be enhanced for both researchers and practitioners. Their interpretation of the field to others will be clarified, and the quality of their professional decisions affecting people in varied environmental settings will be improved.

Therefore, theory is always tentative, fluid, and subject to evolution as new evidence becomes available. Ultimately, theory represents the most accurate and complete current record of man's understandings and comprehensions about himself, the world, and the universe in which he lives.

Hence, we have come full circle in this brief overview of what theory is and how it is generated and employed to serve man's philosophical, scientific, humanistic, and practical needs, drives, and interests. Theory is essential for man to learn, understand, and control (through prediction) his own destiny in the incessant, on-rushing, compelling human struggle for a life of purpose, fulfillment, and personal dignity.

CONCEPTUAL THEORY AND PHYSICAL EDUCATION

The words *concept* and *theory* have many connotations. For the purpose of clarification and parsimony, *concept* will be defined as *sensate information, comprehended and classified, but not necessarily analyzed. Theory* will be considered as a *systematic organization of concepts* into a logical scheme of relationships.

Hence, the *conceptual theory* of physical education is concerned with the interrelationship of all of the components which are generally considered as belonging to the body of knowledge of physical education. The conceptual theory of physical education deals with the relationships which characterize the field of study and its body of knowledge; the relationships of the school, college, and other institutional experience as contrasted with life experience; the process-media-result relationship, and the interaction of *how-to* and *what-for*.

In attempting to find a rationale for its framework, physical education has sought to organize and utilize factual concepts such as *human movement phenomena, play, sports and games, recreation, human engineering, movement education, fitness, behavioral domains, holistic man,* and *education*. An attempt to sort out these concepts and their relationships may offer a tentative design which will facilitate understanding and provide a guide to needed research and improved educational practices. This structure represents the *translation approach* and, as such, is subject to the new facts and ever-changing laws and hypotheses.

DISCIPLINE-BODY OF KNOWLEDGE RELATIONSHIP

A discipline which could be titled *Human Movement Phenomena* is the broad category under which the body of knowledge labeled *physical education* can best be subsumed. Other bodies of knowledge, such as human engineering, physical therapy, recreation, educational athletics, dance, physical medicine, professional athletics, and human ecology also are integral parts of the context of the disciplinary organization of the phenomena identified as *human movement*.

Each of these areas (and others which could be named) has an individual focus for its study of human movement, yet each is sensitive to the basic concerns of all. For example, *human engineering* looks at human movement in relationship to material products. Time-motion analysis, the adaptability of man to machines and machines to man, and the structuring of materials to accommodate man, are all concerns of human engineering. *Physical therapy* is based on the utilization of specific movement patterns to correct functional disabilities. *Recreation* is concerned with patterns of human movement as they relate to a leisure time sequence. Recreation utilizes movement patterns already acquired by the individual and seeks to find ways by which such patterns can enhance the individual's life style. Both *educational* and *professional athletics* as specialized organizations of sport, relate human movement to game organization. Athletes and coaches are concerned with movement and its identification with the structure of the game. Important values may emerge from the game which are concomitant to the event itself. *Dance* relates movement to time and space in symbolic patterns of presentation. *Physical medicine* sees human movement as a therapeutic device to restore the individual to a healthful state. *Human ecology* seeks to use human movement in effecting a symbiotic relationship between the physical environment and *Homo sapiens* a relationship which will abet and augment the quality of life on this planet. Meanwhile, physical education focuses on the development of human movement through various pattern processes to help the individual identify his nature, his potential, and his limitations.

It is possible to depict the discipline-body of knowledge relationship, as in Figure 1.

Physical education shares its concern about human movement with other areas. The specific concerns of these areas are not mutually exclusive, but have a meaningful relationship with each other. Athletics and recreation are

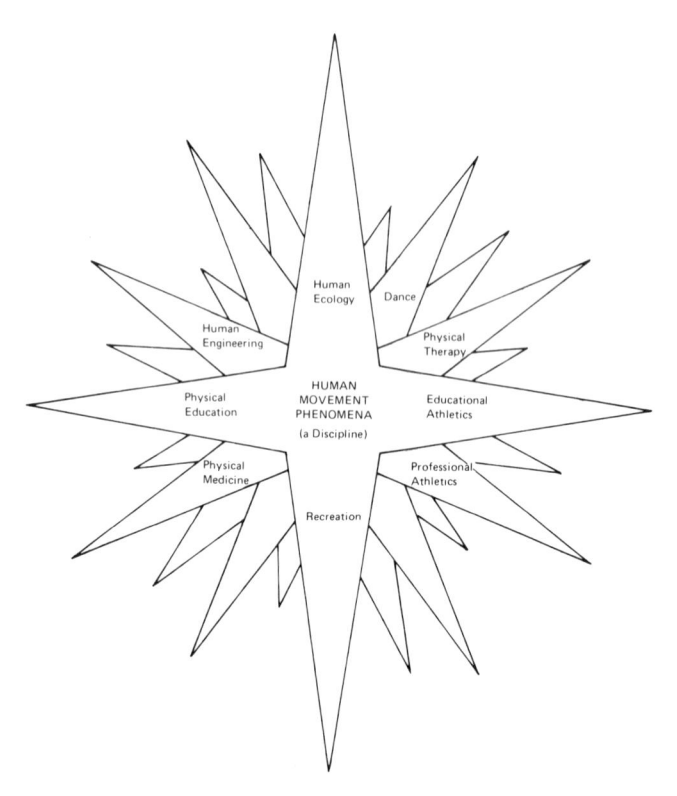

Figure 1.

both sensitive to physical education and physical education shares a portion of their special focus on sports and leisure. Physical medicine utilizes some of the techniques of movement which are also used by physical education. However, physical medicine and physical therapy are remedial and cater to the pathological, the prevention of the pathological, and the atypical rather than to the typical or normal individual. Human engineering and human ecology both are concerned with the harmony of man, movement, and material aspects of the physical environment; they share methods of effecting such harmony with athletics, recreation, and physical medicine, as well as with physical education.

The model of the star need not be interpreted as indicating that the discipline dealing with human movement phenomena has only nine points. Stars have many points in a three-dimensional model. There is the opportunity and flexibility in the discipline pertaining to human movement for multifaceted design.

LIFE-EDUCATION RELATIONSHIP

As one of the bodies of knowledge related to the human movement discipline, physical education has a commitment to influence the understandings, practices, and directions of that discipline. Traditionally, this responsibility has been accomplished through the social institution of the school, thus connecting physical education with the educational process. However, in a larger context, physical education has extended its concern with self-understanding to all people of all ages and dispositions, through many social institutions. Physical education tends to divide its concerns mainly in relation to process and product and then finds implications for those concerns in developmental and organizational syndromes (patterns, sets, forms, designs). Historically, such syndromes have related to age, sex, and aptitude classifications. Such stratification has limited the insights, although it has acutely sharpened some understandings within specific categories.

The life-educational relationship thrusts are depicted in Figure 2.

It is obvious from the model in Figure 2 that the usual way of looking at physical education can diminish the thrust of the arrowhead. If physical education, as a body of knowledge, relates only to young skilled males, or young unskilled females, or any combination of discrete wedges, a portion of the arrowhead is missing and the thrust of the physical education interpretation of human movement phenomena is lessened. Additional wedges could be added to the arrowhead to hone the point to a finer, more precise end. Wedges representing morphological characteristics, psychic readiness, and social aptitude are all potential additions. Other arrows of the human movement phenomenon exist for other bodies of knowledge, each capable of making an

52 Ulrich and Nixon

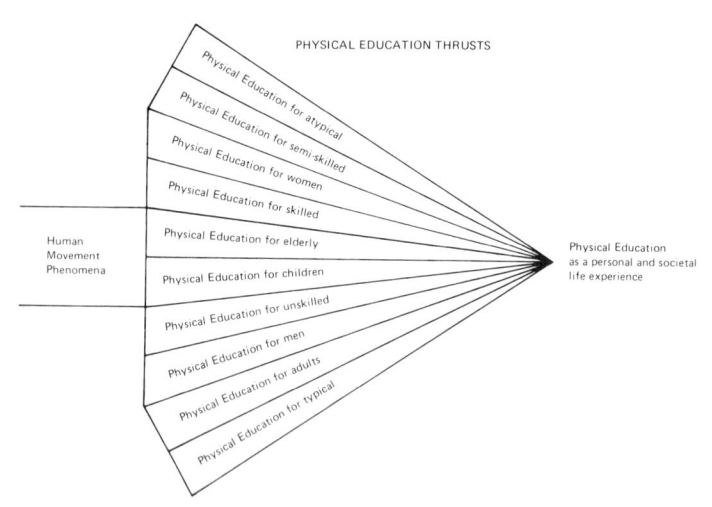

Figure 2.

impact on the personal and societal life experience. The human movement phenomenon has a quiver of arrows.

PROCESS-MEDIA-RESULT RELATIONSHIP

If that part of the arrowhead which deals primarily with physical education in an educational milieu is extracted, it is possible to structure the process-media-result relationship. Such a relationship *may* have implications for the life-experience concerns of physical education, but the process-media-result pattern essentially is predicated upon the school experience.

The processes which are used by physical education in such a setting deal with types of movement. These, as described by Jewett (3,4) are:

Generic
movement— includes those processes which facilitate the development of effective and characteristic motor patterns: these may be regarded as movement fundamentals and are typically exploratory operations.

Ordinative
movement— includes those processes which organize, refine, and perform skillful movements; these may be regarded as specific patterned acquisitions and are perceptual-motor abilities with a view to solving particular movement tasks or requirements.

Inventive
creative
movement— includes those processes of inventing or creating skillful movements which serve the immediate and individual purposes of the learner;

these movements may be regarded as styles and are directed toward discovery, integration, abstraction, idealization, emotional objectification, and composition.

These three types of movement are processed through the behavioral domains of the individual. Such processing often is structured in play-like situations. The domains of behavior are:

Cognitive domain— that aspect of behavior which deals with understandings, knowledges, and intellectual abstractions.

Affective domain— that aspect of behavior which deals with feelings, interests, attitudes, appreciations, sensations, and visceral involvement.

Motor domain— that aspect of behavior which deals with kinesthetic awareness, motoric abilities, and sensory-motor patterning.

The means used in the processing deal with activity, which is carefully structured as to kind, and always conducted as to outcome. The media, or life-stuff, of physical education has a participation aura which demands active involvement and being, not just passive understanding and becoming.

The results of activity reside in its effect upon the desires, needs, and nature of the individual and his ability to recognize and accommodate his own actualization potential. The ultimate result could be described as total well-being in the most macro-cosmic connotation of the concept and could be classifed, as Jewett has done, through the "purpose-oriented concepts of movement." These are:

1. *Individual development through movement* (man as master of himself)—man develops through his movement.
2. *Environmental adaptation and control through movement* (man in space)—man adapts to his environment through movement; man controls or modifies his environment through movement.
3. *Expression and communication through movement* (man in a social world)—man expresses himself through movement; communication affects his movement.

It might be possible to depict the relationship of process-media-result in the model given in Figure 3. The threads of process are funneled via voluntary, purposeful human movement situations which are synthesized for each individual through a conduit of activity which emphasizes involvement and being and results in purpose-oriented ends which meld into a composite of interwoven relays resulting in human well-being. Such a relationship among process-media-result clarifies the *how-to* and *what-for* interaction with regard to physical education.

54 Ulrich and Nixon

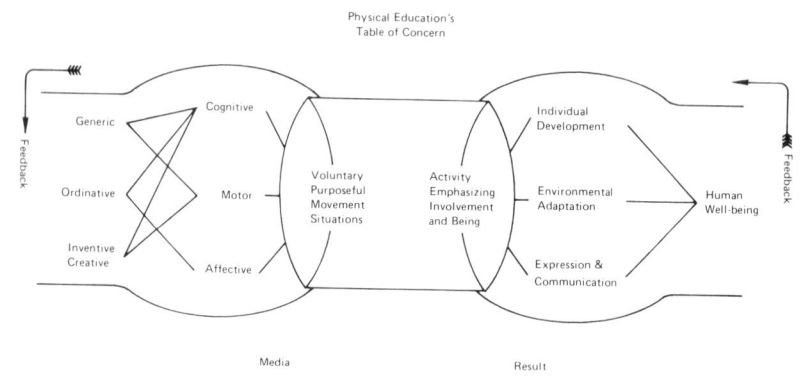

Figure 3.

The conceptual theory of physical education resides in its relationship to the discipline concerned with human movement phenomena; it finds its structure in both the total life experience and the school experience; its operational plan is structured in terms of movement processes, behavioral domains, activity, and the resultant recognition of the nature, needs, potentials, and limitations of the individual within his world (Figure 4).

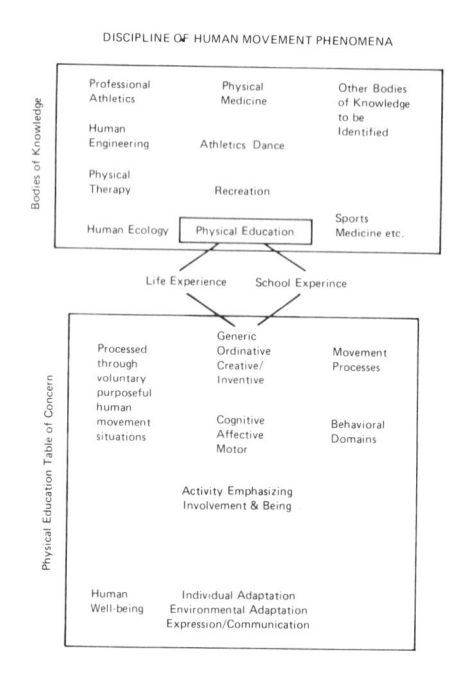

Figure 4.

PHYSICAL EDUCATION KNOWLEDGE

Conceptual theory provides the framework on, and within, which evolving knowledge can be structured. Knowledge, in this reference, is defined as general substantiated evidence used in analyzing and validating concepts. Thus, knowledge elucidates concepts even as concepts suggest a structure of knowledge. There is a cyclic relationship between conceptual theory and knowledge.

Physical educators identify their body of knowledge in reference to both the discipline of human movement and the conceptual theory of physical education. They are responsible for both broad understandings and specific factual evidence.

The knowledge implicit to the discipline of human movement is generalized knowledge which is shared by all of those areas which hold human movement within their purview. This knowledge is traditionally categorized according to content. As such, it may be located in many bodies of knowledge which are relevant to the discipline of human movement. However, the interaction of all knowledge pertaining to the human movement phenomena is the unique responsibility of the discipline of human movement. It alone is responsible for the structuring of disciplinary design, and it alone is held accountable for omissions, faulty logic, and flimsy patterns.

The disciplinary knowledge of human movement concerns itself with content areas, such as the following:

1. Biomechanics of movement
2. Human developmental patterns
3. Physiology of activity
4. Motor learning
5. Behavioral components of human movement
6. Meaning and significance of human movement
7. History of human movement meaning
8. Theories regarding the meaning of human movement
9. Social-cultural aspects of human movement
10. Symbols of human movement (art, sports, dance, aquatics, etc.)

The above content areas, structured upon factual evidence, filter through all bodies of knowledge which identify with the discipline of human movement. Thus, the human engineer, the doctor of physical medicine, the human ecologist, the coach, the recreator, the physical therapist, the dancer, the athletic director, and the physical educator should be sensitive to the generalized understandings afforded by study of the above content areas. Moreover, in an educational setting, such knowledge should be available to all students of human movement in order to enhance self-understanding and adaptation.

Physical education knowledge relating to the conceptual theory of physical education deals with both *process* and *product*. The student of physical education must understand how to process movement and how to utilize the product of movement. Hence, the *process, knowledge of physical education* (which is associated with specific sorts of activities), is found in the following content areas:

1. Acquisition of skill patterns through ordinative movement
2. Self-actualization through generic, ordinative, and creative movement
3. Creative patterns of activity emphasizing individual style
4. Conditioning and training regimens
5. Decision making and its movement patterns
6. Experience in behavioral situations which foster interaction, social stratification, social control, self-realization, motivational understandings, social processing, interpretations of ethics and morality, making value judgments
7. Behavioral opportunities for nonverbal communication
8. Utilization of cognitive learning commensurate with motoric development

These *process* knowledge areas have been historically labeled according to the activity sponsoring the process. Thus, labels of archery, bowling, tennis, football, field hockey, body mechanics, weight training, judo, basketball, and many others have contained the process knowledge of physical education. However, it should be noted that many times the process knowledge was incidental to the outcomes of activity, that is, process became a concomitant rather than a focus.

The *product* knowledge areas are clustered around the outcomes of activity. *Product knowledge in physical education* is concerned with:

1. Worthy use of leisure time
2. Ability to participate adequately in sports and games
3. Understanding of rules, strategies, and tactics
4. Organic integrity—usually called optimum physical fitness
5. Desirable behavioral attitudes
6. Emotional satisfaction gained through involvement
7. Maximum work results with minimum mechanical effort

It is to be noted that many of the *product* knowledges of physical education support a connotation of value. Thus, the products of activity have often been value loaded, tending to give physical education knowledge a moral flavor. Value knowledges are always subject to the fluctuation of cultural interpretation. Because of this, physical education knowledge (i.e., the subject matter of physical education) has been both in and out of favor with the times. It has been endorsed as a positive value and cursed as an unnecessary evil. Had the knowledge of physical education centered around process instead of product, such vacillation might not have occurred. It is still possible to remove the value from the product, if such a maneuver seems desirable.

All of the above knowledges are requisite to a clear understanding of physical education's relationship to the discipline of human movement. Understandings of the factual evidence support the conceptual theory of physical education, which, in turn, provides rationale for gaining additional knowledges and ascertaining new relationships.

In addition to human movement knowledge, and physical education process-product knowledge, there is *teaching-learning* knowledge. This knowledge is incidental to the consumer of physical education (the student) but absolutely essential to the purveyor of physical education (the teacher). Teaching-learning knowledge has certain generalized constructs found in nonspecific educational content. However, the teaching-learning knowledge of physical education is specific to that particular body of knowledge. The area of physical education can support technical artisans (specialists who can *do* but do not understand *why*); however, the worth of physical education depends upon the teaching-learning knowledge of behavioral artists (teachers who can structure activity to enhance knowledge). The areas of content imperative to teaching-learning knowledge in physical education are found in:

1. Kinesiology
2. Philosophy of physical education
3. Teaching methodology for motor skill acquisition
4. Motor learning
5. Physical education curriculum construction
6. Evaluation in physical education
7. Administration of physical education
8. Adapted physical education
9. Practicum in teaching physical education

Such teaching-learning knowledge has direct reference to the conceptual theory of physical education. It provides the operational know-how, the "how-to" design.

It behooves physical educators to continually seek congruency between conceptual theory and knowledge. On such congruency rests the future of the body of understanding which is physical education. It is possible to depict the relationship of knowledges, as in Figure 5.

In the bell of knowledge that is physical education, knowledge concerning human movement provides the handle for manipulation of the bell. The metal body of the bell has both an inside and outside aspect which accommodates the *process* and the *product* knowledges of physical education. The clapper, which is the *teaching-learning knowledge,* imparts action to experience and sets the tone as it hits specific areas of the bell's body. The interplay

PHYSICAL EDUCATION'S BELL OF KNOWLEDGE

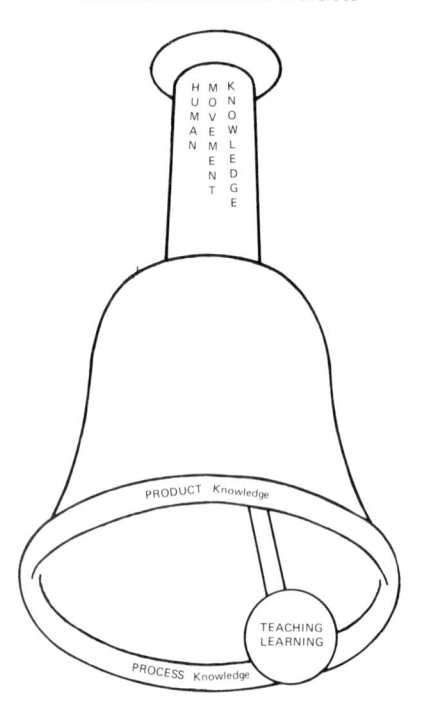

Figure 5.

of each of the bell's segments provides intellectual integrity and assures that the bell's ring will herald a meaningful experience.

REFERENCES

1. D. B. Gowin, "A Trial Set of Distinctions and Definitions of Terms Used in Structure of Knowledge Analysis," (Ithaca, N.Y.: Cornell University, May 28, 1969), 4 pp. (mimeographed)
2. Warren P. Fraleigh, "A Prologue to the Study of Theory Building in Physical Education," (San Jose, Calif.: San Jose State College, undated). 11 pp. (mimeographed)
3. Ann E. Jewett, "Implications for Curriculum Theory for Physical Education." *Academy Papers 2* (1968): 10–18.
4. _____, *Curriculum Handbook* (American Association for School Administrators) 1972.

The Content of Sport Pedagogy as a Theoretical Field of Sport Science

H. Haag

The fast development of sport science and the observable strong differentiation of this scientific discipline require a discussion of scientific theory as it relates to one central aspect of sport science, namely, sport pedagogy (1).

In order to develop a concept of sport pedagogy as a part of sport science, it is especially important to understand the genesis of sport pedagogy from the theory of physical education. Mester has described these relationships very clearly (2):

1. In the 1950s, the ideas of reform-pedagogy were adapted into the theory of physical education.
2. In the 1960s, there was a change from the educational aspect of physical education to sport pedagogy as it related to society.
3. In the 1970s, sport science originated, with one part called sport pedagogy.

The dimension of methodology has become a horizontal dimension within science, in which there are similar perspectives for many scientific disciplines with regard to the application of scientific methods. Therefore, the determination of the content of a science or of a scientific subdiscipline has become more important (3). Whether or not one can speak of an independent science is dependent upon the dimension of content, themes, etc. The content dimension, therefore, has to be seen as central to the discussion of the nature of a scientific discipline. Based on four available models, another model is used in this chapter to describe the content of sport pedagogy. The chapter discusses and examines whether or not this model can be applied as a description of the body of knowledge of sport pedagogy.

Reprinted by permission from: Haag, H. 1976. Zur inhaltlichen Konzipierung der Sportpädagogik als Aspekt der Sportwissenschaft. In: H. Andrecs and S. Redl (Hrsg.), *Forschen—Lehren—Handeln,* pp. 23-33. Österreichischer Bundesverlag für Unterricht, Wissenschaft und Kunst, Wien.

THE CONTENT DIMENSION OF
SPORT PEDAGOGY ACCORDING TO K. WIDMER (FIGURE 1)

One of the few newer systematic publications pertaining to questions of the nature of sport pedagogy is the publication of K. Widmer, *Prolegomena zur theoretischen Begründung der Sportpädagogik as Wissenschaft* (4). Four central themes are discussed:

1. Search for a scientific sport pedagogy.
2. The foundation of sport pedagogy.
3. Remarks on the problem of scientific theory in sport pedagogy.
4. Theory in practical application of sport pedagogy.

The theoretical foundation of sport pedagogy as a science is based on scientific methodology and on the content dimension, which will be further explained. Widmer used the term *formal object* in order to describe sport pedagogy. The term is: "the young generation, which should be interested and enabled to participate in sports (5)." The term sport pedagogy is defined by Widmer on the basis of this formal object in the following way:

> The term sport pedagogy includes all educational efforts directed at the young, who should be interested in and enabled to participate in sport. It includes the basic theoretical educational thinking, as well as the sport pedagogical behavior that should be related to practice and founded in theory: the anthropological question, the problems of aims and objectives, the curriculum trends, and the

A) Pedagogically relevant aspects of sport			B) Sport-relevant aspects of education		
A 1	A 2		B 1	B 2	B 3
Movement as basic sign of sportive activity	The levels of interdepence of sportive activity	Physical and psychic functions	Aims and objectives of education	Education as interaction process	Education as result
		Sport and social environment			
		Sport and value system			Fields of education
		Learner and teacher			Responsibility of education
		Sport and institution			Pedagogical behavior and pedagogical "means"

Figure 1. The content dimension of sport pedagogy according to K. Widmer.

educational efforts for socialization and individualization of the young generation through sportive activity'' (6).

Widmer tries to clarify the content of sport pedagogy by asking two questions, namely: What are the pedagogically relevant aspects of sport (7), and What are the sport-relevant aspects of education?
  I. Pedagogically relevant aspects of sport:
     A. Movement as a basic element of sport activity
     B. Levels of interdependence of sport activity (five levels of interdependence: physical and psychic functions, sport and social environment, sport and value system, learner and teacher, sport and institution)
 II. Sport-relevant aspects of education:
     A. Aims and objectives of education
     B. Education as an interaction process (fields of education, responsibility for education, pedagogical behavior, and pedagogical "means")
III. Education as a result

This attempt to formulate the content of sport pedagogy from two aspects (sport and education) and from the complementary relationship of these two aspects, however, has the disadvantage that there is a certain overlapping of the content description of sport pedagogy. Nevertheless, this is a very interesting way to explain the nature of sport pedagogy from the point of view of an educational scientist; this approach goes a lot farther than the approach of Roehrs (9), who tries to categorize sport pedagogy as one field of the educational sciences. Roehrs interprets sport pedagogy as the pedagogy of physical education, a discipline of the science of education, which also includes the history of education, school education, didactics and methods, social education, remedial education, economic education, and comparative education. The inclusion of sport pedagogy in this content concept seems to be very promising and indicates the importance of sport pedagogy. If one examines this concept more closely, one can see several unsystematic dimensions within the said disciplines of education.

THE CONTENT DIMENSION OF SPORT PEDAGOGY AS PRESENTED BY J.N. SCHMITZ (FIGURE 2)

The argument of Schmitz is based on a relatively unclear and different usage of the terms sport pedagogy, sport didactic, and theory of the curriculum (10). Schmitz attempted in his article "Special didactics and curriculum theory within sport science," (11) to clarify the content and concept of sport peda-

Sport pedagogy (as part of the discipline of sport science)

| Scientific theory and methodology | Anthropological foundations | Sport didactics | History of physical education and sport instruction | Institutions and organizations | Comparative sport pedagogy |

Sport didactics

| Theory of curriculum (sport curriculm) | Theory of learning | Theory of teaching |

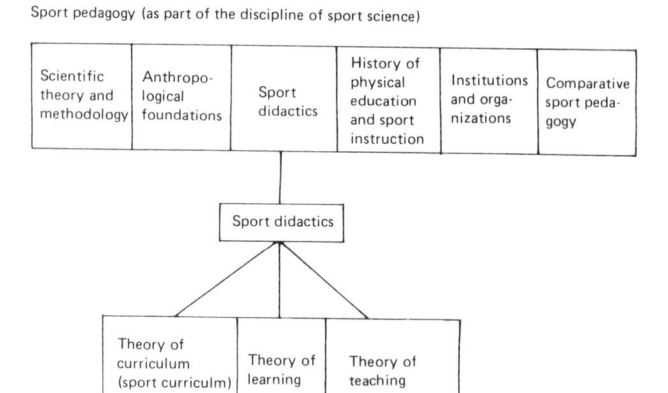

Figure 2. The content dimension of sport pedagogy according to J. N. Schmitz.

gogy on the basis of the actual discussion of didactics and curriculum within the Federal Republic of Germany. He tried to create a proper understanding of terminology by interpretations of the history of terminology and the use of analytical models for terminology. Schmitz contradicts the thesis that there is a difference between curriculum theory and the old theory of specific didactics. By trying to clarify the terminology, Schmitz develops the following concept of the content of sport pedagogy as part of sport science. Sport pedagogy is "the science that deals with the educational foundations and problems of sport as an educational field in teaching and research" (12). In connection with the term sport pedagogy one must also deal with the not yet answered question on the relationship between theoretical and practical pedagogy as well as the distinction made in regard to scientific theory between hermeneutic and empirical analytical education. Such questions, especially those on the relationship between theory and practice, also have to be discussed in sport pedagogy, because these are the foundations for understanding the nature of sport pedagogy. The content dimension has to be clarified in order to get an understanding of sport pedagogy.

According to Schmitz, sport pedagogy is characterized by the following themes: scientific theory and methodology, anthropological foundations, sport didactics, history of physical education and sport instruction, institutions and organizations, and comparative sport pedagogy.

The term sport didactics, which is not clearly used, is further divided into theory of curriculum (sport curriculum), theory of learning, and theory of teaching.

Schmitz's explanation is limiting in that no request for absolute truth of a concept is contained in this model. Nevertheless, the themes constituting sport pedagogy are of a different quality, and can be misunderstood in the manner used (13).

THE CONTENT DIMENSION OF SPORT PEDAGOGY AS SEEN IN THE GERMAN DEMOCRATIC REPUBLIC (FIGURE 3)

H. Schwidtmann describes sport pedagogy within the informational material on results of the sport science research and development in the German Democratic Republic during the period from 1964 until 1972. Sport pedagogy is seen as "the theory of guidance and creation of the aim oriented, planned and continuous process of socialistic education of people and collectives engaging in sport under the concrete conditions of exercising and training in sport within its basic aspects and forms" (15). The main tasks of research and development so far described have been the following: clarification of the dialectical mutual relationship of education and sport and the exact determination of the function and effect of physical education in forming socialistic personalities. Results of research in sport pedagogy are presented in two main areas, along with their respective subfields:

I. Research results for foundations of sport pedagogy
    A. Socialistic personality
    B. Content of physical education
    C. Leadership and self-activity
    D. Influence of sport collective

```
                    Foundation of sport pedagogy
   ┌──────────┬──────────┬──────────┬──────────┬──────────┬──────────┐
Socialistic  Content of  Leadership  Influence   Sport in    Historical
personality  physical    and self-   of the      free time   questions
             education   activity    sport
                                     collective
```

```
         Methods of sport within and outside of instruction
   ┌──────────────┬──────────────┬──────────────┐
   Realization of  Intensification of  Effective formation
   sport curricula the process of      of competitions and
                   exercising and      of the systems of
                   training            competition
```

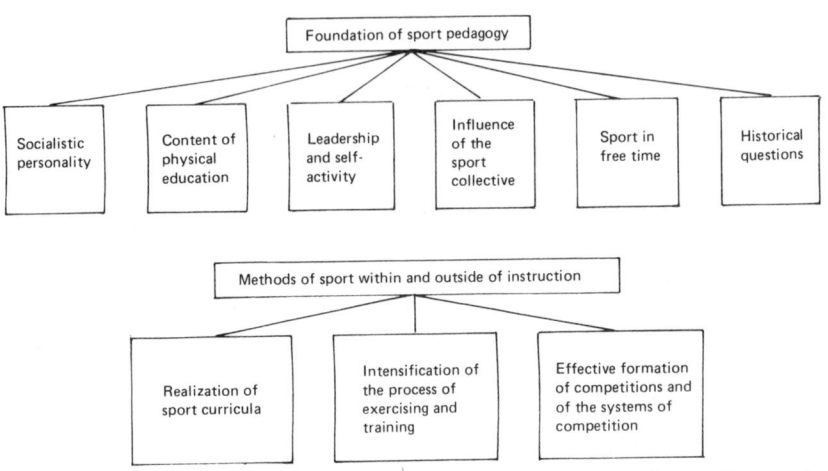

Figure 3. The content dimension of sport pedagogy as it is seen in the German Democratic Republic.

E. Sport in free time
F. Historical questions
II. Research results for methods of sport within and outside of instruction
   A. Realization of sport curricula
   B. Intensification of the process of exercising and training
   C. Effective formation of competitions and of the systems of competition

The content dimension of sport pedagogy can probably be derived from the given system of research results within sport pedagogy. However, this system does not seem to be very useful within the foundations of sport pedagogy, since the historical dimension is seen on the same level as the other aspects. This specific listing of methods as one complex in addition to the foundations is stressed too much and shows great identity with questions within the theory of training. From the results of various research projects, which are referred to as single research results, a more precise foundation of the educational science can be seen as related to sport; this also contributes to the changes in the practical work within physical education (16).

This basic position assumes the following: physical education is a recognized part of socialistic education; physical education is realized in a uniform way as an obligatory faculty teaching-learning process in sport; physical education is used to create a consciousness for society; physical education influences the over-all development of the socialistic personality. Thus, it is clear what the normative basis of sport pedagogy is, and that this can be used as the starting point for a detailed content description of aspects of teaching and research in sport pedagogy.

THE CONTENT DIMENSION OF SPORT PEDAGOGY AS SEEN WITHIN SPORT SCIENCE (PHYSICAL EDUCATION) IN THE USA (FIGURE 4)

According to the present status of the discussion of scientific theory in the United States, one can assume that there is no visible theoretical field of sport pedagogy that is a component of sport science with the other theoretical fields. Physical education, however, is the nucleus, the process, and the reality on which different scientific theoretical fields should concentrate their work; it is not seen as an independent scientific theoretical field. In the *Big-Ten Body-of-Knowledge-Project in Physical Education* the following content concept has been developed for the American theory of physical education:

1. Physiology of exercise
2. Organizational theory
3. Sociology of sport and physical education
4. Biomechanics

Content of Sport Pedagogy   65

```
                    ┌──────────────────┐
                    │ 2. Organizational│
                    │    theory        │
                    └──────────────────┘
┌──────────────┐                            ┌──────────────────┐
│1. Physiology │                            │ 3. Sociology of  │
│   of exercise│                            │ sport and physical│
└──────────────┘                            │    education     │
                                            └──────────────────┘
                    Physical education
┌──────────────┐    (Sport pedagogy)        ┌──────────────┐
│6. History    │                            │4. Biomechanics│
│   philosophy,│                            └──────────────┘
│   comparative│
│   physical edu-│
│   cation, and │
│   sport       │
└──────────────┘
                    ┌──────────────────┐
                    │5. Movement theory│
                    │   and sport psy- │
                    │   chology        │
                    └──────────────────┘
```

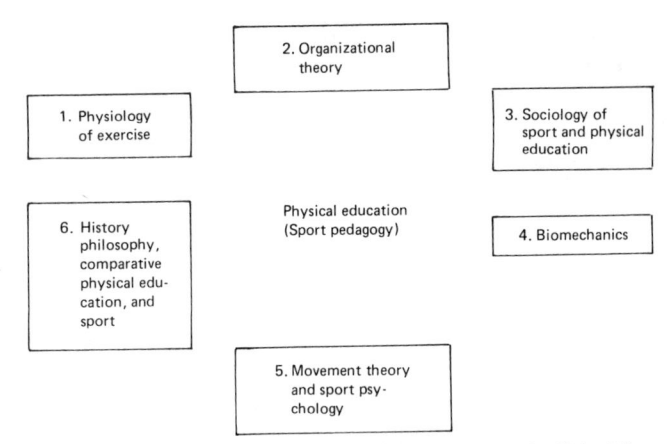

Figure 4. The content dimension of sport pedagogy as it is seen in the United States.

5. Movement theory and sport psychology
6. History, philosophy, comparative physical education, and sport (17).

A new publication with the title *Physical Education—An Interdisciplinary Approach* (18) shows, how physical education and sport pedagogy are seen as focal points for different scientific and sport science endeavors. In this publication, the results of the theoretical fields of sport science, physiology, physics, psychology, sociology, anthropology, and philosophy build the interdisciplinary scientific framework for the investigation of the process of physical education. From this a large content description can be derived for physical education (nearly comparable with the theory of physical education in the Federal Republic of Germany).

Thus, it can be understood that a basic volume of American sport science literature, Bucher's *Foundations of Physical Education* (19), deals with the following topics:

1. Nature and character of physical education.
2. Philosophy of physical education as part of general education.
3. Relationship of physical education to health, recreation, camping, and outdoor education.
4. History of physical education.
5. Scientific foundations of physical education (biology, psychology, sociology).
6. The physical education teacher.
7. The profession of the physical education teacher.

Taking these facts into consideration, it is very difficult to introduce the term sport science, or sport sciences, into a professional discussion in the United States. Currently, the main focal point for work in sport science in the

United States is physical education; from this it follows that within professional discussions in the United States sport pedagogy is not seen as a scientific theoretical field of sport science; instead, physical education serves as the focal point for the different scientific and sport scientific endeavors. This development is astonishing because, especially in the United States, education has found a broad and empirical scientific foundation. The aspect of physical education, or sport pedagogy, however, is not viewed as a theoretical field with its own scientific existence.

CONCEPT FOR DESCRIBING THE CONTENT DIMENSION OF SPORT PEDAGOGY (FIGURE 5)

On the basis of the content concepts developed by Widmer, Schmitz, the German Democratic Republic and the US, the content of teaching and research in sport pedagogy can be described as questions and problems dealing with the teaching-learning processes involving movement. These are realized in different forms of social reality called sport, including the conscious treatment of this reality.

On the basis of the discussion of models of general didactics, influenced especially by Blankertz (21), the six factors of the learning theory–didactic

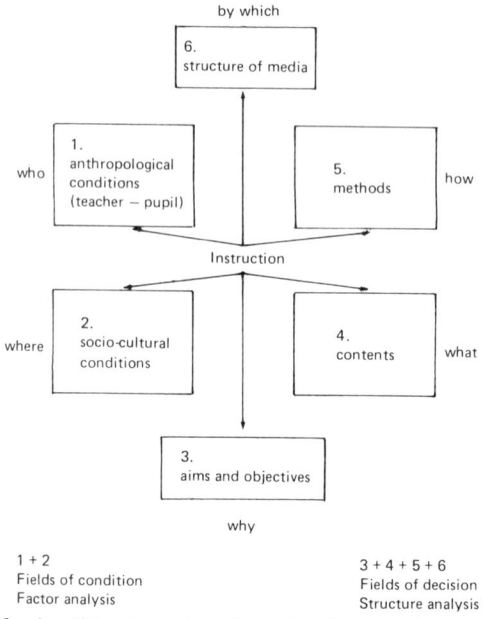

Figure 5. Concept for describing the content dimension of sport pedagogy.

model (22) are useful categories for the description of the content of sport pedagogy:
1. Anthropological conditions (teacher - pupil)
2. Socio-cultural conditions
3. Aims and objectives
4. Contents
5. Methods
6. Media

The didactic models of educational theory (23) and of information theory (24) are also mentioned, particularly by Blankertz. They are part of the learning theory model, and therefore can be used for a more precise content description of sport pedagogy (aspects of educational theory are relevant, especially for points 3 and 4, aspects of information theory are especially applicable to points 5 and 6). Such models have to be viewed with caution; nevertheless, they seem to give criteria by which a discussion on the scientific preconditions of, and on the nature of, sport pedagogy can be pursued with regard to the content dimension of this scientific theoretical field. With this model one can determine all those factors that constitute the teaching-learning processes within and outside sport instruction. One has to see teaching-learning processes within and outside school. Thus, the aspects of sport pedagogy beyond sport instruction in school are acknowledged.

The starting point was the hypothesis that the foundation of the scientific character of a discipline like sport science is dependent on the dimensions of content and research methods.

This chapter attempts to define the content of one theoretical field of sport science, sport pedagogy. Within the dimension of research methods one can distinguish between basic research methods (e.g., experiment), techniques of data collection (e.g., interview), and techniques of data treatment (e.g., statistics). In this regard only small differences can be found among the scientific disciplines. Within the techniques of data collection, certain specific aspects have to be regarded as dependent on the scientific discipline. Beyond this, one can assume that the dimension of research methods is similar within all scientific disciplines.

REFERENCES

1. Compare: Kurz, D. 1973. Sportpädagogik, Sportdidaktik, Theorie des Sportcurriculum. (Sport pedagogy, sport didactics, theory of sport curriculum.) In: E. Jost (ed.) Sportcurriculum. Entwürfe, Aspekte, Argumente, pp. 117–125. Karl Hofmann, Druckerei und Verlag, Schorndorf; Begov, F. and Kurz, D. 1972. Sportpädagogik in Westeuropäischen Ländern. (Sport pedagogy in the states of Western Europe.) In: H. Baitsch et al. (eds.), Sport im blickpunkt der Wissenschaften, (Sport from the Standpoint of Sciences.) pp. 141–151.

Springer, Berlin, Heidelberg, New York; Haag, H. 1972. Sportpädagogik in den Vereinigten Staaten. (Sport pedagogy in the USA.) In: H. Baitsch *et al.* (eds.), Sport im Blickpunkt der Wissenschaften. (Sport from the Standpoint of Sciences.) pp. 173–180. Springer, Berlin, Heidelberg, New York; Widmer, K. 1973. Zur methodologischen Problematik der Sportpädagogik als Theorie. (The methologically problematic nature of physical education as theory.) *Int. J. Phys. Ed.* 1:28–35.
2. Mester, L. 1973. Wechselbeziehungen zwischen Sportpädagogik und Erziehungswissenschaft. (The correlations between sport pedagogy and the science of education.) Int. J. Phys. Ed. 1:15–20.
3. Willimczik, K. 1968. Wissenschaftstheoretische Aspekte einer Sportwissenschaft. (Aspects of the Scientific Theory of Sport Science.) Wilhelm Limpert-Verlag, Frankfurt.
4. Widmer, K. 1974. Sportpädagogik. Prolegomena zur theoretischen Begründung der Sportpädagogik als Wissenschaft. (Sport Pedagogy. Prologue for the Theoretical Foundation of Sport Pedagogy as Science.) Karl Hofmann, Druckerei und Verlag, Schorndorf.
5. Ibid., p. 16.
6. Ibid., p. 32.
7. Ibid., p. 18ff.
8. Ibid., p. 22ff.
9. Röhrs, H. 1970. Allgemeine Erziehungswissenschaft. (General Educational Science.) Julius Belz OHG., Weinheim.
10. Kurz, (1973), pp. 117–125.
11. Schmitz, J.N. 1973. Fachdidaktik und Curriculumtheorie in der Sportwissenschaft. (Special didactics and curriculum theory in sport science.) *Sportwissenschaft* 3:251–276.
12. Röthig, P. (Red.) 1973. Sportwissenschaftliches Lexikon. (Sport Science Dictionary.) 2nd Ed., p. 238. Karl Hofmann Druckerei und Verlag, Schrondorf.
13. Schmitz (1973), p. 274.
14. Schwidtmann, H. 1972. Sportpädagogik (Sport pedagogy.) *Theorie und Praxis der Körperkultur.* Beiheft 3:25–31.
15. Ibid., p. 25.
16. Ibid., p. 26.
17. Haag (1972), p. 174.
18. Singer, R., Lamb, D.R., Loy, J.W., Malina, R.M., and Kleinman, S. 1972. Physical Education. An Interdisciplinary Approach. The Macmillan Company, New York.
19. Bucher, C.A. 1968. Foundations of Physical Education. 5th Ed. C.V. Mosby Co. St. Louis.
20. Compare the interesting discussion in: Quest IX. The nature of a discipline. Tucson, 1967; further literature see Haag (1972), p. 198 ff.
21. Blankertz, H. 1969. Theorien und Modelle der Didaktik. (Theories and Models of Didactics.) Juventa-Verlag GmbH., München.
22. Schulz, W. 1968. Grundzüge der Unterrichtsanalyse. (Fundamentals of the Analysis of Instruction.) In: G. Dohmen and F. Maurer (eds.), Unterricht. Aufbau und Kritik, pp. 57–63. R. Piper & Co. KG., München.
23. Klafki, W. 1967. Studien zur Bildungstheorie und Didaktik. (Studies Concerning Educational Theory and Didactics.) Julius Belz OHG., Weinheim.
24. Compare: Cube, F.v. 1968. Kybernetische Grundlagen des Lernens und Lehrens. (Cybernetic Foundations of Learning and Teaching.) Ernst Klett OHG., Stuttgart.

Scientific Research Methods in Sport Pedagogy

The Methodological Problem of Physical Education as Theory

K. Widmer

Today the two methodological tendencies, the hermeneutic-phenomenological and the empirical, are completely separated from one another. This is shown particularly clearly by the many anthologies which have been published in recent years (e.g., those from Klöhn, Plessner, Groll and Tscherne, Grupe) as well as reports from various congresses and meetings, e.g., that from Recla (1). In these anthologies articles representing both tendencies stand next to one another without any internal connection. The question may be asked why physical education, which is seeking to become a science, does not have to deal with fundamental methodological problems. In other words, should meta-theoretical considerations not also be counted as requirements for a scientific study of physical education? We find such considerations to be necessary.

HERMENEUTIC-PHENOMENOLOGICAL AND EMPIRICAL METHODS

The science of sports increasingly asserts itself in theory and practice, not the least stimulated by physical education work. It may be said that a scientific study of physical education exists. The science is, however, primarily based on the personal questioning and interests of the researcher and on the more or less reflected preliminary methodological decisions that he makes. An interesting task would be to attempt to integrate different types of sciences. In this sense, the following examples are to be understood as mere attempts. It is especially important to define the fundamental question as to whether empirically gathered data or the recognition of a hermeneutically achieved philosophical anthropology should form the bases of physical education theories.

Reprinted by permission from: Widmer, K. 1973. The methodologically problematic nature of physical education as theory. *International Journal of Physical Education,* 1: 21-27, 35.

HERMENEUTIC-PHENOMENOLOGICAL METHODS

Hermeneutic thinking is "the exposition of texts using knowledge gained from already understood texts. It leads to new processes of acquiring knowledge built upon other processes which have already been completed; it is a stage of socialisation, attached to the socialisation that has already taken place, in that it adjusts itself to tradition while at the same time continuing that tradition" (2). The hermeneutic approach attempts to understand the reality of education as it has developed and, on the bases of this understanding, to explain the purpose and structure of pedagogical activity. Norms and rules for behaviour, to which validity is attributed in the logical substantiation, are to be derived from this exposition. In coordination with anthropological findings, the hermeneutic approach has a legitimate role in physical education in the clarification of its task in general education, in the setting of educational goals, in the clarification of the social relevance of physical education, in the exposition of the purpose of the educational conceptions of physical education, and in the analyses of the institution of "physical education" in terms of its historical development. The primary theory-free phenomenological description of the significant general features and of the appropriate specific features of a physical education problem provides assistance for this task.

The danger of one-sidedness of the hermeneutic-phenomenological approach to physical education problems lies in the fact that absolute goals, postulates, and axioms are often set as unalterable standards for research and practice. A danger also results from the tendency to give final declarations of purpose, from which demands are set that can often scarcely be fulfilled. It is questionable whether physical education has not supported itself for too long on idealistic conceptions and has not lost much credit for itself through promises, which were neither empirically provable nor logically reasonable and testable. An example of this is the decade-long maintained claim about the transfer of ethical behaviour in sports to other areas of life. Ideological attitudes and expectations have often been taken over and mixed or even exchanged with exact knowledge.

Empirical-Positivistic Methods

A general trend in scientific thinking can be recognized away from the formulation of hermeneutic-anthropological questions toward the formulation of empirical-positivistic ones. This trend is also apparent in physical education. It can be seen in the changes of the development, the shifts of interest, and the altered value assessments of the individual types of sports by young people, as well as in certain overevaluations of physical education as necessary and justified. The empirical theorists try to question the reality of physical education in terms of causes and regularities, in order to gain testable perspectives on experience, or in order to come up with empirical theories. Educational reality should be made objective through empirical-analytical methods. Empirical physical education, then, seeks not to set norms but to clarify them, as well as to determine subject matter and gain certain data. At the center stands the method of collecting and processing data. Accordingly, hypotheses should be tested and when necessary corrected. This empirical method gathers the necessary data with the help of methods validated by the social sciences, methods such as observation, interviews, group discussions, subject matter analyses, individual case studies, and sociometry, etc. In kinematics, on the other hand, it makes use of methods from the natural sciences such as physics, biomechanics, photometrie, etc. Bockelmann distinguishes between two types of empirical researchers in the science of education: 1. the researcher primarily concerned with empirical methods, who begins with observation and reaches inductively valid conclusions, and 2. the empirical theorist, who sets hypotheses which must be empirically tested.

In the field of physical education, the justification and necessity of empirical thinking can be seen in the questions about motor learning processes, motivation, and transfer; in the clarification of attitudes and behavior; in the consideration of the psychological and physical abilities involved in activities in sport; in the problems of socialisation; in the evaluation of the educational concepts of physical education; in the diagnosis of attitudes; in the consideration of the role of environmental influences in relation to behavior in sport; and, especially, in the general curriculum discussion.

It is appropriate here to point out the limits and possible dangers of empirical thinking in physical education. Empirical assertions have a relative value, because they usually only record a particular area (a micro-structure). The danger of undue generalization is also not to be overlooked, because, occasionally, statistical probability is too little tested, and the irrelevant "cases" are left unconsidered, cases which may be educationally particularly interesting. In the survey of reliable data it is often an open question whether subjective or empirically untestable experiences are incorporated in the interpretation. The critical testing of the explanation and interpretation phase is often too short.

The Necessity of a Theory Complex for Physical Education

It is clear from the specified dangers and limits of the two methodological approaches that they may not be uncritically accepted. In any case, they may not be used as alibis to play down the fact that all scientific findings have a validity which is epochal and subject to time. It is also questionable whether, in an empirical science of education, a strict separation between education which works according to empirically analytical conditions (Brezinka) and nonscientific educational theory can be carried through; for, in pedagogical thinking, normative examples and factual reality are unalterably bound to one another.

The concept of experience may not be limited to empirically exact statements. If this were done, many pedagogically relevant problems, for which exact empirical analysis are largely impossible, would have to be excluded from the pedagogical theoretical discussion. An example of this unempirical material would be Freud's handling of sport competition, involvement, and responsibility. On the other hand, pedagogical thinking may not conceive of its role as only the clarification of purposes, nor as the analysis of the given educational facts and conditions in terms of their historical development, nor as the setting of norms which attempts to remove itself from the necessity of verification. We see two possibilities for the relationship between the hermeneutical and empirical approaches.

Clarification of the Appropriate Area of Research for Each Method It will always be necessary to determine which area of research is to be studied with which of the two methods. In macro-structural problems, e.g., in the questions about educational conceptions or about the educational goals of physical education, the hermeneutical methods have their place. However, researchers using this approach will always have to be ready to have their results subjected to empirical evaluation and, if necessary, to correct and modify them. The empirical methods have their unalterable place in the micro-structural problems. Researchers here must be ready to consider particularly carefully those critical points in the research process in which the work necessarily goes beyond pure empiricism. For example, in the setting of hypotheses, they must study the literature of previous research in the field as well as its explanation and interpretation. It is important that each research method employed be named and substantiated in relation to the object of the research. As a result, rather than a monism of methods in the scientific study of physical education, there is a pluralism in which the methodological approaches do not deny or ridicule one another, but in which the basic relation between object and method is clearly substantiated and maintained.

In this sense, the hermeneutical and empirical approaches are not inimical to one another but operate as partners, each caring for its limited area of effectiveness.

Integration of the Methodological Approaches in a Theory Complex There are many issues under discussion in the dispute between the empirical and hermeneutic approaches in modern education as well as in physical education. Among these issues are the function of the pre-scientific understandings of education and experience, the relation between testable statements of fact and interpretative statements of value, the question about a generally valid language for science, and the question concerning the breadth and time limits of a theory's validity. The issue must also be raised whether it is possible to find an integration in the sense of a normative physical education thinking that is also capable of working under testable conditions. We have already seen that goals may be hermeneutically determined on the basis of their connection with an anthropological explanation of human existence and that empirical investigations may, within the framework of defined problems, achieve exact statements and prognoses for similar behaviour under the same conditions. Because of this, the two methodological approaches can and must be coordinated with one another, and their place in defined stages of the research process must be maintained. Pedagogical factual research takes for granted hermeneutically achieved prerequisites when the problem statement must be modified or the meaning of a pedagogical problem or the conception of education must be given. The interpretation of data requires certain criteria for the effective carrying out of its function, criteria which cannot be derived from the data itself. So we find hermeneutical thinking at the beginning of empirical research, in the final phases of interpretation, and in the attempt to make the findings useful for the practice of education. And vice versa, hermeneutically achieved concepts of education and goals require empirical correction and evaluation, if they do not want to move as promising theories in a utopian vacuum in constant and unsolvable conflict with the realities of education.

Here, we believe that a theory complex can provide some help. Leinfellner speaks of three basic philosophical positions for gaining knowledge: from rationalism, which sets up an axiomatic science; from empiricism, which reduces all conceptually theoretical assertions to empirical ones to be tested by experience; and from pragmatism, which places all knowledge in relation to men. A theory complex consists of the union of rational, empirical, and pragmatic thinking. "Modern science and epistemology require all three basic philosophical attitudes" (3). A theory complex signifies that "only systematically related constructs of concepts which may be operationally and strategically substantiated have any value for science and knowledge" (4). We do not intent to use this principle in the strict sense that Leinfellner does, when he calls for a transposition of all assertions into a meta-theoretical formal speech in "modified empiricism." Instead, we use it in the broadest sense of a possible integration of methodological approaches as far as that is feasible for a scientific study of physical education (5).

SCIENTIFIC DEMANDS ON PHYSICAL EDUCATION ASSERTIONS

Leinfellner understands a theory as "a strictly logical and coherent system of principles, that is valid for a specific area D." The basic area D of physical education is the educational reality of sports (6). It consists of both the sociological-social and the psychological-biological relevance of sport activity for young people. Learning and behaviour goals are derived from reflection on this educational reality. They contain primarily the improvement of physical performance in sports with reference to all the involved psychological variables such as cognitive, emotional, and motivational factors, attitudes, and behaviour. The function of experience and the social function of sport activities are also included in the learning goals. In the following didactic and organizational reflections, learning goals are transferred into instructions for behaviour for all persons and institutions participating in sports for young people. After the concrete execution of a project influenced by the preliminary reflection process, follows of necessity the critical reconsideration of the way of behaviour, of the success or failure of the efforts. From this reconsideration clearly results the confirmation or correction of the goals or behavioural instructions. A scientific study of physical education seeks to combine the knowledge that it and other sciences have gained about the educational reality of sports into a system of correct conclusions. It is a branch of the science of education which tests physical education problems in the field of sport activity with modified problem formulations and a defined methodology. The scientific study of physical education takes the problem formulation and methodology from educational science and makes use of them in the field of youthful athletic activity. By way of definition, one could say that a study of physical education based on educational science seeks to make logically or empirically testable assertions about physical education behaviour and to organize these statements to a system of connected scientific findings. The scientific study of physical education will, therefore, analyse, describe, and explain the educational reality of sports, so that forecasts can be made, as far as the conditions remain the same or at least similar (7).

To Which Conditions Must Physical Education Theories and Statements Correspond?

Newer efforts are directed toward providing meta-theoretical criteria as substantiation for scientific educational assertions. In other words, the attempt is made to subject theories and methods to general scientifically theoretic and epistemologically theoretic conditions (8). According to Leinfellner, knowledge means the symbolic representation, i.e., the representation in colloquial and formal language, of a segment of the world. "Scientific knowledge is present everywhere where the objects, characteristics and relations to be represented are derived from the basic area D (e.g., observations and/or their measurement) in connected sentences, respectively systems of sentences and sequences of sentences, comprising theoretical terms" (9). The starting points for pedagogical theory formation are the concrete problems of educational reality, which are described in modified problem formulations.

These problem formulations are then recast in theoretical constructs.

Theoretical constructs are the assumptions about the functional correlations of reality, which are further formulated as hypotheses. Hypotheses are the assumed principles which contain defined problem formulations. These assumptions are developed into theories through observation, description, clarification, and interpretation. Without an expressed connection to theory purely descriptive data is not yet the same as scientific results. Theories are developed formally from valid evidence about conditions and connections of a defined pedagogical problem, whose hypotheses are logically and empirically tested. According to the positivistic perspective only that which is expressed in empirical elementary and protocol principles has scientific validity. Popper broadened this positivistic perspective in his critical rationalism; according to him, research begins with the first step of setting of hypotheses, which must be rationally tested and can be empirically falsified but never verified. In other words, the hypotheses may claim validity, so long as no new empirical data contradicts them. The subjection of all theories to time results from this perspective.

The Criterion of Intersubjective Testability

The deciding criterion for theories and hypotheses is to fulfill intersubjective testability. "If a theory can be qualitatively and quantitatively confirmed by experience, then it fulfills operative criteria. If it can be proved that a completed theory is free from contradiction, then the theory fulfills the operational criteria" (10). In the study of physical education, especially the empirically achieved theoretical conclusions must be subjected to logical testing; while the hermeneutical-anthropological conclusions must undergo empirical testing in the sense of the operative criteria.

A further criterion in newer scientific theory is usefulness. It implies that theories must show some practical connection. This does not mean that unalterable behavioural instructions can be derived from every theory, but that a theory is objectively informative about a defined set of problems (11).

PARADIGM FOR THE DEVELOPMENT OF A RESEARCH PROJECT IN PHYSICAL EDUCATION

We are of the opinion that an integration of the various methodological approaches within a physical education theory complex is possible and necessary on the basis of valid analyses of theory formation. This may be clarified with an example. We have chosen as a paradigm the question concerning the attitudes of sixteen-year-old high school students toward physical education instruction.

Problem and Problem Formulation

The point of departure is the concrete experience that the attitude toward physical education changes in different developmental phases, but that the learning involvement and success are motivationally dependent on that attitude. The likewise concrete pedagogical concern to gain influence over the students' attitudes results from this realization. This problem situation leads to the transcription of the problem formulation: What does attitude mean? Are the attitudes of a sixteen-year-old toward physical education dependent on his age or are they all individually determined? What do we know in general from developmental psychology about sixteen-year-old high school students? What do we know from experiments that have already been carried out about the attitude problems in this age group? When we answer these questions, what conclusions can we draw about the motivational responsibilities of the physical education teacher? The answers to these preliminary questions require a hermeneutic-phenomenological mode of thinking. The available literature is to be analysed according to hermeneutical standards, and there are preliminary decisions to be made, for example, which concept of "attitude" should be chosen as a basis. The choice may be in favour of the hermeneutic concept taken over from the literature, or "attitude" itself may be set up as a working hypotheses. Also, the question must be answered as to which results from the various aspects of developmental psychology should be taken as bases. Each of these preliminary decisions must be carefully made and substantiated. The success of this phase of research planning depends on the use of hermeneutic-phenomenological methods and attention to anthropological preliminary decisions.

Theoretical Construction and Hypotheses Formation

The significant factors affecting attitudes must next be discriminated, for example, the emotional involvement, the cognitive understanding, previous experiences of success and failure, developmentally specific and individual psychological status, as well as the environmental factors such as teacher-pupils relationships, the influence of group experiences and group pressures. In the theoretical construction, the functional correlation of these discriminated factors is sought out as an assumption and, from there, the hypotheses to be tested are derived. The following could be possible examples of such hypotheses:

—The attitude of sixteen-year-old high school students is dependent on individual development status, as well as on that status that is specific to age. It is also dependent on previous sports experiences, on the level of demand exercised on the student up until this time, and on the performance level of the student in general and in individual sport branches.

—The attitude is changeable and therefore may be influenced by personal encounter between teacher and student, by stimulated reflection on the significance of sport activity, and by learning success.

—The attitude toward physical education is also dependent on the personality of the teacher, particularly on his ability to motivate students, and on his didactic skill.

The creation of the theoretic construction and the derivation of hypotheses require an inclusive, hermeneutically handled study of literature and an hermeneutic interpretation of psychological insights.

Preliminary Methodological Decision

There are preliminary methodological decisions to be made which are not only empirically substantiated, but which are based on the capacities of the research project and the interest of the researcher. We are thinking about the preliminary decisions concerning the methods to be used: for example, the methods of interviewing the students, methods of attitude research, the inclusions of grade comparison, analyses of instruction by physical education teachers, the choice of the classes in which the experiment is to be carried out, interviews of physical education teachers about their more or less reflected behaviour in terms of influencing the attitudes of their students, etc. When the methodological decisions are primarily based on the recognition of the claims for validity of the individual empirical methods, decisions and methodologically normative evaluations must be completed for the abundance of possibilities. The complexity of our example makes a preliminary decision necessary on methodological grounds, namely, to choose some or perhaps only one factor to be separated from the others and tested alone. A choice might be the significance of the previous level of sport success on the attitude or the effect of the group, or the influence of the didactic skill of the physical education teacher. This issue also concerns preliminary decisions which grow either out of the methodological possibilities or the specific interests of the researcher.

The Collection and Presentation of Data

With the exception of the question of representation (i.e., a selection of test participants), the empirical work in a more narrow sense begins with the collection and presentation of data. The collection of data takes place in the implementation of the experiment with the help of operative observation and measurement. This implementation must be organizationally planned in all details, a process that usually requires much work and time. Among the tasks here may be: concerns about maintaining constant test conditions, schedule, training of interviewers, instruction of co-workers, etc. In the presentation of the data, the results of the experiment dealing with the chosen factors are described and, finally, analytical evaluations are completed.

Interpretation and Theory Formation

The first step in the interpretation is the transposition of the measurement and observation data, i.e., the transposition of the statements expressed in characteristics of probability theory into assertions in scientific language. This transposition demands more than purely empirical thinking. The problem of the relationship between the statement and the implied reality, a central problem of scientific logic and semantics, is also involved here and must be reflected. Descriptive speech forms must be found which represent clear assertions about the completed measurements and observations, as well as about the connections of characteristics and relations, because a sentence is only true when the implied content is also correct (Leinfellner). In the attempt of theory formation in the area of research it is important considering the semantic and linguistic premises to explain the concepts taken as working hypotheses and to theoretically define them anew. The final step is to achieve a logical structural picture from the conclusions of the interpretation. The empirical assertions of the interpretation about the significant effective factors of the attitude toward physical education are attached to one another and confronted with the assumptions in the theoretical construction. In this way it becomes clear whether the assumed factors really exist and in what way. In other words, the assertions about the actually discovered effective factors and their interdependence result in a theory about the attitude of sixteen-year-old high school students toward physical education. The structure of the valid assertions is expressed either logically and deductively or according to probability theory (the measure of validity under these or those conditions). Such a theory about the attitude of high school students could prove, for example, that the experience of learning success has more effect on the attitude than the motivational influence of the physical education teacher, or that cognitive insight into the significance of sport activity affects the attitude only under defined conditions, or that group experiences and group pressures contribute only a little to the attitude.

The Connection of the Theories to Practice

The necessity that a theory be connected to practice results in the following consideration: the usefulness of a theory is set up as the criterion for a good theory. Theories and hypotheses make forecasts possible which are valid for a representative sampling and are also valid for the entire population under identical or similar time and social conditions (with the exclusion of further effective factors or possible disturbances). After all, education always stands under the basic demand to attempt to influence a desired change in attitude or behaviour. As a result, it is right to ask the question as to the possible pedagogical consequences of an achieved theory. This connection of theory to practice, which is not based primarily on empirical working modes but on logical deduction in terms of pedagogical knowledge and experience, occurs first in the setting of goals. In our example, the connection to practice is based on the necessity of motivational influence on the attitude, as far as the theory has proven that this influence really exists. From there, possible behavioural instructions may be deductively derived. When the analysis of effective factors and their interrelation has been presented, then the question of possible pedagogical influence may be raised, for example: How does a possible influencing of cognitive attitude or of emotional involvement occur? How can the level of performance demand be raised? How can negative group pressures be compensated for? All of these issues may be dealt with under the condition that the theory of attitude has clearly proven such effective factors and their interplay.

Such deductions occur on the basis of a logical and pedagogical if-then relationship. Because all of the variables in the complexity of the pedagogical reality can never be covered, these deductions may not be declared to be infinitive norms and pedagogical postulates. They should, at most, be understood as clues, as chosen instructions for pedagogical behaviour. Behavioural instructions are values which include anthropological and general education experience. In these instructions, values are completed even when they have logically already been substantiated, i.e., values in which preferential decisions have been made.

Evaluation and Correction of the Theory

Every theory must be subjected to evaluation. This may occur empirically, in that the same experiment is carried out one or several more times in other groups, or in that the findings are fundamentally falsified by another theoretical hypothesis. However, in a pedagogical evaluation, it is most important to test the outlined connection of the theory to practice. The basic question must be asked, whether a pedagogical theory can be tested at all, with the exception of the repetition of the experiment, when the theory expresses no behavioural instruction. The effectiveness of these pedagogical behavioural instructions should be checked. A pedagogical evaluation would, in our case, imply that a possible change in attitude could be determined through tests on the basis of the behavioural instructions. The following questions result from this: Can the suggested theory of the attitude toward physical education be maintained as legitimate, or must it be corrected or criticised? do the derived behavioural instructions have to be changed in order to maintain the theory? (If the theory is not false, have we presented it falsely or should we test it differently?)

The following may be said in summary: Theories, as results of the research process, must be value-free and non-normative. However, in the research process there are always places and situations which require the inclusion of the hermeneutic-anthropological mode of thinking beside the empirical mode. The former is especially to be included where values and decisions must be made: in the discovery and formulation of a problem, in the creation of a theoretical construction, in the interpretation of the data, in the connection of the theory to practice, and in the individual phases of the pedagogical evaluation.

Therefore it is important to indicate the scientific theoretical prerequisites. They must be pointed out and substantiated as working hypotheses and bases for scientific discussion and scientific communication, just as the theoretical description of the key concepts. One individual scientific and theoretic standpoint, such as that of critical rationalism or of a hermeneutical-anthropological normative methodology, should not be made absolute. The intolerance that grows out of absolutes and rejects all further conclusions as pseudo-objective or unscientific is unacceptable for research.

REFERENCES

1. Examples: Klöhn, G. (ed.) 1963. Leibeserziehung und Sport. (Physical Education and Sport.) Julius Belz OHG., Weinheim; Plessner, H., H.-E. Bock, and O. Grupe (eds.) 1967. Sport und Leibeserziehung. (Sport and Physical Education.) Piper, München; Groll, H., and F. Tscherne (eds.) 1964. Ideen und Gestalt der Leibeserziehung von heute. (Idea and Form of Physical Education Today.) Osterreichischer Bundesverlag, Graz.
2. Habermas, J. 1967. Zur Logik der Sozialwissenschaften. (Concerning the logic of social science.) p. 159. Suhrkamp, Verlag KG., Frankfurt.
3. Leinfellner, W. 1965. Einführung in die Erkenntnis- und Wissenschaftstheorie. (Introduction to the Theory of Knowing and Science.) p. 22. Bibliographisches Institut, Mannheim.
4. Ibid., p. 20.
5. Bokelmann, H. 1969. Pädagogik, Erziehung, Erziehungswissenschaft. (Pedagogy, education, educational science.) In: Handbuch pädagogischer Grundbegriffe. Bd. 2, p. 255. Kösel-Verlag, München.
6. Leinfellner (1965), p. 20.
7. Brezinka, W. 1971. Von der Pädagogik zur Erziehungswissenschaft. (From Pedagogy to Educational Science.) Julius Belz OHG., Weinheim.
8. Bokelmann (1969), p. 255.
9. Leinfellner (1965), p. 13.
10. Ibid.
11. Brezinka (1971), p. 34.

Considerations of the Scientific Character of Sport Pedagogy

St. Grössing

THEORY OF PHYSICAL EDUCATION AS A SCIENCE

Groll's (1957) position on scientific theory will only be covered briefly here as far as is necessary in order to distinguish his position from my own position on the scientific character of sport pedagogy. We both consider this discipline (theory of physical education, or sport pedagogy) a part of education, a specific science within a traditional basic science. I have learned Groll's position through various articles, lectures, seminars, papers, and symposia, and by direct discussion with him. His position is based on the tradition of German *Hermeneutik*. The *geisteswissenschafliche Pädogogik* (Nohl, Spranger, Litt, Bollnow, et al.), as well as an existentialism oriented towards religious philosophy (Marcel, Gabriel, and Guardini) provided the basic principles for his theoretical position.

The theory of physical education is a relatively independent discipline within education because of its research objectives, its specific questions, and its methods. The subject field is "the cultural phenomenon and social problem of physical activity with its many relationships to the education field" (Groll, 1962, p. 77). The problems of this field include the definition of the nature of physical activity, the investigation of its historical development, its biological and biomechanical foundations, its theoretical system, and the applied art of exercising. With regard to methodology, Groll opted for a multiple application of research methods taken from the natural sciences and from the humanities, because physical education is a cross between these disciplines. The development of a system was viewed as a unique problem area (this was attributable to the influence of Gaulhofer) that was not comparable to any other science.

Reprinted by permission from: Grössing, St. 1976. Überlegungen zum Wissenschaftscharakter der Sportpädagogik. In: H. Andrecs and S. Redl (Hrsgs.), *Forschen - Lehren - Handeln*, pp. 13–22. Österreichischer Bundesverlag für Unterricht, Wissenschaft und Kunst, Wien.

The scientific endeavors of Groll indicated physical education had a theoretical basis in the *Hermeneutik,* which has become a basic point of view for the educational thinking of this century. Until the mid-1960s all concepts of a scientifically justified theory of physical education remained within the framework provided by this basic scientific viewpoint. In the years from 1928 to 1936, the theme of the scientific character of physical education was dealt with in the literature in a very modest way (Recla, 1960, has named 13 titles). During this time the system of school gymnastics of Karl Gaulhofer was one of the most prominent programs. After the Second World War, a discussion of the scientific character of physical education started once again. Grell, Zeuner, Fetz, Vopel, Recla, Grupe, and Groll were principal leaders of this period. The clarification of scientific theory in physical education was related to the intentions of scientific politics. It was intended that full academic acknowledgment should be given by the university to physical education as a part of the discipline of education. This movement met with strong resistance from the so-called established sciences. Groll, Fetz and Recla struggled with this opposition in Austria. The academic work of Groll is adequate testimony to the difficulties of this plan. Besides creating full professorships at German and Austrian universities, the leadership of sport science has done the following during this period in order to define the scientific theory of physical education:

1. The position of physical education as a science within the other disciplines was defined, and most of the authors included the new science within educational science.
2. The subject field of the new science was clarified, even if it was not defined in a unique and complete way. For example, the statements include movement, the moving human being, and educational possibilities through physical exercise as parts of the field.
3. Aspects for research and problem areas were defined. As a result, the impression exists that the tasks of physical education teacher training were considered to a greater extent than the criteria of scientific development.
4. Research methods were not considered to a great extent, so that a so-called methodological vacuum seems to have been created in this area.

CONCEPT OF A CRITICAL-RATIONAL SPORT PEDAGOGY

By the end of the 1960s sport science theory had become more varied and differentiated. In addition to the term physical education, or movement education, the term *sport science* was often used. Dialectic and analytic thinking were included in discussion of the *hermeneutic* position. Today, all three classical European ways of thinking (Albert, 1972), hermeneutical, dialectical, and analytical, are used to clarify the scientific character of physical education or sport science. From the point of view of scientific theory, my position concerning the foundation of sport pedagogy could be called analytical. The term *critical-rational sport pedagogy* leads to Popper (1966, 1973), because his critical-rationalism is the basis for the given definition of the field of physical education, the definition of the problem area, and the methodology of sport pedagogy. The following considerations, however, are only a first attempt; they are not complete and systematic. This contribution is only the first outline for a larger investigation.

SCIENTIFIC THEORY

Sport pedagogy is seen as part of the discipline of educational science on the basis of the analytical-empirical interpretation of science. Sport as an educational means is its subject; therefore, sport instruction stands in the center. Instruction, however, is not the complete subject field of sport pedagogy; but it is a central thrust, and a problem area with great deficiencies with regard to research. Sport pedagogy, therefore, is considered mainly as a science of instruction.

It is not possible to present the scientific theory of Popper in detail, because it includes his ideas on the aim of analytical science, on the method of critical examination, on theory and reality, on falsification, on intersubjectivity, etc. This chapter deals with topics that were selected because of their close relationship to sport pedagogy as an analytical science.

Popper (1966, 1973) defines the task of science as determination of theories that are in fact true through the method of critical examination. The advancement of science (at least within the social sciences) is not reached by induction, i.e., the formation of general laws from singular observation data. Induction is now a useful method for examining the truth of theories of social science. Therefore, the real task of an analytical science is obvious. It is not so much the discovery of theories but their classification. Theories in certain subject areas (e.g., sport instruction) have different conditions and sources for their development. These include: (a) knowledge from people working in the practical field, which can be taken as primary ideas that have been written down (these are based on experience and intuition that is often gained from single cases and in specific situations); (b) text interpretation; (c) observation of results, which often come from accidental perception; (d) knowledge gained from scientific surveys utilizing systematic observation; and (e) questionnaires or experiments. None of these kinds of data for formulating theories guarantees that the theory is true. The degree of truth is exemplified by the degree of correspondence between theory and reality and can only be proven by justification, which is the task of science. Science is the investigation of theories as assumptions of reality, using scientific methods to test their value and their truthfulness (validity).

Nevertheless, it is doubtful that a clear division exists between the origins and the rationale for educational theories, which Brezinka (1971, p. 63 ff.) requires in accordance with the viewpoint of Popper, but such admission is necessary, and is equivalent to the essence of scientific work. Theories on the facts of education originate not only from intuition, practical experiences, and brave speculation, but also from investigations employing scientific methods. Science not only begins with examination of validity, but also integrates each of the original theories, thus providing rationale for these theories, and examines the validity as well as the aspects of the rationale that in turn contribute to the development of new theories.

How can the degree of truth of a theory be examined? Through the method of critical examination, a theory is exposed to experience. This means an attempt is made by scientific techniques to show that a theory is false according to the facts related to it. If a theory cannot be proven wrong, the theory is assumed to be valid, at least for a certain period of time. The major criteria for proving a theory false as outlined by Popper were contraindicated and later viewed differently by himself, but they were never discarded. Saying that the success of science only depends on the disproving of available theories or laws (hypotheses), makes a negative criterion (selection, proof of falseness) become the criterion for the development of science.

Ströker (1973) states that theories are seldom completely contradicted and abolished, but that normally theories are limited in their validity because they can only be partially refuted:

> In analytical-empirical science there is no intent to achieve developed theoretical concepts strictly and dogmatically by introducing experiences into this framework. In analytical-empirical science norms that have become critical are not discarded without any reason or by immediately abandoning these norms in favor of a newly developed theory; it does not accept the dictates of empirical data in order to discredit such theory without reason. (Ströker, 1973, p. 108).

This statement was made about natural sciences; however, it is also valid for social science. Theories in social science do not reach the same exactness of results as theories in natural science; therefore, the evaluation of their validity is even more difficult. As a result, it usually will not be possible to contradict an entire theory with just one empirical procedure. The result of such an examination can only place restrictions on the validity of a theory and indicate the contradiction of a single thesis. An alternative theory is then developed.

Theory II is distinguished from Theory I by its greater truth and by its greater approximation of reality. The new theory, however, cannot render Theory I false except in some cases. It is only more applicable in explaining part of the reality and in making statements of a prognostic nature.

There is no fixed methodological scheme for the examination of the realities of a theory. Disproving a theory is not done according to a fixed set of rules, but is accomplished through critical discussion by experts. Even Popper cannot name another method. Theories or parts of the theory (hypotheses) are not limited or refuted through empirical data, but through an alternative and competing theory. Theories or hypotheses (as part of theories) under a certain aspect or reality are examined if this phase of reality has become a problem. Science begins not with data, but with problems. This also has been stated very precisely by Popper (1966, 1973). From this foundation of scientific theory, inquiries in sport pedagogy can be derived that should be recognized if sport pedagogy understands itself as an empirical science oriented towards the social sciences. For the reality of sport instruction, many theories are available that are derived from different sources. The framework of an original theory does not provide any statements on the degree of truth. Several theories or hypotheses are available for a problem field and therefore there is an immediate impulse to examine their validity. As analytical-empirical science, sport pedagogy will examine the validity of such problem-oriented theories by using methods like observation, interview, or experiment.

SYSTEM OF SPORT PEDAGOGY

Every science develops a system for its subject areas and research aspects. The following system of sport pedagogy is similar to the categories developed for education science by Brezinka (1971), but his strong division between scientific and practical pedagogy is not used anymore.

Metatheory and Philosophy

Each science reflects its research subject, its methods, the kind of knowledge gained, etc. Themes of this nature, which comprise scientific theory, include: theory of acquiring knowledge, methodology, philosophy of education, and anthropology. Important detailed aspects are: (a) the problem of normal freedom of results from sport pedagogy, (b) norms, aims, and objectives of sport instruction, (c) anthropological foundations, including social and cultural questions, (d) the problem of body and soul, and (e) the definition of the nature of play.

All questions of scientific theory and methodology covered in this chapter belong to the problem area of sport pedagogy.

History of Sport Education

As problem and fact, the history of sport education is mainly concerned with physical education within school. The range of possible themes reaches from the idea of physical education in early cultures and classical Greek antiquity up to the present position of school sport. The background of cultural history and economy as well as the relationship to the educational aims and objectives of the respective periods would have to be presented.

Sport Didactics

The task and duty of sport didactics is to investigate scientifically all aspects that are relevant to teaching and learning in sport (description). Furthermore, the task is to transmit these aspects to the practical field (prescription).

This double function makes sport didactics a part of the scientific discipline of sport pedagogy as well as a technology. In its descriptive function instruction research is realized. The results and knowledge of the research are transformed into action recommendations for practical work. Because sport didactics also has to play the prescriptive role, it is very important that the basics for action are recommendations secured through scientific research. The themes of sport didactics include the following aspects: framework of condition (anthropological and social-cultural preconditions like development, motor behavior, motivation, performance ability, etc.) and all elements of sport instruction (learning goals, learning contents, teaching methods, media for teaching, interaction, forms for organization, evaluation, etc.).

Methodology

Each science is judged on its scientific performances, which depend on the status of its research methods. Therefore, methodology is a basic problem for every science. An empirically oriented sport pedagogy requires the methods of empirical research used in social sciences in order to examine the validity of its theories and hypotheses. Observation, interview, and experiment are the three most important empirical methods, which should be touched upon very briefly. Theories can be gained as well as examined by all three methods. This does not mean that other research methods are not thought to be scientific. Hermeneutic, dialectic, and phenomenological methods are also used by Röhrs (1968) for educational science, and can be used to develop theories and to formulate hypotheses. Sport pedagogy as an analytical-empirical science especially stresses the examination of hypotheses and therefore mainly utilizes the methods of empirical research employed in social science. The examination of the validity of theory is done by using observation, experiment, and oral or written questioning by presenting the content of each theory in the practical situation to which it is related. However, these research methods imply different problems in following this procedure. Observation, experiment, and questioning do not provide direct access to real educational situations. Each situation is seen by the observer in light of a given theory. Therefore, empirical research methods are not discovering realities, but theories concerning a certain reality are examined for their validity. The examination of the validity of theories by observation, experiment, and questioning results in other theories that have a higher degree of truth in comparison to the initial theories, because they have met the challenge of being exposed to reality. (This chapter does not consider the problems of scientific language, statistical questions, and the many possibilities for committing errors during data collection, data analysis, and data interpretation.)

Each empirical research method has its advantages and disadvantages, its specific questions and possible answers. The *written questionnaire* is an adequate instrument for investigations with large populations; however, one has to consider many restrictions using this procedure. There is often very little feedback when sending out questionnaires and the selection of the person answering the questionnaire presents a bias, since often only a certain type of person is willing to answer a questionnaire. If questionnaires are answered in closed groups (e.g., school classes), a cumulative effect can be observed. A single person answers on the basis of the group atmosphere, which results in similar answers from other individuals. The results of questioning single members of the group would probably deviate from the results obtained by the questioning of the entire group all together. The questionnaire normally is given to a subject not prepared for this procedure. Spontaneous answers are desired in some cases, but normally there are standardized answers. Anonymity is usually assured, which sometimes leads to wrong answers; some questions are often not answered because of laziness; closed questions influence the direction or the kind of thinking. Subjective aspects often interfere with questionnaire preparation because the researcher can easily introduce his opinions about the given topic. After he has answered the first few questions, the person answering the questionnaire develops certain expectations, which again change the result.

There are some problems with preparing the record of interviewing. The direct influence of the person giving the interview also influences the result.

Within pedagogy, as in sport pedagogy, each *experiment* is a trial with human beings. This is the most important restriction, or disadvantage, in using this scientific method. Each experiment needs comparison of an experimental and a control group. People, or groups of people, however, can only be compared to a certain degree, even if a very careful selection has taken place. Experiments within social science do not reach the degree of exactness of experiments within natural science; furthermore, the experiment seldom is carried out in the laboratory, but primarily in a field situation. This is especially true for pedagogical experiments in which many uncontrolled variables exist. The experiment as a research method within social science has various ways in which it may be employed. Some of the ways it can be used are as follows: (a) to formulate working hypotheses (pilot study), (b) to examine the validity of theories (verification experiment), (c) to establish a position on a certain problem if several hypotheses are available (position experiment), or (d) to present a hypothesis that has been examined already (demonstration experiment).

The method of *observation* is least utilized and developed in sport pedagogy. Systematic observation as scientific method is distinguished from observation in daily life through fixed observational criteria, which are related to the subject field and are defined exactly. For a complete description of this procedure, which is also differentiated to a great extent, the following forms should be mentioned: (a) free and standardized observation, and (b) participating and non-participating observation. A specific form of observation is the observation of instruction, which should become the central research method for sport pedagogy. Before dealing with the task and the difficulties of observation of instruction, some general problems of instructional observation should be indicated.

Each participating observation changes the situation to be observed. Original sport instruction is not observed, but rather what is observed is the sport instruction as it is changed by the observational situation. The behavior of the teacher and that of the pupil are changed by the presence of an observer. The normal situation of school life does not exist anymore.

Instruction is a very complex undertaking, and this complexity makes observation difficult—true perception is restricted, and observation of instruction can only deal with certain aspects of instruction. These aspects can only be perceived with the help of given characteristics and categories. In this way the freedom for observation is restricted to given details. These details, however, are evaluated with the required precision. The observation is fixed in a record. The analysis, usage, and evaluation of instructional records, however, are not easy. The requirements for testing both validity and reliability, as well as the training of the observers, have to be fulfilled.

The systematic observation of sport instruction often creates problems that surpass the usual framework of instructional observation. The instructional procedures are highly dynamic and exhibit a mobility of all participants that are different from those of other school subjects. Situations, actions, compositions of groups, and structures of organizations change very rapidly; many verbal and non-verbal behavior patterns of the pupils and the teacher can be observed; the use of equipment furthermore confuses the situation.

Even though difficulties and deficiencies have been mentioned for all three research methods, this does not mean that these methods cannot be used for sport pedagogy. On the contrary, these are the research methods most suitable for sport pedagogy and its tasks. It is important to improve the research methods of observation, questioning, and experiment by using these methods separately or in combinations. Furthermore, it is important to begin and to continue a discussion on scientific theory within sport science. The lack of discussion of scientific methodology is a great deficiency within sport pedagogy.

THEORY AND PRACTICE

It is astonishing that a science like sport pedagogy, depending as it does on practice, has not done more research to investigate the relationship between theory and practice. Because sport pedagogy is a scientific discipline of empirical nature, this relationship is a very important aspect. The problems come from the practical work in teaching and learning in sport, and, therefore, theories and hypotheses can be derived from these problems. They are then exposed to validation in the practical situation by using scientific methods in order to evaluate their degree of truth. As accepted theories, they change the reality of instruction in order that new problems can originate from these situations. The practice of sport instruction is the basis for theory formation. At the same time, it is the field for testing theories as well as for the application of theory.

REFERENCES

Albert, H. (Hrsg.) 1972. Theories und Realität. (Theory and reality.) Ausgewählte Aufsätze zur Wissenschaftstheorie der Sozialwissenschaften. Mohr, Tübingen.
Brezinka, W. 1971. Von der Pädagogik zur Erziehungswissenschaft. (From pedagogy to educational science.) Julius Belz OHG., Weinheim.
Fetz, Fr. 1961. Zum Wissenschaftscharakter der "Theorie der Leibeserzeihung" (Concerning the scientific character of the "theory of physical education.") Leibesübungen-Leibeserziehung 3:1.
Groll, H. 1957. Die Stellung der Wissenschaft der Leibeserziehung zu den Leibesübungen. (The position of the science of physical education towards physical exercises.) Wissenschaft und Weltbild. p. 281.
Groll, H. 1959. Vom Wissenschaftscharakter der Theorie der Leibesübungen. (Concerning the scientific character of the theory of physical exercises.) In: J. Recla (Hrsg.), Bibliographie und Dokumentation der Leibesübungen, p. 56. Selbstdruck, Graz.
Groll, H. 1961. Was ist der Forschungsgegenstand der Theorie der Leibeserzeihung. (What is the topic of research in the theory of physical education.) Leibesübungen-Leibeserziehung 3:23.
Groll, H. 1962. Möglichkeiten und Grenzen einer Wissenschaft der Leibeserziehung. (Possibilities and limitations of a science of physical education.) In: H. Groll (Hrsg.), Idee und Gestalt der Leibeserziehung heute, p. 73. Osterreichischer Bundesverlag, Wien.
Grupe, O. 1965. Über das Problem einer Wissenschaft oder wissenschaftlichen Theorie der Leibeserziehung. (Concerning the problem of a science or a scientific theory of physical education.) In: O. Grupe (Hrsg.), Studien zur pädagogisch Theorie der Leibeserziehung, p. 5. Karl Hofmann, Druckerei und Verlag, Schorndorf.

Landsheere, G. 1971. Einführung in die pädagogische Forschung. (Introduction to educational research.) Julius Belz OHG., Weinheim.
Popper, K. R., 1966. Logik der Forschung. (Logic of research.) Mohr, Tübingen.
Popper, K. R. 1973. Objektive Erkenntnis. Ein evolutionärer Entwurf. (Objective perception. An evolutionary design.) 2nd Edition, Hoffmann & Campe Verlag, Hamburg.
Recla, J. 1960. Wissenschaft der Leibesübungen. (Science of physical exercises.) Leibesübungen 11:3.
Röhrs, H. 1968. Forschungsmethoden in der Erziehungswissenschaft. (Research methods in educational science.) Verlag W. Kohlhammer, Stuttgart.
Ströker, E. 1973. Einführung in die Wissenschaftstheorie. (Introduction to scientific theory.) Dr. Dietrich Steinkopf, Darmstadt.
Widmer, K. 1974. Sportpädagogik, Prolegomena zur theoretischen Begründung der Sportpädagogik als Wissenschaft. (Sport pedagogy. Prolegomena concerning the theoretical foundation of sport pedagogy as science.) Karl Hofmann, Druckerei und Verlag, Schorndorf.
Willimczik, Kl. 1968. Wissenschaftstheoretische Aspekte der Sportwissenschaft. (Aspects of the scientific theory of sport science.) Wilhelm Limpert-Verlag, Frankfurt.

Research Concepts for Sport Pedagogy

Typology of Research Tasks Concerning School Physical Education and Definition of Priorities of Research in School Physical Education

H. Nupponen

TYPOLOGY OF RESEARCH TASKS CONCERNING SCHOOL PHYSICAL EDUCATION

The research tasks of school physical education may be based on the theories and methodology of several disciplines. The framework of the research into school physical education might thus be constructed in several ways. The list of research tasks presented in the following is only one way of viewing the research area. It is by nature a typological approach and is based mainly on educational considerations, since school physical education is regarded to be most closely connected with the educational institution. The starting points of the typology have been the organizational framework, special features, recent problems, and changes of school physical education, on the basis of which there has been drawn up a list of research tasks in school physical education, which was designed to be as exhaustive and systematic as possible.

The research tasks are classified according to three categories, which are:

1. OBJECTS OF RESEARCH
2. TIME
3. LEVEL OF APPLICATION

The classification according to *objects of research* indicates the part of the *organizational framework* that research is aimed at. The main parts of the

---

Reprinted by permission from: Nupponen, H. 1976. Plan for a program of research on school physical education in Finland in 1975–1979. In: *Reports on Physical Culture and Health 14*. Jyväskylä, Finland. (Pages 17–34 reprinted here.)

organizational framework are (a) the social framework of school physical education, and (b) the internal framework of school physical education. The former includes research tasks, which examine the *functions* of school physical education. The functions of school physical education have been divided into valuation functions and factual functions. Valuation functions concern the position and tasks of school physical education in different institutions, at different levels of administration, at different levels of education, in school and in the development of pupils' personalities. Factual functions refer to the real significance of school physical education for different institutions and for the pupils' personality development as well as to its effects on the development of social relationships within schools, and on the pupils' physical, mental and social development.

The research tasks derived from the internal framework of school physical education concern *objectives, planning, implementation and evaluation*. Studies on objectives deal with the setting, specification and review of objectives. Studies on planning focus on curricula and the planning practices. Implementation studies take up teaching contents, arrangements, process and products. Evaluation studies may deal with the methods of collecting data, the use of evaluation data and marking.

It should be noted that research topics need not always comply with the above classification. They may be selected along the horizontal dimension of the typology and from various points of the typology. Thus it is possible, for instance, to select some objective of school physical education as the research topic and to follow all stages in its attainment: specification of the objective, planning of teaching, teaching process and evaluation of the attainment of the objective.

Time classification means the grouping of research tasks so that we study the earlier development, present state and the reasons for the present state of the research object, the need for change as well as the means and preconditions of change. Research proceeds from a historical to a futurological examination of the research topic. More specifically, we seek answers to the following questions:

1. What has happened in school physical education to date
2. What is the present situation
3. Why is the situation such as it is; should it be changed
4. How can the situation be changed, if necessary
5. What are the prerequisites for changing the situation.

When these questions are examined by object of research we obtain the general research tasks (Table 1).

The general research tasks can be specified by applying the *level of application* classification, i.e. by dividing the research tasks according to institutions connected with school physical education, region, level of admin-

Table 1. Research tasks concerning school physical education

Objects of research	Time					Level of application					
	Earlier development	Present state and comparisons	Reasons for present state, need for change	Means of change	Prerequisites of change	Collective Institution	Level of Administration	Level of education	School community		Individual
1. Functions of school physical education											Individual
1.1. Valuation functions	Development of position and tasks	Position and tasks today	Factors which have influenced present state Need for changing tasks	Means of improving present situation	Prerequisition of improving present situation Possibilities of changing present situation	In education in physical culture, during leisure in health care	at national level, at municipal level	in/pre-school/ primary/ secondary/ teacher education →	in school community in developing social relations between pupils		In pupils' personality devel.
1.2 Factual functions	Change of position	Position today				in education in physical culture, in work & production, in leisure activities					in pupils' personality devel.
		Effects	Reasons for effects observed						on devel. of social relations in class		on pupils' physical mental and social devel. and health
2. Objectives											
2.1. Setting of objectives	History of definition of objects	Structure of prevailing objectives	Factors affecting the definition of prevailing objectives			with the objectives of education, physical culture, and health care	at national level	in different countries	at school level at class level		
		Comparison of P.E. objectives							with the objectives of different groups within school community		with teacher's and pupils' other objectives
2.2. Revision of objectives			Need for revising objectives	Means of revising objectives	Prerequisites of revision of objectives		at national level				
2.3. Specification of objectives		Generality/ specificity of prevailing objectives	Need for specifying objectives	Taxonomies of objectives	Prerequisites of constructing taxonomies of objectives		at national level at municipal level		at school level at class level		at individual level

(continued)

Table 1. Continued

Objects of research	Time					Level of application				
	Earlier development	Present state and comparisons	Reasons for present state, need for change	Means of change	Prerequisites of change	Collective Institution	Level of Administration	Level of education	School community	Individual
3. Planning										
3.1. Curricula	Comparison of earlier P.E. curricula	Prevailing curricula Comparison of prevailing P.E. curricula	Factors which have affected curricula, need for change	Means of changing prevailing curricula	Prerequisites of changing prevailing curricula	with general curricula	at national level at municipal level			
3.2. Use of planning	Use of planning to date	Present objects of planning Comparison of planning in P.E.	Reasons for present state of planning	Means of making planning more effective	Possibilities of making planning more effective	with educational planning with planning of health care	at national level at municipal level		at school level at class level	by teacher by pupil by teacher and pupil
4. Implementation										
4.1. Teaching contents	Use of various teaching contents to date	Use and weighting of contents at present	Reasons for prevailing weighting of contents Need for changing teaching contents	Improving congruence between objectives and contents Taxonomies of teaching contents	Prerequisites of selecting and using different teaching contents		in national curricula in local curricula		at school level at class level	
4.2. Teaching procedures	Use of various teaching procedures to date	Weighting of teaching procedures at present Comparison of teaching procedures in P.E.	Reasons for present weighting of teaching procedures Need for revision of weighting	Improving congruence between objectives and teaching procedures	Prerequisites of selecting and using different teaching procedures	with teaching procedures recommended in general education			in teaching group	

4.3. Teaching-learning process	Development of teaching-learning process to date	Basic elements of teaching-learning process Comparison of teaching-learning processes in P.E.	Factors influencing teaching-learning process Need for changing teaching-learning process	Significance of goal-orientation in teaching-learning process	Prerequisites of changing teaching-learning process	with general educational process	in teaching group	between teacher and pupil
4.4. Products	Development of products to date	Level of products at present Comparison of products	Factors influencing products Learning difficulties	Means of overcoming learning difficulties	Possibilities of overcoming learning difficulties	at national level at municipal level in different countries	in different teaching groups and circumstances	at individual level
5. *Evaluation* 5.1. Collection of data	Development of evaluation methods to date	Objects and methods of evaluation at present Comparison of objects and methods of evaluation in P.E.	Reasons for present state of evaluation Need for comprehensive system of evaluation	Creation of a system of evaluation	Requirements in regard to eval. methods set by evaluation functions Possibilities of developing eval. methods	at national level at municipal level	at school level at class level	at individual level
						with the objects and methods of evaluation in general education		
5.2. Use of evaluation data	Use of evaluation data to date	Use of evaluation at present	Reason for present use of evaluation Need for improving evaluation	Improving utilization of evaluation system	Possibilities of using evaluation data	in national quality control in developing local curric.	at class level in improving teaching	at individual level, in improving learning
5.3. Pupil evaluation	Stages in pupil evaluation to date	Present system of pupil evaluation Comparison between systems of pupil evaluation	Need for revising pupil evaluation	Revision of pupil evaluation	Possibilities of revising pupil evaluation	with general pupil evaluation	at national level at municipal level	in improving teaching	in improving learning

istration, level of education, level of school community, and individual level. Table 1 defines as relevant institutions education, physical culture, work and production, leisure time and health care. Region and level of administration are represented by states, national level and municipal level. Level of education includes pre-school, primary stage, secondary stage and teacher training. School community is subdivided into the entire school community, class, teaching group and other social groupings at school. At the individual level research tasks are examined mainly from the teacher's and pupil's point of view. The general research tasks are illustrated by *examples* which are written in the application column in Table 1.

Research tasks can also be specified by dividing them into subproblems on theoretical, logical or practical grounds. The list of research tasks concerning school physical education is not exhaustive. However, it is designed to illustrate the problems of school physical education. It may be used as the basis of defining priority areas of physical education research. One of its weaknesses is the fact that the listed research problems are of different extent and that the research tasks are not independent of each other.

Another purpose of the list is to suggest research topics for researchers, students and those who are planning to start research on school physical education. Problems should then be divided further into more clearly defined subproblems, since there are not sufficient resources to start several major projects, which means that we are often compelled to limit substantially our research problems.

DEFINITION OF PRIORITIES OF RESEARCH INTO SCHOOL PHYSICAL EDUCATION

The typology of research tasks does not indicate what are the most important problem areas and what is their relative order of urgency. The order of importance and urgency of research tasks is hereafter referred to be the term *priority areas of research into school physical education*. The definition of the priority areas does not imply an absolute concentration of research. Its main aim is to co-ordinate research so that topical and important problems will be studied. It is also hoped that it might help researchers in the selection of research problems.

Priorities can be defined at least in two ways:

1. The criteria of priority areas are defined and they are used in deciding what topics should mainly be selected.
2. General statements on research priorities are taken as the starting point and by means of specification and elaboration the priorities of research into school physical education are obtained.

The two approaches are discussed briefly in the following and previous priority statements are described.

Criteria for Defining Priority Areas

There are no universally accepted criteria for the definition of research priorities. The present work on research priorities took as its point of departure criteria defined in national research programmes. They were modified to suit the more specific problem area of school physical education. Figure 1 presents side by side the criteria of physical education sciences defined in 1971 and 1975 by the Finnish Research Council for Physical Education and Sport and those proposed by the Advisory Council for Research into School Physical Education in 1975.

The Advisory Council has attempted to indicate in Figure 1 how its criteria are related to more general criteria. (Some criteria have been left out and some new ones have been introduced.) The following criteria are proposed for the definition of research priorities:

1. Scientific relevance of the research task
   —Does the solution of the research task indicate new problems?
   —Does it possibly solve other problems beside the one(s) investigated?
   —Does it contribute to the accumulation of knowledge? Does it contribute to theory construction?
2. Existing knowledge base
   —What is already known of school physical education? In what areas is the need for research-based information greatest?
   —Is there a need for basic research?
   —Is the same information available abroad?
3. Available research resources
   —Economic, human, space, equipment and practical resources
4. Social significance
   —Scope and coverage
   —Concentration on such social functions which are important from the point of view of physical education at school, e.g. education, physical culture, health care, economy
5. Topicality
   —Pending decisions concerning education
   —Can the phenomenon be influenced at the particular time?
6. Practical relevance of the research task for education
   —Effects of the completion of the research task and consequences for work in the field
   —Can the particular phenomenon be influenced at all?
7. Investigatability of the problem
   —Can the particular problem be solved by the methods of research?

The criteria have not been presented in the order of importance. They have, however, been divided into three groups: internal scientific criteria

Finnish Research Council for Physical Education and Sports (1971)	Finnish Research Council for Physical Education and Sports (1975)	Advisory Council for Research into School Physical Education (1975)
Scientific significance of the problem		INTERNAL SCIENTIFIC CRITERIA
Connection with other disciplines	Does the branch of study give data suitable for application?	1. Scientific relevance of research task
Need for basic research	Is it mainly a problem of information?	2. Existing knowledge base
Practical conditions for the solution of the problem	What are the conditions for the solution of the problems?	3. Available research resources
	Is it possible to train experts needed by society in the branch of study?	
Significance of the problem for physical culture	What is significance of solutions made in the field for general welfare?	CRITERIA EXTERNAL TO SCIENCE
		4. Social significance
Social and economic significance of the problem	What are the social consequences of results obtained in the branch of study?	
Topicality	How urgent are the decisions and proposals to be made in questions having to do with the branch of study?	5. Topicality
		6. Practical relevance for education practice
Special relevance for Finland	How does the branch of study comply with and promote recommendations issued by the national Science Policy Council?	
	Is it an internationally significant branch of study?	CRITERIA PERTAINING TO INDIVIDUAL PROBLEMS
		7. Investigatability of the problem

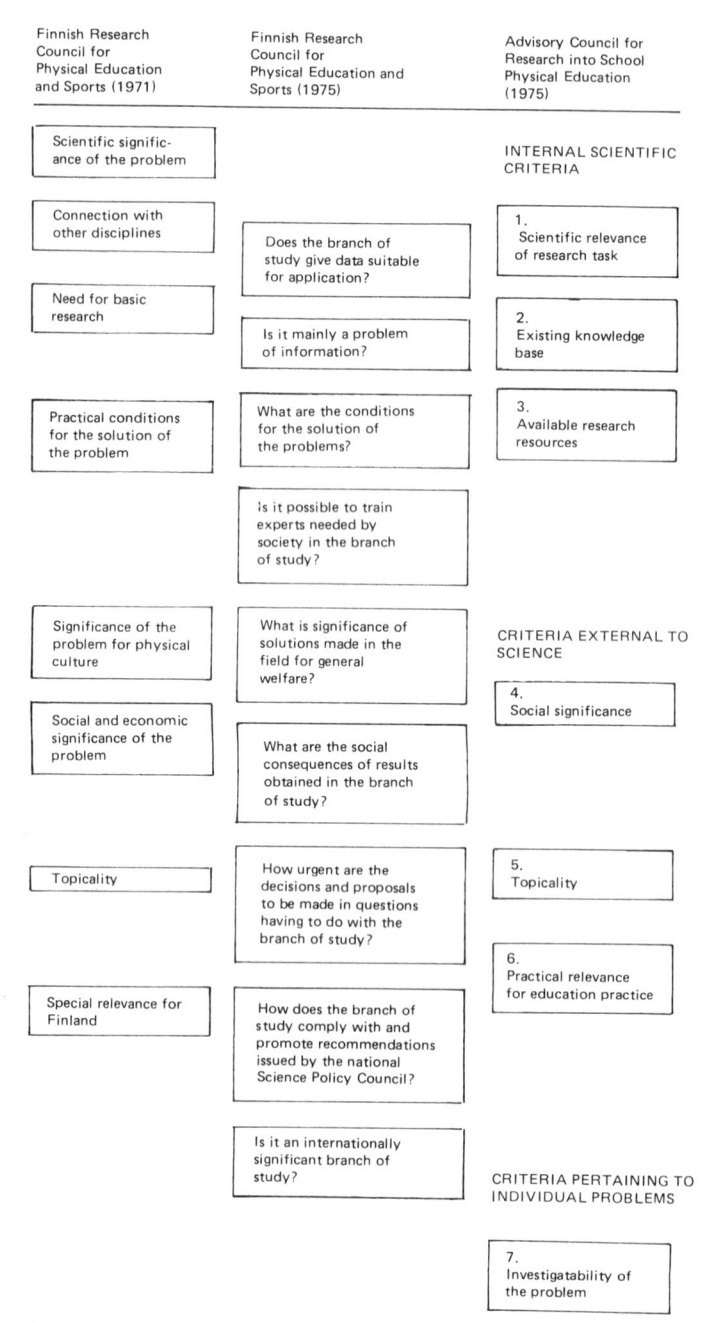

Figure 1. Criteria for research priorities proposed by the Finnish Research Council for Physical Education and Sport in 1971 and 1975 and by the Advisory Council for Research into School Physical Education in 1975.

(1–3), criteria external to science (4–6) and criteria pertaining to individual problems (7). The use of external criteria is facilitated by knowledge of social and educational phenomena. The use of the criterion concerning the investigatability of a problem is based on logical considerations. The criteria can be used in two ways in defining research priorities:

1. The research tasks are set in the order of importance using one criterion at a time. When all criteria have been applied, the data are collected.
2. The research tasks are set in the order of importance by applying all the criteria at the same time.

The first approach has not been used in the preparation of science and research programmes. Since it would have required some time to try it out, the latter method has mainly been used in the present work as well.

The use of criteria is not limited to the construction of research policy documents. They make it possible *to evaluate research proposals, in connection with the allocation of funds and thereby channel research in desirable direction.*

Since criteria are not the sole bases for the definition of research priorities, the general research priorities are presented first and thereafter priority areas within research on school physical education. *Criteria are used in justifying the selection of research priorities.*

Priority Areas Defined in General Research Policy Programmes

National priority areas of research have been outlined by several bodies, e.g. the Science Policy Council in 1973 and the Finnish Research Council for Physical Education and Sports in 1971 and 1975. These priority areas are presented schematically in Figure 2. Related Priority areas are presented, as far as possible, side by side.

There are few links between the Science Policy Council's programme and the 1971 document published by the Research Council, for the obvious reason that the Science Policy Council's more general statement of priorities was published later. The priority areas suggested by the Finnish Research Council for Physical Education and Sports in 1975 are connected with the Science Policy Council's priority areas of public health, general welfare and working life. A common feature of the Research Council's proposals from 1971 and 1975 is the emphasis on the study of physical behaviour, *school physical education,* the effects of physical activity, physical activity of exceptional groups, physical exercise in work and sports. The 1975 proposal gives relatively more attention to the study of physical capacity, follow-up systems, factors affecting physical activity habits, the effects of physical activity and the methods of physical exercise.

State Policy Council 1973	Finnish Research Council for Physical Education and Sports
	1971	1975

State Policy Council 1973:
- Research on public health
- Research on general well-being and the development of the national production system
- Research on the realization of democracy and equality
- Research on the development of methods for the protection of nature and for an effective and minimally damaging use of natural resources
- Research on working life and working conditions

Finnish Research Council for Physical Education and Sports 1971:
- Study of physical behaviour in Finland
- School physical education
- Study of motivation of physical activity
- Planning of physical education and culture
- Study of the structure and functions of physical culture
- Study of the effects of physical activity
- Physical activity of special groups
- Physical exercise in work
- Top and competitive athletics

Finnish Research Council for Physical Education and Sports 1975:

Research on the physical behaviour and physical functioning capacity of the general public
— survey of the public's physical behaviour
— survey of the public's physical functioning capacity
— formation of system of evaluation for a continuous monitoring of the public's physical behaviour and physical functioning capacity

Research on factors affecting physical activity which is significant for general well-being
— study of school physical education, especially its objectives and its effect on the formation of permanent habits of physical activity
— study of other factors influencing the formation of permanent habits of physical activity
— study of the use and effects of public physical services in different social groups
— study of the role of sport and sport associations for general physical activity
— study of social problems associated with the occupational career of active athletes

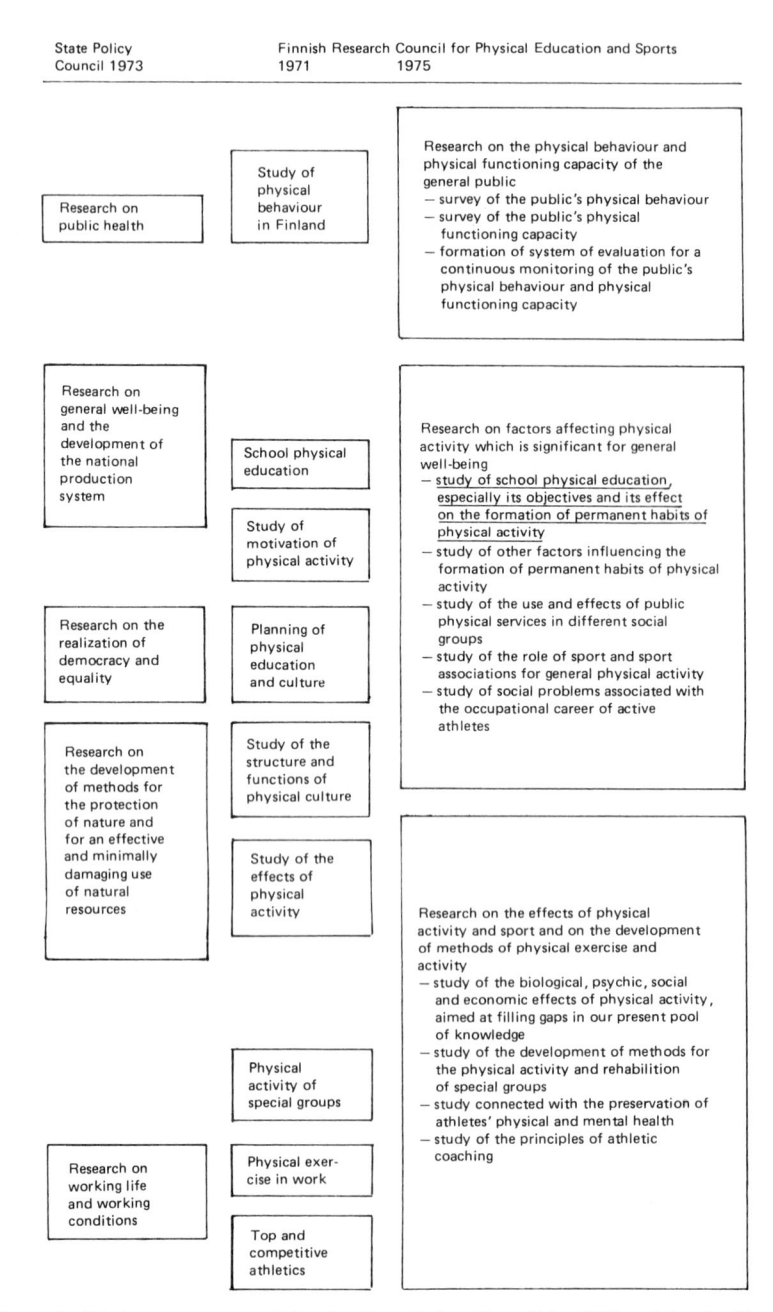

Research on the effects of physical activity and sport and on the development of methods of physical exercise and activity
— study of the biological, psychic, social and economic effects of physical activity, aimed at filling gaps in our present pool of knowledge
— study of the development of methods for the physical activity and rehabilitation of special groups
— study connected with the preservation of athletes' physical and mental health
— study of the principles of athletic coaching

Figure 2. Priority areas proposed by the State Policy Council in 1973 and by the Finnish Research Council for Physical Education and Sports in 1971 and in 1975.

The Research Council has also paid attention to the internal priorities of school physical education, as which it suggests *educational objectives and the effect of school physical education on the formation of permanent habits of physical activity*. The Research Council has also divided the overall societal framework into four sectors with a view to directing research. The Council has proposed the following priority areas within the educational sector:

1. Review of objectives in pre-primary and secondary education.
2. Structuring and specification of the objectives of comprehensive school and the search for concrete intermediate objectives.
3. Position of physical education at different levels of the educational system.
4. Development of curricula and teaching methods in line with educational goals.
5. Teaching circumstances.
6. Development of evaluation methods.

General definitions of research priority areas are used as a second source in the determination of priority areas of research on school physical education, since they are explicitly stated. They are not, however, detailed enough in regard of the entire domain of research on school physical education. Neither are they sufficiently well-grounded from the point of view of school physical education.

Proposal for Priority Areas in Research on School Physical Education in 1975–1979

In the presentation of priority areas some general characteristics of the prioritisized research on school physical education will be briefly described. Thereafter the priority areas will be listed and reasons will be given for their selection. It is, of course, not necessary that studies to be initiated will conform with this classification.

General Characteristics of Prioritisized Research on School Physical Education Special support should be given in the next few years to studies, which focus on

1. the significance or functions of school physical education
2. the goals of school physical education

One special priority area might be the study of the significance of school physical education for various social institutions and pupils' overall development. Since this kind of research would take the lion's share of all resources available for research on school physical education and since such research should be a part of a more general study of the significance of physical activity and exercise, it was decided to propose that *within each priority area special support should be given to plans and studies pertaining to the significance of school physical education.*

Goal-orientation means that support should be given to projects, which have *many-sided and well-formulated objectives*. Research may concentrate on the specification of objectives and on all measures undertaken to achieve them, as well as on the relevance and topicality of objectives.

Goal-oriented thinking has gained ground in school education. It has been specially prominent in the theory and practice of the mastery learning systems. Whereas in traditional school teaching all pupils are given more or less similar instruction and the achievements vary, in the mastery learning system the aim is to help all pupils to learn as much as possible but at least to master the basic objectives, which presupposes a variety of teaching strategies. This principle has been presented in the report of the 1971 Educational Committee, and the Cabinet decision of May 30, 1975 means that the comprehensive school curriculum will be revised in accordance with such principles. The application of the principles of mastery learning to school physical education presupposes research, which on the one hand examines what that basic level of objectives might be and on what grounds the level can be set, and on the other hand analyzes by which teaching arrangements the objectives can most effectively be reached; in other words, goal-oriented research is needed.

The main objectives of school physical education are widely accepted, and it is unlikely that the review of objectives will materially change them in the next few years. These main objectives are: promotion of physical fitness and creation of permanent interest in physical activity and exercise. They are, however, general statements which can act only as guidelines. The two types of goal-oriented research should be carried out within the main objectives set for school physical education.

Priority Areas For the guidance of research it is proposed that studies of school physical education should be concentrated on the following priority areas (areas are not presented in the order of importance):

Research on the Revision of the Objectives of Physical Education This means two main lines of study:

1. specification of present objectives, and
2. search for new objectives, checking their relevance and comparison with more general social objectives

Urgent objects of research within the priority area of the revision of objectives are:

1. specification of the objectives of physical education in the comprehensive school and in secondary education
    —analysis of objectives and creation of a taxonomy of objectives
    —study of the definition of basic objectives

2. study of the attainment of objectives and of improving teaching
   —effect of class size and composition, available time and teaching methods on improving physical capacity
3. significance and objectives of physical education in early grades
   —significance of early physical education on children's general development
   —significance of early stimulus environment and systematic physical education for pupils' physical behaviour
   —objectives and contents of physical education in early grades
4. objectives of the training of physical education teachers and its significance for the achievement of the objectives of school physical education
   —consideration given to the objectives of school physical education teachers (class teachers and specialist subject teachers)

Rationale Objectives have a central role in the organizational framework of school physical education, because they are reflected in all stages of physical education carried out at schools. If the objectives are found to match poorly general social objectives, the existence of the system of school physical education is questionable. The periodical revision of objectives should be based on research knowledge of their relevance and attainability. Objectives are important from the point of view of the entire teaching-learning process.

The objectives of school physical education have been studied hardly at all. In educational sciences the study of objectives has increased in recent years. The Finnish Research Council for Physical Education and Sports has also recommended the investigation of objectives.

According to goal-oriented thinking, objectives form a cognitive pivot on which may depend the solution of several problems. The study of objectives is, for instance, a condition for the didactic study of physical education. The study of objectives does not require large-scale practical arrangements.

The study of objectives is topical especially in those levels of the educational system where objectives will be defined in the near future.

A fully specified, hierarchical system of objectives makes it possible to see how well the objectives cover the whole domain of objectives. Similarly, moving sufficiently low in the hierarchy of objectives we can easily go over to teaching. Individualization is advantageous both from the point of the teacher and the pupils.

The objectives of physical education in the comprehensive school have been stated in a dimensional manner; in other words, it has not been stated clearly when the pupils may be considered to have reached the objectives. Some countries have defined basic objectives in physical education and there have been similar aspirations in Finland. Basic objectives would give firmer bearings to teaching and make it more easy to see to it that all pupils possess certain basic knowledge and master basic skills on leaving school.

Certain teaching arrangements, e.g. teaching methods, available time, the size and composition of class, have become the objects of interest and even of debate. We do not have enough research-based information about the effect of these factors on the attainment of objectives. The information cannot be obtained from abroad, either, and even if it were, it could not be used as such. Research in this area is fairly explicit and can be arranged by administrative decision. Research on teaching methods would contribute to the relatively weak theory of the didactics of school physical education. There would seem to be resources in this area on account of the reform of teacher education and the system of sabbatical term for teacher educators after every seven years of service.

Since some teaching procedures, such as group work and the reduction of the class size, have in some connection been mistaken for objectives, there is reason to show by research how these arrangements, valuable as they are, are to be related to the main objectives of school physical education.

Early stimulus environment and exercise may be of great importance to later behaviour and to the development of physical skills and habits. More research-based knowledge is needed as regards physical education. There are some indications that development can be fostered by early exercise and potential learning difficulties can be averted.

It is the task of early education and early teaching to reduce differences in children's learning readiness due to the growth environment. The goals and practice of physical education in early grades may be of central importance to all later education.

The goals and contents of teacher education are taking shape. Since the teacher is a central factor in the teaching—learning process, it is not inconsequential what the new teacher education will be like.

There are good possibilities of conducting research on teacher education at the Faculty of Physical and Health Education and also in other teacher education units now that teacher education is linked with the Faculties of Education.

Research on Pupils' Physical Functioning Capacity   Urgent research objectives are:

1. match between teaching contents and the physical-motor objectives in the comprehensive school
   —relationship between teaching contents and physical-motor objectives at different developmental levels
   —taxonomy of teaching contents
2. permanent follow-up system for monitoring pupils' physical functioning capacity
   —validation of measurements
   —use of evaluation data
   —pupil evaluation (marking)

Rationale   The available information of pupils' physical functioning capacity is only partly sufficient. Since physical fitness is the central goal of school physical education, the gaps of research in this area should be filled.

Physical functioning capacity is an important goal from the point of view of several social institutions (work, production, health care, physical culture, leisure). Therefore, the assessment of *at least* the goal attainment in the area of physical fitness should be continuous.

In seeking to reach the objectives the first step is to select the teaching contents, and so the question is: what will be taught? In the Comprehensive School Curriculum of 1970 the relationship between objectives and contents is not very clearly indicated. Working out such relations would be useful for the projected Curriculum 1980 and for the realization of goal-oriented physical education at present.

A selection of relevant teaching contents is important also because it is, at least in principle, easy to do something about it, and because the selection has practical consequences also for teaching procedures and evaluation methods. Besides, some of the teaching contents are clearly of national interest only, which means that we cannot expect to be able to draw on information from other countries alone.

Successful education presupposes pertinacious activity. Persistence and constancy of purpose are enhanced if the output of physical education is assessed by the same, reliable methods. Research on evaluation is generally well-defined and does not require unduly large resources.

A *reliable* measurement of the level of physical functioning capacity solves several related problems (Is there a need to improve teaching?) or gives rise to new ones (How can teaching be improved?). Since knowledge of this area is surprisingly scarce (it is debated whether pupils' physical fitness is good or bad), there is a need for basic research on the applicability of measurement methods and for longitudinal studies, which would make it possible to see what effects school physical education has on individuals. This kind of information is of special relevance at the present time when educational reforms are underway at all levels of the educational system. It would permit the follow-up of the influence of the reform on pupils' physical development.

Research on Pupils' Physical Activity Interests   Urgent research objects are

1. specification of the taxonomy of objectives
2. possibility of school physical education to build permanent interest in physical activity and permanent habits of physical exercise
    —contribution of the teacher, teaching conditions, teaching methods and teaching contents to the formation and stability of physical activity interests
3. methods of evaluating the physical activity interests of school children
    —methods of evaluating physical interests in the comprehensive school and in secondary education

Rationale   The promotion of public health is one of the most important social functions of physical activity and exercise. Since the goal of physical interests aims at forming life-long habits of physical activity, it does not only concern school physical education but the health of the whole population. Research on factors affecting the formation of permanent habits of physical exercise is also mentioned as one priority area in the report of the Finnish Research Council for Physical Education and Sports.

Research which contributes to the formation of active interests in physical activity is of topical interest to educational policy, because permanent interest in physical activity is a major objective of physical education in the comprehensive school and knowledge of this area is needed in the development of the comprehensive school curriculum. Permanent interest in physical activity and exercise is likely to be set as a major goal of secondary education in the forthcoming secondary education curricula, and therefore it would be useful to have information about factors affecting the attainment of objectives in the development of such curricula. Work on the revision of the plans of early grades is also under way, and for this reason there is a need of knowledge of the effects of early stimulus environment on the formation of physical activity habits.

The existing knowledge of factors influencing the formation and preservation of permanent physical interests is not sufficient to give a solid basis for school curricula. In addition to the study of physical interests, research on school physical education should focus on the investigation of the effects of those environmental stimuli that can be arranged in systematic physical education or can, in general, be influenced by physical education. The study of stimuli which affect the formation of interests would give new possibilities for didactic study aimed at curriculum development.

Since one of the two major objectives of school physical education is the formation of permanent interest in physical activity and exercise, the changes in pupils' behaviour in this area caused by teaching should also be evaluated. Although final products are visible years after the end of the school, some parts of the taxonomy of objectives should be specified so that it would be possible to evaluate some sub-areas during school especially during secondary education. Such sub-areas might be, for example, activeness in school physical education and participation in extra-curricular and possible out-of-school physical activities. There is a particular need for reliable and valid measures in this area. One central and topical question is the use of interest in pupil evaluation.

The Sport Pedagogy Research Program of the Federal Institute of Sport Science

A. Kirsch

So far, three research programs for the field of sport science have been established within the Federal Republic of Germany: the first one was initiated in 1969 by the Central Committee for Research in Sport; the other two were begun in 1972 and in 1976 by the Federal Institute for Sport Science (BISp). The educational themes of the research program from 1976 are presented in this chapter. Other aspects of the research plan not dealt with here concern research in sport medicine, psychology, sociology, science of coaching and movement, and facilities and equipment for sport and recreation, as well as documentation and information in sport. Philosophy of sport, history of sport, sport and politics, sport and law, and sport and economy are mentioned as possible research areas within the program; however, no themes are named yet for these fields.

There are certain criteria that are used in selecting the research areas from the field of sport science and that will be predominantly developed by the BISp. These include: the meaning of the practical aspects of sport, the available research potential, the character of innovation, and the economic possibilities. Because sport science is an interdisciplinary, or integrated, science, interdisciplinary research programs are especially important. The program has nine main aspects: coaching, development of talents, diagnostic tests for sport, facilities and equipment in sport, movement, social behavior in sport, sport for all, sport for the handicapped, and sport-science film. Sport pedagogy should contribute to most of these themes, if useful results are to be obtained.

Every research program must set priorities. This is necessary not only because of limited financial resources but also because of the specific struc-

---

Reprinted by permission from: Kirsch, A. (ed.) 1976. *Bundesinstitut für Sportwissenschaft. Schwerpunktprogramm der sportwissenschaftlichen Forschung*, Köln. (Pages 10–12 reprinted here—the introduction is an original contribution.)

ture of the institution that is granting the money and functioning as a coordinating agency. In the BISp, the priorities are given to themes concerning performance and improvement of performance, because the Federal Government has a special function in the support of top-level athletics. In the Federal Republic of Germany cultural responsibility is based in the eleven states, which support, in cooperation with the Federal Ministry for Science and Education, research in sport pedagogy, with the main concentration being on school sport. Within the program of the Federal Institute of Sport Science, the following educational topics are included in the list of priorities: play and sport in preschool, role of the physical education teacher and coach, cooperation of school and sport club, field of concentration in sport within the upper level of high school (Sekundarstufe II), and sport for the handicapped.

The support of research is realized through research requests and research grants. Requests are made by sport scientists either alone or in groups. These are examined by a specific committee to evaluate their importance for sport science, their concept of research methodology, their possibility of realization, and their underlying financial plan. Research grants are announced by the Institute and given to the respective applicants. This method guarantees, on the one hand, that research is done in the field, which was not previously considered to a great extent, and, on the other hand, that sport science does not lose its relationship to the actual problems of sport.

EDUCATION

Status and Development

The present status of research support is mainly characterized by the discussion in previous years that has led from the revision of sport curriculum to the necessity for developing instructional models and to the examination of these models on the basis of the respective theoretical construction of the curriculum. According to the Federal Institute of Sport Science, research on talent support within school as well as on conceptualization of youth sport on educational criteria has to be given preferential support. The consequences of these research results for the relationship of school sport and sport in clubs are of special significance with regard to questions of content and organization.

The future fields of concentration can be divided into the three following aspects regarding the previously mentioned fields of concentration:

1. Theory and methods of sport instruction
2. Theory of sport curriculum
3. Theory and organization of specific aspects of sport, especially of youth sport

The enlargement of the current program from the program of 1972 has to consider that the fields of concentration in research so far fixed have to be dealt with further. This applies especially to the improvement of teaching and learning programs, and to the development of learning - aim - oriented test procedures, as well as to the empirical foundation of basic qualifications, which are necessary for the pupil.

At the same time it has to be shown that through changed and enlarged perception of problems within practical aspects of sport and through the enlargement of educational questions, new tasks have been formulated for research. On the one hand, sport aspects outside of school sport are becoming more important because of increasing free time, the changing of the age structure, and the use of sport exercise and training within preventive and rehabilitation functions. On the other hand, questions of educational research have been enlarged within the discussion of socialization theory in regard to social action. As a result, school and instruction have become a problem within the overall relationship with other fields of social action. As a consequence and as a part of this problem, it can be seen that school sport and sport instruction have to be interpreted and investigated with regard to the relationship resulting from the enlarged social importance of the practical aspects of sport. It will be necessary to investigate the action field of sport (in school and outside of school) on the basis of new social science theories of action and communication and to ask questions about the perspectives of educational research.

Questions related to the educational concept of coaching are getting more and more important because of critical comments about athletics, which are widely known. In order to overcome the critical uncertainty of top level athletes, models have to be developed first of all for securing their professional careers. The large and extensive changes of sport instruction also require a structural reform and qualitative improvement of physical education teacher training. This is concerned especially with the problems of action competencies, which define the behavior of physical education teachers and which should be reached through studies in sport pedagogy and sport science. Therefore, it is necessary to do research in structural problem areas, which will determine the training of physical education teachers.

Fields of Concentration

In accordance with justifications given above, the following are fields of concentration for research:

Theory and Methods of Sport Instruction

1. Multidimensional evaluation methods of sport instruction as well as evaluation instruments and tests within instructional research

2. Development of methods for counselling about talent and for the determining of talent by the physical education teacher, including measures of talent support
3. Behavior and behavior change of the teacher; conditions of physical education teacher training, and their consequences for sport instruction
4. Plans for extended study for physical education teachers
5. Optimization of the usage of media within sport instruction
6. Evaluation of situations and influencing factors in sport instruction (learning surroundings)

Theory of Sport Curriculum

1. Movement games for infant and preschool children
2. Empirical foundation of basic qualifications for sport instruction
3. Evaluation instruments for curricula and their parts, especially in primary schools and grades 5 to 10 (Sekundarstufe I)
4. Models and concepts for sport in grades 11 to 13 (Sekundarstufe II), especially the field of concentration "sport".
5. Interaction and communication analysis of the action field sport under aspects of sport pedagogy

Theory and Organization of Specific Aspects of Sport

1. Investigations of the educational planning of coaching in sport clubs and sport associations
2. Comparative investigations of the concept, content, and effectiveness of fitness programs
3. Development of model concepts of sport for older people
4. Didactic models of therapy and rehabilitation within sport for the mentally and physically handicapped as well as in measures of social work
5. Plans for sport for all

Other Aspects Included in This Section

1. Philosophy of sport
2. Sport history
3. Sport and politics

International Symposium on Sport Pedagogy

Introduction

Introduction

E. Beyer

Upon the occasion of the 150th anniversary of the Karlsruhe University, the Ausschuss Deutscher Leibeserzieher (ADL) sent out invitations for an "International Symposium on Sport Pedagogy." The Institute of Sport and Sport Science of the Karlsruhe University was responsible for the local organization of the Symposium, which took place in the Conference Hall of the Karlsruhe Nuclear Center. Here were to be found all the facilities for simultaneous translations into English, French, and German, which were important from a technical standpoint for the success of the Symposium. Fifty specialists in sport pedagogy from 17 countries accepted the invitation of the ADL. The number of participants was limited to maintain the desired atmosphere of the Symposium.

The Organizing Committee chose one main topic from the theoretical field of sport pedagogy for each of the three days of the Conference. In the morning there were lectures, one main and two short papers on each topic; in the afternoons these lectures were discussed in plenary meetings.

The main topics were:

1. The relationship between teacher and pupil in sport instruction
2. Sport in the institution called school
3. Aims and objectives of physical education

These three main topics were expected to be dealt with under three aspects:

1. The subject matter of sport pedagogy
2. Methods of research in sport pedagogy
3. The position of sport pedagogy within the realm of sciences and humanities

In discussions of the *relationship between teacher and pupil in sport instruction,* different concepts were proposed. Specifically, the questions dealt with the problem of pedagogical interaction and interaction as a problem of instructional research in physical education. These are interesting aspects because it is questionable whether or not the choice of one or the other concept of interaction is scientifically justified. The discussion also asked if the teacher-pupil interaction in physical education is in danger of losing its characteristic traits because of the tendency to intellectualize physical education lessons. This tendency, it was stated, causes the process of interaction in physical education instruction to approach that of other school subjects.

The second topic, *sport in the institution called school,* provided an interesting outlook on reform programs of physical education at school as far as the content, structure, and organization are concerned. On the one hand, the relationship between physical education and school was investigated; on the other hand, it became evident that there are also strong ties between physical education at school and outside of school. The consequences of the reform of physical education at school for the teacher training programs were also discussed.

Interesting discussions were stimulated by the third topic, *aims and objectives of physical education.* One of the main problems was whether or not aims and objectives are fixed by prescientific or nonscientific decisions, or whether they could be defined by a research process implying rational and empirical criteria.

It is certainly true that the first two topics could not be thoroughly discussed without touching on the problem of aims and objectives in physical education. In spite of this fact the Organizing Committee of the ADL had decided to put the topic of aims and objectives at the end of the Symposium. This proved to be a wise decision, because otherwise the discussion of this problem would have dominated the other two topics.

Unfortunately, not all the specialists that had been invited could accept the invitation. Nevertheless, the lectures and discussions displayed a broad spectrum of controversial and converging positions and opinions.

The ADL hopes that the Symposium will have helped to strengthen the communication between sport scientists from the theoretical field of sport pedagogy all over the world and to intensify research in sport science, especially in sport pedagogy.

The Relationship Between Teacher and Pupil in Sport Instruction

The Problem of the Teacher-Pupil Relationship in Sport Instruction

K. Widmer

LEGITIMACY OF THE QUESTION POSED

Teacher-Pupil Interaction as a Concern in Sport Pedagogy

The school is a subsystem of society. Physical education instruction is a part of this subsystem. Society, i.e., its dominant groups, have certain of their own expectations to be realized with respect to the school. These have to be realized either in the form of continuity and advancement of already accepted values and apparent values in the various classes of society, state, culture, politics, sciences, and the arts, or in the form of changes in values already accepted by the present class system of society. The school has the job of preparing the young person for his future, however one may understand this term; the pupil is to be regarded as a potential adult. In European class society, at least since the time of Comenius through Pestalozzi up to present day pedagogical anthropology, it can be shown that society looks to the school for continuity and at the same time for innovation. The school provides an environment for the child in which the development of the various dimensions of the individual's personality takes place. The problems that the child might be confronted with later in life are fully explored, and he is encouraged in a special way. This should be accomplished in accordance with the individual's specific rate of development and abilities. With this in mind, the school assumes the responsibility for the individual in the school, not in opposition to society, but in active involvement with society. Both requirements, continuity and innovation, involve values and responsibilities that can be identified clearly in the main activity of learning. Learning needs the stimulation and the systematic development of psycho-physical qualifications in relation to specific problem areas. Stimulation and development occur through the process of teaching. Learning and teaching complement each other in a process of complicated interacting structures. Not only are there factors of organization, administration, and judgment, but also there is the relationship between those doing the teaching and those being taught. All forms of learning, in addition to the learning that takes place in a physical education class, not only are dependent upon direct relationships between the personality structure of the ones being taught and the structures of the material being taught, but also are dependent upon the ways and means by which interaction between pupil and teacher is realized. Learning in physical education, as far as it happens in a physical education class, cannot, therefore, be excluded from the context of the teacher-pupil relationship, i.e., it cannot be explained without the inclusion of the personal interacting structures (Widmer, 1974, pp. 749–753). In this respect the problem of interaction is an essential ingredient of educational science and therefore also a part of sport pedagogy. Therefore, the question arises: Do the teacher-pupil relationship and interaction in physical education instruction follow the same pattern, or rules, as does the interaction that occurs in typical classroom instruction carried out with the direct and frontal approach. Or, under special circumstances, can other structures be identified that apply to the teacher-pupil interaction in sport?

The Deficiency of Theories about Teacher-Pupil Relationships

By examining the available sport pedagogy literature as extensively as possible, it becomes apparent that there are relatively few scientific studies about the specialized theme of teacher-pupul relationship in physical education instruction and that there are hardly any empirically proven theories to be found. So it must be recognized that there is a deficiency of theories in the area of this problem. Since Lewin, Lippit, and White, who introduced the idea of the style of leadership, thought has in recent times shifted from this idea to the single dimension of the teacher relationship and its influence on achievements and behavior in regard to motivation of the pupil. These are points that are discussed today, especially by Flanders (1970), Bales (1950), Tausch and Tausch (1972), Langhurst (1973), and Nickel (1974), who are among the leaders in this field. The common factor among these researchers is that they examine the teacher-pupil relationship mainly among lessons given in the direct frontal form in the canonical subjects. They have also chosen the linguistic aspect as principal indicator of this relationship. Therefore, a direct application of these research results to physical education instruction is only possible under certain circumstances. It would be scientifically more helpful to indicate the applicability of our problem area of personality theories (Ausubel, Guilford, Allport, Lersch and others), a socialization or interaction theory [Parson's (1959) symbolic interactionalism, Mead, Krappmann, Strauss, Habermas, etc], psychological theories (Freud, Adler, Jung, Fromm, Erikson, Mitscherlich) or defense mechanisms (projections, neurotic suggestions, regressions, etc.). Such theories can result in very fruitful interpretations. However, they still have to be modified through empirical examination of the specific teacher-pupil relationships in a physical education lesson.

The Position of the Author's Work

In this regard one can conclude from the pedagogical point of view that recognizably advanced pedagogical philosophies are based on the following precept: Through analysis of the teaching position against a background of a normal theoretical framework one begins to develop modifiable innovations. Here educational science becomes an active science—comparable to the science of medicine—and has self-achievement as its central aim. Therefore, it must be recognized that the goals of education are not unilateral changes in society (sociological reduction), nor are they unilateral changes of the individual (psychological-anthropological reduction). Both aspects have to be taken into consideration.

In view of the deficiency of theories, these ideas can only be regarded as having limited value. After all, they only perform the function of a descriptive pilot study for a theoretical structural framework of the interactive pattern of the teacher-pupil relationship in a physical education class. Furthermore, there are limitations to the immediate relationship of the teacher to the pupil; there is a long list of variables that cannot be disregarded, for example, the pressure exerted on behavior through time restrictions and similar aspects, as well as the external conditions of a physical education lesson. In the same way, it is not possible to discuss the total problem of socialization, with its internal problems of values and norms and their transformation. Nor is it possible to consider the interaction of specific roles and changes in opinions. Even with the knowledge that the resulting material presented is limited by these rather narrow boundaries, it is still difficult to define pedagogical interaction and the central variables of "teacher," "pupil," and "interaction." From these definitions and descriptions some ideas should be obtained for a new theoretical framework.

EXPLANATION OF PEDAGOGICAL INTERACTION

Basic Example of Interaction

Interaction comes about in socially changing forms with acting partners. In order for an *interaction* to take place, common preconditions have to be present in all the partners. For example, one partner sends out signals, which the other partner must be able to understand. Assuming the other partner understands, one can anticipate a possible reaction of the other individual and by this anticipate his own subsequent reaction. The same process takes place in the other partner. As a result, interaction has three main characteristics: reciprocation of, anticipation of, and interpretation of each other's expectations and behaviors between individuals (Mollenhauer, 1972, p. 848). Another precondition of interaction is a common repertoire of signals, with significant symbols on which the interpretation of strange behavior and one's own behavior is based. Therefore, a system of rules for communication that represents a cognitive structure and that becomes a reality during actual interaction has to exist for all those taking part. The significant symbols of communication are mainly linguistic and semantic. However, in the teacher-pupil relationship, the averbal, the meta-communicative, and the paralinguistic symbols (Watzlawik, 1974) all have a part in forming the basis for communication. The general understanding of the significant symbols initially allows the interaction as a *conditio sine qua non*. Reciprocation, anticipation, and interpretation of expectations become possible as parts of the interaction because of an "ownness and singularity of the significant symbols" (Grell, 1974; Watzlawik, 1974, p. 54). The actual release in the speaker provokes the same reaction in the listener. This, and nothing else but this, is called *understanding* (Mollenhauer, 1972, p. 85). If interaction takes place at the same time among several people, then many rules have to be taken into consideration. The "I" person has to have the expectations and anticipations of the others and those of himself at the same time. Therefore, the "I" person comes to understand his position within the structure of interaction. In more or less constant contexts of interaction with relatively lengthy and lasting interacting structures, for example in the family and in the school, the "I" component eventually develops, namely the knowledge of one's position in the system of social relationship. If, in the interaction, the understanding of self agrees with the understanding of others, the identity of the individual remains intact. If, however, the incompatability is too great over a long period of time, the danger of an identity crisis becomes apparent. This entails the loss of identity or the end of communication (Mollenhauer, 1972, p. 86).

Pedagogical Interaction as a Special Form of Interaction

Interaction, as a complex form of action and counteraction in socially changing structures, does not occur in a pedagogical field involving a free-wheeling form of activity. Sport pedagogy or physical education lessons and their interactions, therefore, is determined through a list of specific factors, namely, institutional, intentional, and personal determinants.

Institutional Factor Interaction in physical education lessons happens in the field of education within the school. Therefore, the interaction is determined through the organizational structure of the school, and because it is frequently hindered from further development, it only takes place during the actual physical education instruction. In the same manner, interaction is influenced by the consistency of the surroundings, e.g., the gymnasium, sport field, ski and touring areas, or camps. The typical classroom surroundings create an obstacle to interaction, and may lead some special subject teachers to form limited pedagogical aims and possibilities, which are all too often painfully felt. On the other hand, tour and ski camps provide opportunities for more interpersonal meetings in a way that no other type of teacher other than a physical education teacher can experience or realize.

Intentional Determinants The physical education lesson's interaction is to a great extent determined by the attempt to purposely lean towards certain aims (Dieckert, 1972; Dietrich, 1972; Grössing, 1973; Kirsch; Kurz, 1971; Schmitz, 1973; Seybold, 1973). These aims are extensions of the training and educational aims. Training and educational aims are the normal ideals that present a positive position that can be attained through pedagogical influences. There are changes in the experiences that come about through the teaching process—changes in attitude and in readiness for behavior changes—for which teachers are continually striving (Grupe, 1969, 1973; Mester, 1964; Haag, 1974; Bernett, 1970; Beyer, 1967; Klafki, Groll, and Fetz, 1972; Hecker, 1971; Rieder, 1971; Jost, 1973; Koch and Mielke, 1974; Lutter, 1972; Paschen, 1970; Röthig, 1977).

Readiness for Experience Readiness for experience is the depth of the consciousness of one's bodily experience in an awareness of movement; i.g., identity experiences such as psycho-physical-social entities. It is the experience of control of the bodily existence in sport skills, an experience of a social role and structure in sporting activities.

Readiness of Attitude Readiness of attitude includes: reflection and experience of a positive attitude about one's sporting activities (health, fitness, etc.); an attitude towards sport as a social phenomena; and social aesthetic attitude toward an opponent, one's teammates, the physical education teacher, and, naturally, oneself.

Readiness for Behavior Readiness for behavior might be referred to as psycho-physical achievement potential, i.e., the development of the cognitive structure of controlling movement behavior in sport through social-ethical convictions.

Even if the psycho-motor achievement in the major categories of training, competition, games, and gymnastics remain the focal point, hardly anyone will dispute the fact that a physical education lesson also plays an important part in the individualization and social learning of the pupil, at least in the context of the sport activities (Egger, 1975).

The intentional interaction is further controlled in a physical education lesson through achieving or gradually making operational the aims related to the learning objectives, the curricula, and the procedure regulations. The closer the physical education teacher manages to adhere to these determinants, the more efficient his interaction becomes, and the possibilities for interaction become greater.

Personal Determinant In physical interaction, one partner, the physical education teacher, exhibits his maturity, experience, and usually, his advanced achievements as compared to the other partner—the pupil. This head start, which is a question of age and training, manifests itself in the qualifications of the physical education teacher, which put him in the position of being able to cope with the relevant situations that often arise. His psycho-motor competence, his competence in questions of didactics and methods (including his competence in verbal explanations and instructions), his qualities of leadership, his psychological competence (understanding and observing the personalities of the pupils and the interactional structures), and his knowledge of the political and social class system of society are all factors that enable the physical education teacher to gain authority. This authority, however, cannot be justified within the realms of evaluation and sanction, which are given to the teacher by the school as a societal system. Thus, the power of the teacher has to be proved or justified in front of the pupils. In the problem of personal determination of interaction there are three things that have to be discussed:

1. The interaction within physical education instruction does not proceed in any direct manner, in that an active teacher influences a more passive and waiting object, the pupil. The interaction is a process of reciprocity, based on reciprocation, anticipation, and interpretation of expectations and behavior patterns. This means that not only does the pupil change within the interactive structuure, but also the physical education teacher experiences changes and should alter his own attitudes toward his experiences, opinions, and behavior patterns. The need for personal change through reflection, as a result of experiences, is an educational task required of the teacher for his entire teaching career.

2. The limited opportunity for interaction in physical education instruction develops on the part of the teacher as well as within the pupil, a pattern of mutual determination of self and of others. The institutional, intentional, and personal determinations often act as a hindrance to outward influence on the pupil. The institutional and intentional determinations restrict the teacher in his own determination of self. The new tendencies are toward more open objectives of learning and an action-oriented curricula, thereby showing the teacher the way to greater self-determination, and by this to a greater opportunity for didactic and educational creativeness (Moser, 1974). The pupil, more so than the teacher, is subjected to a multitude of environmental and personal limitations, which he often experiences solely as external influences. In physical education instruction the pupil receives a certain amount of freedom in

which he can develop his personal identity, and in which a broad range of interacting experiences can be encountered. Physical education instruction, therefore, can contribute to a reasonable relationship between necessary external influences and the sought-after, allowed-for, and experienced self-determination.

3. Anticipation, reciprocation, and interpretation of expectations and behavior patterns as signs of interaction also happen in physical education instruction according to the personality structures of those taking part. It can be expected that some inconsistencies, such as misunderstandings, refusals, or even opposition, arise, and that some of these conditions manifest themselves as conflicts. Because of the problem of the relationship between external influences and self-determination, it must be stated that such inconsistencies are not only necessary but desirable. They must not be disregarded, and must not be suppressed through one-sided external influence, but must be clarified in thought and in discussions.

INTERACTIONAL ANALYSIS OF THE TEACHER-PUPIL RELATIONSHIP IN PHYSICAL EDUCATION INSTRUCTION

The deficiency of theories with respect to physical education instruction has already been mentioned. The majority of the interaction analyses concern theoretical instruction and choose verbal communication as the central indicator. Therefore, teacher behavior is often the independent, and pupil behavior the dependent variable. Thus, Tausch and Barthel (1969) in their work *The Effect of Encouraging Teacher Comments on the Performances of Pupils in Track and Field* determine that planned verbal encouragement and reinforcement lead to better achievements. As valuable as such investigations are, they are still a rarity in physical education instruction. Often they are also based on a theoretical scientific point of view from a simplified inductive theoretical model. Occasionally, the field-theory model of Lewin, in which the whole situation has to be considered is also neglected. This means that all too often the feedback process of the influence of the pupil on the teacher, the group processes, and the institutional and intentional determinations are not thoroughly considered.

We would like to attempt to identify some of the differences between physical education instruction and normal classroom instruction. Under the term classroom instruction we include all those subjects that are tested in the canon form in the *Arbitur*, the examination taken when a student is leaving the German school for entry into the university. These subjects include native language, mathematics, natural science, history, foreign languages, etc. The external distinguishing factors of classroom instruction are, according to Tausch et al. (1969), the frontal form of giving instruction in a small classroom and the overstress on verbal interaction. (This comparison does not in any way represent the total picture.)

Differences Between a Physical Education Lesson and a Classroom Lesson

Organizational Structure

P.E. Lesson	Classroom Lesson
No Promotion Subject: Influence or the motivation to learn lies within the pupil. No pressure for grades. Sport is counted as one of the "soft" subjects, with a higher than average attainment level (Ziegenspeck, 1973; Ingenkamp, 1977; Roeder and Freemann, 1974).	Promotion Subjects: Pressure or motivation comes through grades. Foreign languages and mathematics are the "hard" subjects. On the average, stricter marking levels prevail.
Immense organizational problems for the physical education teacher: working in the large space of the gymnasium and the field; preparation of equipment; checking of material; working with groups that are separated.	Relatively little organizational problems in frontal teaching.
Organization of out-of-school activities, e.g., school sport, sport meetings, training of interest groups.	Practically no organizational tasks for the teacher outside the compulsory hours.

Structure of Performance

P.E. Lesson	Classroom Lesson
The pupil experiences a feeling of unity through his psycho-physical-social experiences. His complete involvement is required.	Mostly only the cognitive part of the person is used, e.g., knowledge, solving of problems, the development of thought processes.
Permanent demands for achievement during a physical education lesson.	In the perceptive phases of learning there is seldom a manifestation of achievement.
The pupil constantly seeks to show his achievement in front of the teacher, his friends, and himself. Poor results cannot be hidden.	Pupil seldom exerts himself. Poor results are not so immediately apparent.
The fear of participating cannot be hidden; fear eventually can be overcome, because achievement is not important for class promotion; therefore, the possibility of a lesson without fear is created.	Fear of participating is easily hidden; however, among less-competent students the fear of not being promoted is often a motivational barrier (orientation toward disappointment).

Continued

Differences Between a Physical Education Lesson and a Classroom Lesson—*Continued*

Structure of Performance

Protection of engagement (Goffmann, 1973), which allows the individual to pretend participation, is not possible, because of the continuous open participation.	Protection of engagement, hidden through light participation is easily possible. While thinking about other things, there may also be visual activity.
The achievement of the teacher and the pupil can be easily observed and can usually be measured (easy visibility of performance).	Performances often do not show for a long time; they are harder to see openly and to measure. For many performances there is only one form of measurement, i.e. composition (no visibility of performance).
It is possible to make a direct comparison of achievement in almost all cases, with definite measures being available (competition as positive or negative motivational factor).	The lack of comparative measures allows for more rationalizations for the protection of uncertainty.
The positive or negative results are evident at once and work immediately as reinforcements.	Positive or negative results are often provided much later (e.g., return of written work); loss of direct reinforcement.
Demonstrations by the physical education teacher are direct, his competence in the subject area is always evident, and, to an extent, therefore noticeable to the pupils; it is not possible to fake competence in the subject.	The teacher can easily cover his weaknesses.
The teacher can, by virtue of his demonstrable competence, i.e., superior performance level, easily gain authority and prove it.	It is difficult to prove authority through subject competence.
On the contrary: the sport skills of the teacher are often not taken seriously because of the pressure of general criticism of performance.	To be taken seriously in his subject area, the teacher can exert pressure on the grading of performance (which is unfortunately often done).
Values that are basic in physical education often correspond with values in the youth's life and culture, e.g., apparent performance, sharing, participation, team attainment, fairness, physical prowess, especially among boys (a convergence of values). (Coleman, 1969; Widmer, 1966; Widmer, 1970b).	The values of the classroom lesson are often not recognized by the pupil, or they are still (at least for the time being) strange to him.

Continued

Differences Between a Physical Education Lesson and a Classroom Lesson—*Continued*

Differences in Methods

The learning model is secondary to intellectual learning. With this in mind, the methodological principle of verbal demonstration (psycho-motor-verbal learning) and the example become especially important.

Movement pictures as a cognitive movement structure have primary importance for the cognitive control of the development. The quality of the movement is the central objective. Cognitive movement pictures, mental training, etc., are always secondary to the subsequent movement performance.

After the learning phase the conditioning phase must be given special emphasis because conditioned movement patterns are the basis for modified movements and behavior in competitive sports, play, etc. The didactic form of the conditioning phase is important.

In physical education instruction, one strives for higher performance levels; therefore, one is apt to find a multitude of verbal commands, rules, and directives (however, this statement has yet to be empirically proven).

The development of cognitive structures and of problem-solving behavior is the main aim of a classroom lesson. Thought phases are the main emphasis.

Cognitive structures, such as knowledge and the thought processes, are the focal point. The immediate behavior (telling about...) is often only a control factor for the teacher.

Practice and utilization of ideas are usually left up to the pupil and as a rule are only tested in a written examination.

Classroom education requires many consultation and group teaching; there is as a result less necessity for giving orders.

Immediate Interactional Structure

Averbal and paralinguistic interaction have a great deal of meaning (e.g., manifestations of fear, manifestations of strengthening of gestures, posture expression). From the point of view of the teacher, the verbal interaction has a definite instrumental value in the premotivation, the explanation, and the verbal strengthening process.

The activity takes place in a large room. With the organizational problems, the complete engagement in sport activity, and the more free and open communication, the physical education instruction often turns into a place of conflict. Rivalries, differences in performance or interests, and conflicts between various pupils or informal groups can often be seen in competition, in games, or in training.

Verbal interaction is the main instrument for achieving recognition. Averbal and paralinguistic interaction are more readily suppressed by the pupil, and occasionally even faked.

The simple organizational structure and the concentration on cognitive fields in a frontal lesson prevents conflicts and rivalry from manifesting themselves readily.

Differences Between a
Physical Education Lesson and a Classroom Lesson

The personal interaction in physical education is distinguished by its physical nature. A physical education teacher often has to deal with situations of interaction that never confront the subject teacher in the classroom. Teacher and pupil are together when changing and showering; at camp they may possibly sleep in the same rooms; pupil-teacher bodily contact occurs when pupils are given manual assistance (i.e., contact is needed in physical education instruction). Maintenance of restrictions on the physical contact is expected of the subject teacher. If he does otherwise, the pupil regards him with suspicion or refuses to recognize his authority.

The various opposing characteristics of physical education and classroom instruction that have been presented here without any scientific basis show that the structural interaction in the teacher-pupil relationship differs in many ways between the two areas; it differs in questions of organization, in achievement or attainment, in didactics, and in the immediate interpersonal relationships. It is believed that in physical education instruction there is more immediate feedback regarding the self-image of pupils and teachers than in classroom instruction. These differences can explain to some extent the assumptions made earlier in this chapter. It is impossible to apply research results concerning the teacher-pupil relationship that have been obtained in classroom instruction directly to physical education instruction.

Analysis of the Variables of Interaction

Interaction in sport instruction has three main variables: the physical education teacher, the pupil, and the process of interaction. These three variables are examined briefly. At the same time, the preliminary nature of this discussion should be emphasized.

The Physical Education Teacher A considerable amount of literature exists concerning the personality of the coach and the leadership problems of top athletes (Feige et al., 1973, pp. 83-87 and 93-94). However, there is relatively little literature to be found on the personality of the physical education teacher, his self-image, and his interactions in physical education instruction. Such problems have been treated by using personality analyses, through questionnaires about attitudes and changes of attitudes, through the examination of the physical education teacher's outside image, through examinations by superiors, and by "deep" interviews (Koch, 1973; Bastine et al., 1969, 1970; Davis and Vienstein, 1972).

Personality Structure and Socialization through Sport Koch is of the opinion that physical education teachers have already undergone intensive socialization through sport in the family, in school, and in clubs, through which the teacher has made an early and stable decision concerning his profession. However, as a result of this, the danger exists that the physical education teacher has the tendency to reproduce too strongly his own idea of sport in the school and he can only appeal to those pupils who, through "primary and early socialization," like himself are motivated towards, and are ready for, sport. Self-recruiting and early stabilization lead to "a high degree of identification and an insufficient ability for self-criticism, i.e., the physical education teacher does not question the central aspects of the role of the physical education teacher and the substantial conditions of sport at all, or, if so, merely in a rudimentary way" (Cachay, 1973, pp. 387–393).

Hendry and Whiting (1972) point out in their personality analysis of future physical education teachers the dominant outstanding characteristics, as follows: Mesomorphic habitus (muscular), a relatively stable extroverted attitude, social orientation, a slight tendency towards narcissism and exhibitionism, aggressiveness in oral and written expression, emphasis on authority and order, highly motivated towards attainment levels, impulsiveness and emotional expression, interest in activity and a desire for adventure, keenness in planning, leading, and organization, and high male sexual identification. Furthermore, they point out that physical education teachers often regard others with a different physical and psychic constitution as being of very little importance. So the danger exists that their instructional philosophy will be, or will at least be implied, "What I can do, you can do too" (Hendry, 1974; Hendry and Whiting, 1972).

Self-profile of a Physical Education Teacher Hendry (1974) asked 1,000 physical education teachers to name six contributing factors that make up a successful physical education teacher. The self-profile resulted in the following qualities, listed in order of importance: 1) ability to gain the respect of the pupils, 2) ability to communicate ideas, 3) ability to develop confidence, 4) knowledge of material, 5) honesty and integrity, and 6) perseverence, or the ability to engage in continuous hard work. An examination of 132 high school trainers (coaches) in London resulted in a personality profile with high rates of achievement and a strong tendency for dominance, with a lower score in sensitivity towards others and ability to communicate with people. Questioning the teachers about their own behavior (profile) yielded a high score with respect to the ability to establish relationships with others (*Schools' Council Enquiry,* 1973).

There appears to be a gap between the desire to establish relationships with others and to help the pupils, on the one hand, and a high orientation toward achievement, on the other hand. A further discrepancy appears in the question of self-rating with respect to the image of the physical education teacher in family, school, and society. While Koch (1972), as a result of his research, has come to the conclusion that the physical education teacher has a high self-image, Volkamer (1967, 1970) talks about the uncertainty of the status of a physical education teacher. As a result of many discussions with teachers and with the realization that many groups of teachers and also many pupils regard sport as a "soft" subject, i.e., unessential for the child's promotion in classes, this writer believes that in reality the view of Volkamer (1967, 1970) is more likely to be the pertinent one; even if Hendry (1974) does express himself about the teacher of physical education as follows: "He is not a purveyor of life chances via examinations." The truth is that many physical education teachers in high schools do have a feeling of insecurity in their position that must be openly stated. If one considers further the differences between a physical education lesson and a classroom lesson, such as the many roles that the teacher has to assume or to initiate (set of rules), the more intimate contact between pupil and teacher, the continual striving for physical achievement in the eyes of the pupils, and the incidence of conflicts that occur in his lesson, then it is understandable that, with a certain type of personality and under certain conditions, all these factors can weigh heavily upon the physical education teacher.

Definite answers to the question concerning the interaction variable and the *physical education teacher* cannot be given presently because of the contradictory and very generalized research result. We are still missing research results from broader investigations on sport-socialization of the physical education teacher, on his self-profile and outward profile, on personality structures, and on professional motivations, and, above all, from investigations on his role as a socializer (i.e., on the question of how the various dimensions of personality, attitudes, and changes of attitudes affect specific circumstances). The role of the physical education teacher in the process of interaction has hardly been examined. Tausch (1970) is of the opinion that there is such a thing as a behavior of an educator, independent of the subject of teaching. Many authors, such as Rumpf (1969), Ulich (1977), Grell (1974), Flanders (1970), Combe (1971), Kirsten (1975), and others, warn of the tendency to derive interaction and behavior roles totally out of the personality and behavior. The interactional behavior can only be evaluated when it is considered with its didactic connotation, the learning aims, the specific lesson structures, and the personalities of pupils with different levels of intelligence.

The Pupil In a high school (or grammar school) with decentralized subject teaching, one can regard every pupil as a sports pupil. In this situation he is also under a certain handicap, because he is subject to many outside influences. The same applies to the teacher, who has to initiate and control the pedagogical interaction. From the comparison of physical education lessons to classroom lessons presented earlier, one may observe that the pupil is required to exhibit a permanent manifestation of his ability in front of the teacher and his fellow pupils. As a result there is always either a very positive or negative feedback for him, fears can be less easily hidden, the averbal and paralinguistic interactions take on an important meaning, conflicts with the teacher or with his fellow pupils take place openly, and interactions with the teacher and his friends involve a much closer bodily contact than in a verbal instructional pattern. This basic feeling of openness and freedom in a physical education lesson, with its many organizational facets, its wide interactional spectrum, and perhaps its permanent teacher personality structure, all too often lead the young physical education teacher to a stiff and authoritarian instructional style wherein only few opportunities are provided for the self-determination of the pupil.

Thus, physical education instruction is in danger of becoming a total "institution," in which all interactions are strongly regimented according to a set of rules, and which is threatened and controlled with sanctions (Goffman, 1973, p. 75; Heinze, 1974). Often the pupil tries to develop behavior patterns, which Goffman (1973) calls "interpersonal tactics." These are the interactions that take the form of opposition, refusal, and negation of performance or are evidenced by the interactional behavior patterns towards one's fellow pupils, such as apparent refusals, provoked disinterest, misuse of equipment, etc. With these types of interactions he shows his intentions to his fellow pupils and tries to influence them in his way of thinking. In reality, "interpersonal tactics" usually occur in conflict situations to save one's identity. The freedom in physical education instruction presents more possibilities for such tactics than does classroom instruction.

Mollenhauer (1972, p. 93) has drawn our attention to another pupil situation that can occur in physical education instruction. The repeated demonstrated ability of a pupil and the requirement for feedback can sometimes lead the physical education teacher to give too many compliments through praise and verbal encouragement. This tendency may arise as a result of misunderstanding certain aspects of teacher behavior training programs. With too great a frequency of praise, the enforcement effect may become dulled. The pupil may come to feel that this continual praise should no longer be taken seriously; therefore, an inconsistency develops between verbal reinforcement and the importance of it and praise is no longer taken seriously. The pupil is caught in a "relationship pit" (double-blind interaction) or in a "paradoxical communication situation" (Watzlawik, 1974). The inconsistency between verbally explained information and non-verbal gestures and actions, if it occurs too often, provokes "interpersonal tactics" in the pupil. It is still worse if the pupil no longer takes the teacher seriously. Because the identification with one subject is often more extrinsic through identification with a teacher, it is quite likely that will there be a negative attitude not only toward the physical education teacher, but also toward the sport activities with which he is associated.

There are research results available that deal with the interest in sport among high school pupils. The two hypothetically presented examples of possible pupil interaction (for which the empirical proof still has to be found, however) indicate that only a few investigations exist concerning pupil behavior and its effect on interactional structures in physical education instruction. The majority of research material pertains to the pupil behavior as an independent variable, but not vice versa. In this connection, comprehensive studies on the following questions should be started:

1. How do groups within a sports class originate?
2. How do physical education teachers behave in reacting to differently motivated pupils with various abilities to perform?
3. How do physical education teachers change their attitudes toward individual pupils or their profession, based on their acquired professional experience, e.g., accumulated failure experiences?

THE PROCESS OF INTERACTION

The problem of interaction has been a central research problem in educational science since about 1960. Rating scales for observation, analyses of lesson preparations, analyses of lesson procedures with video and tape recordings, and administration of questionnaires to both teachers and pupils, are all available as techniques for collection of data. Out of the many research results, a few have been selected at random and are presented in the following excerpts (Klausmeier and Ripple, 1974; Nickel, 1974; Kirsten, 1973; Flanders, 1970).

Flanders (1970) presents a scheme for interpretation and observation of teacher-pupil interaction in which only verbal behavior is examined. Assuming that this is an adequate pattern for total behavior, he differentiates between direct and indirect influences; the former increase the amount of freedom allowed to the pupil, and the latter decrease this freedom. Indirect influence accompanies higher school attainments and a positive attitude of the pupil toward the teacher and toward the school as a whole.

Nickel (1974) stated that with increased directions from the teacher, the pupil's level of concentration falls off markedly. Furthermore, one has to assume, according to available research results, that motivation for pupil performance is decreased as a result of too many directions.

Soar (1972) has stated that the present research position allows for some preliminary conclusions with respect to the relationship between teacher behavior and pupil development. Non-directiveness in the teacher's behavior tends to correlate positively with creativeness and growth of performance as well as with better pupil attitudes. There is also a positive correlation between teacher flexibility and an increase in the pupil's performance level. Criticism on the part of the teacher, in general, correlates negatively with higher levels of performance. The subtle, rather than readily apparent, behavior reactions of the teacher also show a positive relationship to the development of the pupil (Soar, 1972).

These studies show that the primary research emphasis has been on pattern and its effect on the development of the pupil. What is missing is a specific model of observed interaction for physical education instruction. Such a model not only should try to analyze the verbal interaction, but also should include the averbal and the psycho-motor forms of interaction. It should also present bibliographical data concerning the teacher and the pupil as well as the entire complex of the pupil relationship and its effect on teacher behavior.

There are a large number of very valuable models of observations and interpretations of the interactional process (Tausch and Tausch, 1972, p. 1952). In view of the fact that these examples mainly consider the verbal interaction and the effect of a defined teacher behavior pattern on the performance and motivation of the pupil, an attempt is made in the following sections to present, in a preliminary classification, several interactional patterns of the teacher and pupil in physical education instruction.

Teaching-Oriented Interaction Process

The fact has already been mentioned that interaction in physical education instruction does not present a free form of interaction, but that it is determined by institutional and intentional limitations. The institutional limitations are the organizational structure of the school as a subsystem of society and the ideological expectations of the school held by society. The intentional limitations are the unavoidable task of teaching for the teacher and learning for the pupil.

In the intentional teaching-learning processes there are limitations on free interaction through the more or less structured curricula and the so-called valid learning aims. Learning determined interactional processes are all those that are necessary for the intentional teaching-learning processes. These are the processes through which defined psycho-motor qualifications (strength, flexibility, control of game, tactics, cognitive control of motor patterns, psycho-motor automatism, etc.) and defined movement patterns in the various sport disciplines are taught and learned.

The actions of the teacher consist of: verbal motivation; catching pupils' interest; encouraging; being ready to assist; reinforcing gestures and actions; encouraging half-semantic verbal expressions; presenting; demonstrating; verbal explanation and justifications; giving commentaries and directions that accompany the movements (Volpert, 1977; Hildenbrandt, 1973; Ungerer, 1973; Drexel, 1975); interaction involving tactile contact when assisting; giving correlations by demonstration and verbalization; verbal reinforcement through praise or reprimand, averbal reinforcement through gesture and actions; space, time, and intensity commands, such as "now," "over there," "still more," etc.; and, finally, formulating and justifying decisions.

The pupil's actions take the form of verbal and averbal expression of interest and readiness; verbal and averbal signs of having understood; posing questions; asking for a new explanation; discussing; carrying out; repeating; tactile bodily contact with the teacher; requesting support and assistance; feedback for the teacher's expression of joy and satisfaction after successful achievements; expression of anger, fear, or feelings of shame after unsuccessful achievement (e.g., exclamation, brightness of the eyes, and posture); or thanking the teacher for his help, etc.

Teaching-oriented interactions are exemplified in a reciprocal process of information exchange, anticipation of the awaited reaction, and anticipation of the subsequent action in the medium of language, gesture, mimicry, and movement patterns. The complete process of interaction results in a flow of interaction, which is controlled by the teaching aim, in a total action or action game (Moser, 1974). In general, in a teaching-oriented interactional process, the physical education teacher will determine the rules of the active game as a result of his knowledge and experiences, his subject, and his methodologic and didactic skill (Widmer, 1975b).

The Inter-Instructional Interaction Process

In addition to the teaching-oriented interaction process, immediate interpersonal contacts are realized by interaction that has been initiated through the learning-oriented interaction process. These contacts are the reactions to this interaction, and come primarily from feelings of empathy. They can involve extreme expressions, e.g., maintaining an attiude of aloofness, or speech and gesture, and various types of behavior, including an actual meeting of minds through a friendly participation in the fate of other individuals. Inter-instructional interaction processes include all those interactions that occur simultaneously and that are expressions of an immediate sympathetic relationship between teacher and pupil.

The degree of reversibility or irreversibility is defined by an understanding of the roles exhibited by the teacher and pupil in their actions. These may be signs of either a negative or positive interaction, and occasionally of an indifferent attitude. They may include: gestures of sympathy; hand shaking; tapping on the shoulder, smiling and laughing; consoling; giving encouragement; appealing to courage, duty, and norms; informing; advising; keeping in mind the many variations of emotional situations; gestures of refusal and mimicry; verbal expression of turning away, of opposition, and of aggression; verbal and motor characterization; and refusal to maintain eye contact.

In the inter-instructional interaction process one can also find reciprocity, anticipation, and interpretation of expectations and observed behavior. These interactions are also determined by the role patterns, that is to say by a hierarchical system of authoritarian dominance. However, these interactions are no longer as strongly directed as in the intentional rule-game of instruction; above all they are directed by sympathy (Claessens, 1972). In this system of sympathy, personality variables can be regarded as playing an especially important role; for example, the unconscious refusal mechanisms, such as projection, regression, and fixation, on the part of the teacher and the pupil (Heyer, 1974). One has to remember at this point the phenomena of "interpersonal tactics" (Goffman, 1973) and the reactions in "cases of relationship" (Mollenhauer, 1972). According to Soar (1972) the importance of inter-instructional interaction must be clear. The subtle, and not the immediately apparent, behavior reactions of the teacher show the relationship to the individual pupil's development.

CONTROL FROM OUTSIDE AND SELF-CONTROL IN THE INTERACTION PROCESS

Questions about teaching-oriented and inter-instructional interaction still remain, and to these questions can be added the pedagogically important question about the degree of freedom of the single interaction, e.g., the question of control from outside or self-control. Physical education instruction is, as previously stated, subject to the control of social and institutional influences that pertain to both the teacher and the pupil. Learning from the control of environmental influences as a pedagogical task occurs in physical education instruction in many ways: space-time conditions, order and question of sports material, clothing used, rules used in the various sport disciplines, etc., all have their influence. Outside controls also result from the intentional aspects, e.g., curriculum, planned or requested teaching and learning aims, laws that occur in the course of psycho-physical activities, necessities of training programs, etc. However, within the intentional aspect the question of possible self-control arises. Self-control, a gradual decision about the kind of interaction, which comes from the personality structure in a given social context, is like the learning control from outside a pedagogical task. In the interaction process between teacher and pupils, mutual degrees of freedom between self- and outward determination can be seen. This concerns the following polarization:

openness	rigidity
permissiveness	repressiveness
room for decision	manipulation
authoritarianism	discussion with partners (co-determination)
reversibility	irreversibility

Some interaction actions are given here that belong to the category self-determination or control from outside:

1. Interactions of the teacher within the limits of self-determination of the pupils: demanding, requesting, not allowing any discussion, giving orders, criticizing, promising, deciding oneself, warning, threatening, refusing answers and reasons, negative strengthening using gestures and actions.

2. Interactions of the teacher with respect to exhibiting self-control: allowing something to be voted upon, discussing, cooperative planning, looking for the consensus, caring for minorities, allowing the possibility of spontaneous learning of movement (interest groups), proving his authority, allowing criticism and questions without threatening with sanctions, giving encouragement.

3. Interactions of the pupils who request self-control: being allowed to vote, asking, discussing, indicating needs and desires, giving their own opinions and justifying them, talking of voluntary abstinence, criticizing (when it is justified) without fear of sanctions.

4. Interactions of the pupils who disturb the self-control of the teacher: insulting, becoming angry, supplying opposition, organizing groups to work against the teacher, criticizing in an unmotivated and unjustified way, refusing to perform, caricaturing the teacher and making fun of him, faking pain or injury, damaging equipment, not looking after equipment, provoking the physical education teacher with questions stemming from other subjects in order to demonstrate his weaknesses.

SITUATIVE INTERACTION AND LASTING INTERACTION

Until now we have spoken mainly about interaction in concrete situations, e.g., before, during, and shortly after physical education instruction. As a result of the personality structures of the teacher and the pupil and as a result of the experiences with interaction one can eventually develop a lasting interaction structure. This means that similar situations always turn out in a similar ways or perhaps even in the same way. Thus, in a lasting interaction, the self-control on the part of the teacher or the outside influence, the acceptance or the refusal, the role played or the meeting, can dominate. The lasting interaction structure is the observable style of leadership or instruction by a teacher. Pupils also may develop interaction structures of a lasting quality or signs of evidence of such structure: refusal or pleasure, openness or defense, opposition or acceptance. Lasting interaction patterns allow the partner to make predictions of behavior with a relative degree of certainty. The teacher is faced with the task of self-examination, namely, to ask himself about such lasting interaction patterns in order to make possible corrections and modifications.

Dimensions of Interaction

An attempt is made here to present in a classified scheme the dimensions of physical education instruction interactions already discussed. In actual physical education instruction these interactions overlap in their dimensions and continually influence each other.

Aspects of the Degree of Freedom	Aspects of Statements of Position
Self-determination (Self-control)	Turning toward confirmation, acceptance
Outward-determination (Outside control)	Refusal, turning away, turning back

Teaching-Oriented Interactions	Inter-instructional Interaction
Motivation Demonstration Verbal explanation and justification Correction Evaluation Reinforcement	Position-determined interaction Meeting-determined interaction

Time Aspect of Interaction	Social Aspect of Interaction
Situation interaction structures Lasting interaction structures	Individual (Teacher: Pupil) Collective and group teacher: group, class

Forms of Communication

Psycho-motor-tactile
Verbal-semantic
Paralinguistic
Averbal

PEDAGOGICAL OUTLOOK

We have seen that interaction in physical education instruction is complex. Many factors interact. The leading recognized fields of thought in this pedagogical area have been taken into consideration. As a follow-up of the discoveries related to pedagogical theories, some preliminary conclusions may be drawn as a consequence of these findings (Widmer, 1974, pp. 109, 119–121).

Research Questions

At the beginning of this chapter, it was mentioned that a deficiency of theories existed for sport pedagogy. Despite the valuable research results available and cited in this chapter, some research questions remain that have to be approached on a broader base. These include: research on the personality of the physical education teacher; research on attitudes and changes in attitude of the teacher and the pupil through the experiences of interaction; investigations of the socialization of physical education teachers and the social effects of physical education instruction; empirical data comparing classroom instruction with physical education instruction; frequency and meaning of averbal interaction in comparison to verbal interaction; investigation of the self-image and the outer image of the physical education teacher; comparison of the self-image of the physical education teacher and the actual interaction patterns; the origin and changes of interaction patterns between pupils and teachers in physical education instruction; influence of the pupil's interaction on the self-image and concrete behavior of the physical education teacher; function and meaning of the styles of leadership in physical education instruction as compared to classroom instruction.

Incentives for Interaction as a Part of Instruction—
Reflection and Observation of One's Interaction

In accordance with the complexity and the meaning of interaction, it would appear to be imperative that the physical education teacher get to know and continually consider this behavior and his own interaction behavior. Reflection on his lessons, observations of instructions, talks with colleagues, and video tapes of his instruction can help him achieve this goal. He should learn to observe and interpret the averbal interactions of pupils, and to keep his own interactions under control.

Meaning of Reinforcement According to Flanders (1970), the meaning of interaction, and therefore of reinforcement, rests upon accepting that one is in a position that involves give and take as well as tolerance of others. Through reinforcement, the pupil experiences the participation of the teacher, which provides feedback and serves as incentive for his subsequent behavior. The genuineness of the reinforcement can especially be seen in the structure of the meeting, which is part of inter-instructional interaction. Providing adequate praise and recognition as well as preventing inconsistencies between verbal reinforcement and actual meaningful reinforcement are continuing tasks of the physical education teacher.

Search for Possibilities of Self-Control Self-control is recognized as a pedagogical aim, even in physical education instruction. Discussion of aims and methods; group activities; possibilities for participating in the planning of instruction; reserving room for decision, etc., all encourage its development. The significance of self-control, as proven empirically, is expressed in the following quotation:

> In the whole one is allowed to acknowledge, that the available results support the statement, that the allowance of independence, the recognition of own initiative, and independently acquired behavior patterns have definite impact on the education towards independence and also on the motivation for achievement behavior (Nickel, 1974, p. 29).

Solving Conflicts The comparison between classroom instruction and physical education instruction has shown that physical education instruction under certain circumstances is more prone to conflicts, e.g., through the many organizational tasks, through bodily contact, and through the openness of the instruction in a large area, but above all through the total engagement in bodily activity. Conflicts should not be allowed to be pushed aside as a result of repression or too much rigidity; they have to be worked out in discussions (Habermas; Mollenhauer, 1972) and in general analysis of interactional conflicts.

Problem of Pedagogical Leadership Style Tausch (1972), Correll (1970), and Klafki (1970), among others, are of the opinion that there is one possible correct style of approach or leadership that results in a positive pupil relationship, and that this style is valid for all situations in instruction: The socio-integrative, cooperative, non-directive, democratic, or participation style. Insight into the complexity of instruction demands certain modifications.

> Apparently differing types of pupils, differing situations, different learning aims require different teaching methods which can no longer be seen under the conventional term *democratic* and cannot be used as a consistent behavior pattern (Reinhardt, 1972, p. 140).

Without a doubt, this is also true for physical education instruction, with its specific institutional, intentional, and personal conditions. Soar (1972) said:

> Many investigations point out that an increase of non-directive teacher behavior leads to an increased rate of development for the pupil, although only up to a certain point, after which there may be a certain degree of falling off in the pupil advancement. Furthermore, the question of an optimal development seems to be a function of the learning aims; the more abstract the task, the more optimal is non-directiveness in the teacher's behavior, the more concrete the task, the more is optimal directiveness (Soar, 1972, p. 516).

Such a generalization should be accepted very carefully; if it is true, it would appear that a direct teaching style would be the best for the physical education teacher, because here one is dealing with concrete aims and learning tasks, along with concise biomechanical and physiological laws and more or less clear cut rules in the various sport disciplines. If one expects that physical education instruction must also provide motivation to sport activity as well as its more obvious task of encouraging attainment in sport, and if it also performs the task of contributing to individualizations, to socialization, and to self-control, then it is apparent that the style of leadership should lean toward non-directiveness and be applied in a non-directive way. In accordance with both the already presented multi-dimensional problems of interaction structures in physical education instruction and the various quotations presented concerning possible demands for modifications in the style of instruction, the following might be concluded for the physical education teacher: Instead of using a utopian style of leadership of non-directiveness, or, for the sake of simplicity, using an authoritarian and unjustified behavior pattern, it may be desirable for one to strive to attain a situational style of leadership. This means that the physical education teacher should decide according to his pedagogical and didactic understandings how he should plan to carry out his instructions and how he will be able to carry them through in a pedagogical way, or how he would like to be able to do it.

FURTHER QUESTIONS

This chapter covers only the immediate interaction process between the teacher and pupil. This approach inadvertently sets aside two questions that should now just be mentioned briefly:

1. The question of the social meaning of the teacher-pupil interaction. The specialized form of interaction in physical education instruction should clarify how one can contribute to the social development of the pupil in society, how well this may become an example of a possible democratic form of behavior, and where the possible boundaries of such intentions lie (Castner, 1969; Heinemann, 1977; Rosenthal and Jakobsen, 1971; Ruhloff et al., 1971; Widmer, 1970a, 1975a).

2. Then there is the question of the meaning of the interaction structure in the basic and more advanced education of physical education teachers. This might include courses in teacher behavior training (Antons, 1973; Argyle, 1972; Becke, 1973; Belschner et al., 1973; Caselmann, 1964; Groothoff, 1972; Luft, 1971; Lutz and Ronellenfitsch, 1971; Rogers, 1951, 1956, 1972; Spangenberg, 1969); incorporation of group dynamics in the training of teachers; role playing of the teaching and planning procedures; socio-drama training of observation of teacher's behavior, not only with respect to the learning-oriented behavior but also with respect to the inter-instructional interaction; and questions of micro-teaching (Allen and Ryan, 1972; Eigler et al., 1973; Gerner, 1972; Grace, 1973, Herrmann, 1972; Lange, 1972; Siegner, 1975; Tausch, 1970; Zöschbauer, 1974).

This chapter concludes with the following two suggestions:

1. The problem of interaction between the teacher and the pupil in physical education instruction should become the subject of future research in sport pedagogy.
2. The problem of interaction between teacher and pupil has to be systematically built into the training curriculum of the physical education teachers in the basic and advanced programs.

REFERENCES

Allen, D.W., and Ryan, K.A. 1972. Mikroteaching. (Microteaching.) Julius Belz OHG., Weinheim.
Antons, K. 1973. Praxis der Gruppendynamik. (Practice of Group Dynamics.) Hogrefe, Göttingen.
Argyle, M. 1972. Soziale Interaktion. (Social Interaction.) Kiepenheuer, Witsch & Co. Gmbh., Köln-Marienburg.
Bales, R.F. 1950. Interaction Process Analysis. Routledge and Kegan Paul Ltd., London.
Bastine, R., et al. 1969. Konstruktion eines Fragebogens zur direktiven Einstellung von Lehrern (FDE). (Construction of a questionnaire in relation to directive attitude of teachers.) Z. Entwicklungspsychol. Pädagog. Psychol. 3:176–189.
Bastine, R., et al. 1970. Beiträge zur Konstrukt-Validierung des Fragebogens zur direktiven Einstellung von Lehrern (FDE). (Contributions to the construct validation of the questionnaire in relation to directive attitude of teachers.) Z. Entwicklungspsychol. Pädagog. Psychol. 1:47–59.
Becke, G.E. 1973. Optimierung schulischer Gruppenprozesse durch situatives Lehrertraining. (Optimization of group processes in school through situation training of teachers.) In: Gruppenpädagogik /Gruppendynamik. Band 3. Quelle & Meyer, Heidelberg.
Belschner, W. u.a. 1973. Verhaltenstherapie in Erziehung und Unterricht. (Behavior Therapy in Education and Instruction.) Verlag W. Kohlhammer, Stuttgart.
Bernett, H. 1970. Grundfragen der Leibeserziehung. (Basic Issues of Physical Education.) 2. Aufl. Karl Hofmann, Druckerei und Verlag, Schorndorf.
Beyer, E. 1967. Begabtenförderung in zentralen Neigungsgruppen. (Support for the gifted in centralized interest groups.) Die Leibeserziehung 16.
Cachay, K., et al. 1973. Bericht zum Kongreß "Sozialisation im Sport." (Report on the congress "socialization in sport.") Sportwissenschaft 4:387 ff.
Caselmann, Ch. 1964. Wesensformen des Lehrers. (Basic Patterns of the Teacher.) 3. Aufl. Ernst Klett OHG., Stuttgart.
Castner, Th. 1969. Schüler im Autoritätskonflikt. (Pupils in Authority Conflict.) Hermann Luchterhand Verlag, Darmstadt.
Claessens, D. 1972. Familie und Wertsystem. (Family and Value System.) 3. Aufl. Duncker & Humbolt, Berlin.
Coleman, J.S. 1961. The Adolescent Society. The Free Press of Glencoe Illinois, Glencoe.
Combe, A. 1971. Kritik der Lehrerrolle. (Critics of the Role of the Teacher.) Verlag das Taschenbuch, Balve.

Correll, W. 1970. Lernpsychologie. (Psychology of Learning.) 10. Aufl. Ludwig Auer, Verlag Cassianeum, Donauwörth.

Davis, E.E., and Viernstein, N. 1972. Entwicklung einer Skala zur Messung von Einstellungen von Lehrern zu Kind und Unterricht (LEKU). (Development of a scale for measuring attitudes of teachers towards the child and instruction.) Z. Entwicklungspsychol. Pädagog. Psychol. 3:194–216.

Diekert, J. 1972. Entwurf eines Curriculummodells Leibeserziehung. (Development of a curriculum model for physical education.) Die Leibeserziehung 7:221–228.

Dietrich, K. 1972. Zum Problem der Lehrplanentscheidung. Eine Analyse der Reformbestrebungen in der Leibeserziehung. (Concerning the Problem of Curriculum Decision. An Analysis of Reform Movements in Physical Education.) Czwalina, Ahrensburg.

Drexel, G. 1975. Sprechhandlungen des Lehrers im Sportunterricht. (Speech behavior of the teacher in sport instruction.) Sportwissenschaft 2:162–184.

Egger, K. 1975. Lernübertragungen im Sportunterricht. (Transfer of Learning in Sport Instruction.) Birkhäuser Verlag, Basel.

Feige, K., et al. (Red.). 1973. III. Europäischer Kongreß für Sportpsychologie. (III. European Congress for Sport Psychology.) Karl Hofmann, Druckerei und Verlag, Schorndorf.

Eigler, G., et al. 1973. Grundkurs Lehren und Lernen. (Basic Course in Teaching and Learning.) Julius Belz OHG., Weinheim.

Fetz, D. 1972. Allgemeine Methodik der Leibesübungen. (General Methods of Physical Education.) 5. Aufl. Wilhelm Limpert-Verlag, Frankfurt.

Flanders, N. 1970. Analyzing Teaching Behavior. Addison-Wesley Publishing Company Inc., Massachusetts.

Gerner, B. 1972. Der Lehrer—Verhalten und Wirkung. (The teacher—Behavior and Effect.) Wissenschaftliche Buchgesellschaft, Darmstadt.

Goffman, E. 1973. Asyle. Suhrkamp Verlag KG., Frankfurt.

Grace, G.R. 1973. Der Lehrer im Rollenkonflikt. (The Teacher in Role Conflict.) L. Schwann-Verlag, Düsseldorf.

Grell, J. 1974. Techniken des Lehrerverhaltens. (Techniques of Teacher Behavior.) Julius Belz OHG., Weinheim.

Grössing, St. 1973. Sport-Curriculum. (Sport-Curriculum.) Universität-Salzburg, Salzburg.

Groothoff, H. 1972. Funktion und Rolle des Erziehers. (Function and Role of The Educator.) Juventa-Verlag GmbH., München.

Grupe, O. 1969. Grundfragen der Sportpädagogik. (Basic Questions of Sport Pedagogy.) Karl Hofmann, Druckerei und Verlag, Schorndorf.

Grupe, O. (Hrsg.) 1973. Einführung in die Theorie der Leibeserziehung. (Introduction to The Theory of Physical Education.) 3. Aufl. Karl Hofmann, Druckerei und Verlag, Schorndorf.

Haag, H. (Red.) 1974. Leistungskurs Sport. (Special Course: Sport.) Karl Hofmann, Druckerei und Verlag, Schorndorf.

Hecker, G. 1971. Leistungsentwicklung im Sportunterricht. (Development of Performance in Sport Instruction.) Julius Belz OHG., Weinheim.

Heinemann, K. 1971. Das Sportengagement von Gymnastikschülern verschiedener Schichten. (The participation of high school students belonging to different social classes.) Sportwissenschaft 2:214–228.

Heinze, R. and Th. 1974. Soziale Interaktion in der Schulklasse. (Social interaction in the school class.) Westermanns Pädagogische Beiträge 5.

Hendry, L. 1974. A Study of Certain Aspects of the Physical-Education Profession. Hum. Factors 16:528-544.

Hendry, L., and Whiting, H.T.A. 1972. General Course and Specialist Physical Education Student Characteristics. Educat. Res. 14:152-156.

Herrmann, Th. (Hrsg.) 1972. Psychologie der Erziehungsstile. (Psychology of Educational Styles.) 2. Aufl. Hogrefe, Göttingen.

Heyer, A. 1974. Psychodynamische Aspekte der Lehrer-Schüler Interaktion. (Psychodynamics of the Teacher-Pupil Relationship.) Juris-Verlag Dr. H. Christen, Zürich.

Hildenbrandt, E. 1973. Sprache und Bewegung. (Language and movement.) Sportwisenschaft 3:55-69.

Ingenkamp, K. (Hrsg.) 1971. Die Fragwürdigkeit der Zensurengebung. (The Doubtfullness of Grading.) Julius Belz OHG., Weinheim.

Jost, E. (Hrsg.) 1973. Sport-Curriculum. (Sport Curriculum.) Karl Hofmann, Druckerei und Verlag, Schorndorf.

Kirsch, A.O.J. Grundriß der Leibeserziehung. (Foundations of Physical Education.) Ferdinand Kamp KG., Verlag, Bochum.

Kirsten, R.F. 1973. Lehrerverhalten. (Teacher Behavior.) Ernst Klett OHG., Stuttgart.

Klafki, W., et al. 1970. Funkkolleg Erziehungswissenschaft. Studienbegleitbrief. Bd. I (Radio-College-Education. Written Material, Vol. I.) 2. Aufl. Julius Belz OHG., Weinheim.

Klausmeier, H.J., and Ripple, R.E. 1947. Moderne Unterrichtspsychologie. (Modern Instructional Psychology.) Bd. II. Ernst Reinhardt, München.

Koch, J.J. 1972. Lehrer—Studium und Berut. (Teacher—Study and Profession.) Süddeutsche Verlagsges. mbH., Ulm.

Koch, K., and Mielke, W. 1974. Die Gestaltung des Unterrichts in der Leibeserziehung. (The Formation of Instruction in Physical Education.) 4. Aufl. Karl Hofmann Druckerei und Verlag, Schorndorf.

Kurz, D. 1971. Curriculumentwicklung als Werkstattarbeit. (Development of curricula as field work.) Sportwissenschaft 2:197-213.

Lange, H., and Garritsen, H. 1972. Strukturkonflikte des Lehrerberufs. (Structure Conflicts of the Teaching Profession.) Bertelsmann, Düsseldorf.

Luft, J. 1971. Einführung in die Gruppendynamik. (Introduction to Group Dynamics.) Ernst Klett OHG., Stuttgart.

Lutz, M., and Ronellenfitsch, W. 1971. Gruppendynamisches Training in der Lehrerbildung. (Training in Group Dynamics in Teacher Training.) Ernst Klett OHG., Stuttgart.

Lutter, H. 1972. Untersuchungen über Formen seelischen Geschehens auf dem Gebiet der Leibeserziehung. (Investigations on Aspects of Inner Actions in Physical Education.) Czwalina, Ahrensburg.

Mester, L. 1969. Grundfragen der Leibeserziehung. (Foundations of Physical Education.) 3. Aufl. Georg Westermann Verlag, Braunschweig.

Mollenhauer, K. 1972. Theorien zum Erziehungsprozeß. (Theories of the Educational Process.) Juventa-Verlag GmbH., München.

Moser, H. 1974. Handlungsorientierte Curriculumforschung. (Action-Oriented Curriculum Research) Julius Belz, OHG., Basel.

Nickel, H. 1973. Probleme und Schwierigkeiten in der Verwirklichung eines nichtautoritären Lehrerverhaltens. (Problems and difficulties in the realization of a nonauthoritarian teacher behavior.) In: H. Nickel and E. Langhorst (Hrsg.),

Brennpunkte der pädagogischen Psychologie (Issues of Educational Psychology), Klett, Bern.
Nickel, H., and Langhorst, E. (Hrsg.) 1973. Brennpunkte der Pädagogischen Psychologie. (Issues of Educational Psychology.) Klett, Bern.
Nickel, H. 1974. Beiträge zur Psychologie des Lehrerverhaltens. (Contributions on Psychology of Teacher Behavior.) Ernst Reinhardt, München.
Parson, T. 1959. The School Class as a Social-System. Harvard Ed. Rev. 29.
Paschen, K. 1970. Didaktik der Leibeserziehung. (Didactics of Physical Education.) 3. Aufl. Wilhelm Limpert-Verlag, Frankfurt.
Reinhardt, S. 1972. Zum Professionalisierungsprozeß des Lehrers. (The Process of Professionalization of the Teacher.) Athenäum, Frankfurt.
Rieder, H. 1971. Sport als Terapie. (Sport as Therapy.) Bartels und Wernitz, Berlin.
Riegauer, B. 1969. Sport und Arbeit. (Sport and Work.) Suhrkamp Verlag KG., Frankfurt.
Roeder, P.M., and Treumann, K. 1974. Dimension der Schulleistung. (The Dimension of School Performance.) Ernst Klett OHG., Stuttgart.
Rogers, C.R. 1951. Client-centered Therapy. Boston.
Rogers, C.R. 1956. On Becoming a Person. Pastoral Psychology 7.
Rogers, C.R. 1972. Die nicht-direktive Beratung. (Non-Directive Counseling.) Kindler Verlag GmbH., München.
Röthig, P. (Red.) 1977. Sportwissenschaftliches Lexikon. (Sport Science Dictionary.) 4. Aufl. Karl Hofmann, Druckerei und Verlag, Schorndorf.
Rosenthal, C., and Jakobsen, L. 1971. Pygmalion im Unterricht. (Pygmalion in Instruction.) Julius Belz OHG., Weinheim.
Ruhloff, J., et al. 1970. Ein Schulkonflikt wird durchgespielt. (Trial for a Conflict in School.) Quelle & Meyer, Heidelberg.
Rumpf, H. 1969. Sachneutrale Unterrichtsbeobachtung. (Object-neutral observation of instruction.) Z. Pädagog. 17:293–314.
Schmitz, J.N. 1973. Lernen in den Leibesübungen. (Learning in Physical Activity.) 2. Aufl. Karl Hofmann, Druckerei und Verlag, Schorndorf.
Schools' Council Enquiry. 1973. Physical Education Report. Her Majesty's Stationary Office, London.
Seybold, A. 1973. Pädagogische Prinzipien in der Leibeserziehung. (Educational Principles in Physical Education.) Karl Hofmann Druckerei und Verlag, Schorndorf.
Siegner, R. 1975. Erziehungspsychologisches Verhaltenstraining für Lehrer. (Educational - Psychological Behavior Training for the Teacher.) Ungedruckte Lizentiatsarbeit, Pädagogisches Institut der Universität Zürich, Zürich.
Soar, R.S. 1972. Teaching Behavior and Measures of Pupil Growth. Int. Rev. Ed. p. 526.
Spangenberg, K. 1969. Chancen der Gruppenpädagogik. (Chances of Group Pedagogy.) Julius Belz OHG., Weinheim.
Tausch, R. 1970. Gesprächstherapie. (Conversation Therapy.) Hogrefe, Göttingen.
Tausch, R., and Tausch, A.-M. 1972. Erziehungspsychologie. (Educational Psychology.) 4. Aufl. Hogrefe, Göttingen.
Tausch, R., and Barthel, A., et al. 1969. Die Auswirkungen ermutigender Lehreräußerungen auf die Leichtathletikleistungen von Schülern. (The effect of encouraging teacher comments on the performance of track and field with pupils.) Z. Entwicklungspsychol. Pädagog. Psycho. 4:241—248.
Ulrich, E. 1971. Gruppendynamik in der Schulklasse. (Group Dynamics in the School Class.) Ehrenwirth Verlag GbmH., München.

Ungerer, D. 1973. Zur Theorie des sensomotorischen Lernens. (Concerning the Theory of Sensomotor-Learning.) 2. Aufl. Karl Hofmann, Druckerei und Verlag, Schorndorf.

Volkamer, M. 1967 and 1970. Zur Sozialpsychologie des Leibeserziehers. (Concerning Social Psychology of the Physical Education Teacher.) Die Leibeserziehung 12 and 4.

Volpert, W. 1971. Sensomotorisches Lernen. (Sensorimotor Learning.) Wilhelm Limpert-Verlag, Frankfurt.

Watzlawik, P., et al. 1974. Menschliche Kommunikation. (Human Communication.) 4. Aufl. Hans Huber, Bern.

Widmer, K. 1966. Entwicklungsspezifisches Erleben und Verhalten des Jugendlichen Mädchens im Turn- und Sportunterricht. (Feeling and Behavior of Young Girls in Sport Instruction according to their developmental Level.) In: Turnen und Sport für weibliche Jugend. Eidg. Turn-und Sportschule, Magglingen.

Widmer, K. 1970a. Der Begriff "Haltung" in der pädagogischen Fragestellung. (The term 'posture' in educational perspective.) Die Leibeserziehung. 4:112–118.

Widmer, K. 1970b. Die Situation der Jugend in einer sich wandelnden Zeit. (The situation of youth in a changing time.) In: F. Tscherne (Hrsg.), Leibesübungen im Pubertätsalter. Bundesanstalt. f. Leibenerziehung, Wien.

Widmer, K. 1974. Sportpädagogik. Prolegomena zur theoretischen Begründung der Sportpädagogik als Wissenschaft. (Sport Pedagogy. Prologue for the Theoretical Foundation of Sport Pedagogy as Science.) Karl Hofmann, Druckerei und Verlag, Schorndorf.

Widmer, K. 1975a. Pädagogische Aspekte der schulischen Leistung. (Educational Aspects of School Performance.) In: J. Buhofer (Hrsg.), Grenzen der Leistung. Walter-Verlag, Freiburg.

Widmer, K. 1975b. Kompetenzprobleme des Sportlehrers. (Problems of the competence of the sport teacher.) In: E. Niedermann (Hrsg.), Salzburger Beiträge zum Sport in unserer Zeit. Universität Salzburg, Salzburg.

Ziegenspeck, J. 1973. Zensur und Zeugnis in der Schule. (Grades and Certificates in the School.) Hermann Schroedel Verlag KG., Hannover.

Zöschbauer, F., and Hoekstra A. 1974. Kommunikationstraining (Communication training.) In: E. Meyer (Hrsg.), Gruppenpädagogik/Gruppendynamik. Quelle & Meyer, Heidelberg.

The Teacher-Pupil Relationship in Sport Instruction

G. Landau

Scientific study of the existing problems in the realm of sport pedagogy has, as yet, hardly been touched upon. One could review the development of studies on instructional theory, but if given too early this could prove to be more detrimental than helpful for sport pedagogy. On the other hand, an overall review of the few available publications in the German language shows that these previous studies of the problem are characterized by a pragmatic adoption of apparently sound concepts or theories without considering the impenetrable theoretical premises for instruction.

Whoever considers seriously the aim of this Symposium, that is, to define the position of sport pedagogy within sport sciences and especially within education as a science, will not be able to take a position of unquestioning acceptance of available concepts. All the more so because, underneath the veneer of a dignified scientific approach, a special idea of sport instruction and an interpretation of the teacher-pupil relationship are presented in an uncritical form for the training of physical education teachers. For a definition of the position of sport pedagogy it would be necessary to clarify certain points: for example, what is the relationship of the problem of the teacher-pupil relationship to instruction theory, and, at the same time, how does the development of a theory of sport pedagogy relate to the theories of educational science? As a result, in this chapter an attempt is made, first, to draw attention to the necessity for clarity in instructional theory through a critical analysis of the points of view presently held by researchers in sport pedagogy. Second, the chapter shows that every instructional or educational theory predefines the position of instruction and the teacher-pupil relationship in a very specific way. At this stage one must ask in what way the definition of instruction is a preconceived research concept related to the teacher-pupil relationship, and what conclusions can be drawn about statements concerning and pertaining to an issue related to sport instruction.

POINTS OF VIEW PRESENTLY HELD
IN DISCUSSION AND EXPLANATION OF INSTRUCTIONAL THEORY

The majority of available publications originate from the models of pedagogical and psychological research, examining the relationship between the educator and children and youth, and discuss the relevance to sport instruction. These are attempts to put forward a behavior training program for teachers of sport. Among these attempts deserving mention are the arguments put forth by Grössing (1972), Schmitz (1972), and Widmer (1974), as well as the behavior training experiments done by Jessen (1974). All of these contributions are based on the foundations developed by Lewin (among others) and try to make use either of his theory of the typology of educational behavior patterns or of the theory of Tausch (among others) who further developed the analytical dimensional model. They discuss the teacher-pupil relationship in sport instruction, particularly in the categories *instruction, teaching method,* and *educational dimensions,* and they try to make it workable in a training concept.

Grössing, Schmitz, and Widmer disagree about the usefulness of the concept of teaching styles in sport instruction. Although all point out that at present there is insufficient empirical certainty of the uses of teaching styles in the area of sport, they all (including Jessen) adhere to the research assumption, that the educator's behavior is the independent variable that influences the experience and behavior of the pupil. Through such a premise the teacher-pupil relationship is presented within an *a priori* definite interaction framework, in which the teacher is the controlling and central figure of instruction, and is presented as the one on whom the pupils must depend in a feedback situation. The teacher-pupil relationship works, as a result of acceptance of this premise, only as far as one may question the example of how a behavior pattern introduced by the teacher dictates the resulting pupil's behavior. The leadership style categories then try to pinpoint what type of relationship the teacher has developed, or will build up, between himself and his pupils. In the analytical dimensional model, Tausch recognized that the kind of relationship should be measured by the degree of directional control and the degree of higher or lower estimation by the teacher with respect to the pupil.

The behavior structures themselves are not the basis for research, but rather the one-sidedness of a teacher's relationship and its results on a pupil's behavior pattern. A first *halved* interaction analysis (Flanders, 1970; Landau, 1974) in relationship to the function of one-sided working structures is the focal point of interest in research. The research results serve in the long run to expose behavior patterns of the teacher that are meeting desired pupil behavior, and consequently to train the teacher accordingly (Jessen, 1974).

The predefinition of the normal teacher-pupil relationship in this research concept (Wilson, 1973), as far as interaction in instruction is concerned, is based on a fixed-role understanding [teacher = subject of the instructional process, gives the content and the method, controls the instruction with sanctions; pupils = objects of the instruction, react to the teacher (Müller-Stephan and Messing, 1974; Hanke and Bucke, 1975)]. The structure of the relationship neglects moments that, above all, are part of the research concept *hidden curriculum.* The ways and means by which institutional context determines the relationship structures are clear. Quite definite socialization patterns correspond to the structures, and at the same time the organization of the relationship is determined by the content and method of the subject field.

Before the conflicts in the instructional or educational theory that arise out of the interpretation of instruction as a basis for this research concept are presented, one must deal with the specific interaction problem of present sport instruction.

Widmer (1974) and Hildenbrandt (1973) especially have pointed out the specific interactional structure of physical education instruction, in comparison to instruction in other subjects. Readily available for discussion is the concept of Hildenbrandt, who outlines the analysis of instruction as an analytical work on instructional language used in sport instruction. As a result of his observations, Hildenbrandt thinks, based on his analysis, that the following basic scheme of interaction is valid:

> The teacher's verbal demands (the presentation of aims, achievements in movement to be obtained, etc.) lead to motor action by the pupils, which is observed by the teacher (visual control), leading to additional verbal instruction from the teacher (correction, new movement directions) (Hildenbrandt, 1973, p. 64).

If one accepts that the proposed basic formula of the example of interaction shows the present position held in physical education instruction, the one-sided dependency of the pupil on the teacher is shown in two ways. On one side, the pupils have to follow the aims of the lesson as given by the teacher, without deviation, as carrier of the wishes of the *establishment,* while on the other hand, there is the order given by the teacher, which is not discussed further, but which results in an even stronger interdependent relationship. As proof of this interpretation of Hildenbrandt, consider the following points he makes about instructional language used in the present form of physical education instruction: Directions that control and concentrate on organization and on drawing attention clearly constitute the major part of all language statements. Communication based on understanding between teacher and pupil plays a relatively insignificant role. Sign language statements are noticeable and are often used... (Hildenbrandt, 1973, p. 65).

Testing the above statements reveals a high degree of validity: In the reality of present-day physical education instruction, it can be documented that an almost dressage-like relationship exists between teacher and pupil (compare: verbal language use to the frequency of organization and control through sign language, i.e., no metacommunication concerning the procedure of the lesson or given aims).

However, it must be critically pointed out that Hildenbrandt, by his descriptive evaluation of language usage in sport instruction, does not discuss further any special structure of relationship, but rather stresses the best way of teaching. In the concept of leadership style, a predefinition of the teacher-pupil relationship is taken out of the normal institutional context, so that one finds in Hildenbrandt's solution a secret predefinition based on an unquestioned acceptance of a subject-specific context. Even if both concepts operate from different starting points, they both follow the same instruction paradigm and the included definition or relationship.

A review of the previous discussion shows that although the relationship problem is treated on the basis of an *a priori* relationship example, this basic relationship structure, which predefines the examples, has not become the focal point of research. This fact is the result of insufficient reflection on the relationship between the conception of instruction, its basic underlying educational understanding, and content definitions of instructional research. Only when this relationship is clear will it be possible to decide on a definite research concept within the realms of sport pedagogy.

INSTRUCTIONAL CONCEPT—ITS EDUCATIONAL/SCIENTIFIC MEANING AND THE RESULTING RESEARCH INTEREST

Two controversial directions of education research are evident. These differ from one another with regard to how the relationship problem should be scientifically approached. At this point the concept to be dealt with is, to a large extent, the basis of empirical instructional research, and also includes the previously discussed concepts of sport pedagogy (Ingenkamp and Parey, 1970–71).

INSTRUCTION/EDUCATION AS A PROBLEM OF INFLUENCE

The following position is held, by Brezinka (1971), within educational research: Under the term education one understands social actions by which people try to permanently better the framework of psychic dispositions of others with psychic and/or social-cultural means, in any direction, or social actions by which people try to maintain their components, which have already been judged to be of a certain value (Brezinka, 1971, p. 613). Education, psychotherapy, social work, and propaganda all agree with one another, that these are experiments to influence other people with psychic and socialcultural means, in order to attain learning aims that are thought to be worthwhile or desirable (Brezinka, 1972, pp. 238–239).

The scientific view of instructional practice is a technological problem (Brezinka, 1972, p. 238) in which the question of relationship arises because of the interest in optimizing desirable influences. The research interest is directed on the one hand to the discovery of laws of nature in the individual. This means that mechanisms that are responsible for the teacher's influence are being sought. On the other hand, one has to examine, with the help of certain methods, how close the teacher is to the knowledge of such laws, and to behaving toward people in an optimal way with regard to this mechanism. The foundational theory models to be mentioned here are the concept of conditional psychology (Skinner, 1972), as well as models of social learning, such as the mechanism of *imitation* and *identification* (Bandura and Parsons).

The heart of the scientific approach presented must be equally adhered to by research and practice, a concept that Smedslund (1973) explains in his critical review of analytical and empirical methods in psychology. The research concepts are related to "the functioning of the direct consciousness which can be understood as influenced without knowledge of the involved person" (Smedslund, 1973, p. 492; Skinner, 1972, p. 233); this can mislead one "to influence people on an automatic and non-reflected level" (Smedslund, 1973, p. 499).

In relation to this point, education can be understood as a manipulative force and can be developed with an increasingly more subtle control of a person, or a counter theory of communicative education can be formulated. This educational concept tries to counteract the general danger of the possibility of total manipulation of people. The concept follows, therefore, the line of thought of the *critical theory,* which points out the danger of a pure technological social science. With the already available knowledge about social processes it is possible to change the living conditions of people in manipulative systems, without the objects (the people) ever realizing the control mechanisms to which they are being subjected (Adorno, 1956; Habermas, 1968; Apel, 1970).

INSTRUCTION AS A PROBLEM OF COMMUNICATION

With regard to the above-mentioned idea of an aim of communicative education, Mollenhauer (1972) formulates a programatic definition of education:

> Education must be understood as a communicative action, with the aim of establishing a communications structure, which makes possible the acquisition of abilities for discursive behavior (Mollenhauer, 1972, pp. 68–69).

Only by defining the category *discourse* will this educational formula become clear. Mollenhauer provided a verbal and content (political) definition of the term: on the one hand, *discourse* means "the level of communication on which language is not only transferring a normative bound meaning, but allows a self-reflective medium communication over communication"; the other view is that of Apel, to whom *discourse* is a meta-institution, "an example of critics of all unreflected social norms" (Mollenhauer, 1972, p. 64).

This definition of education contains (just as does the influence-concept) a regulatory point with regard to the teacher-pupil relationship problem, but in this case one should also add the requirement of forming instruction so that the relationship of the structures can be treated by all those participating in the instruction. However, at the same time, the interpersonal actions of communication cannot be seen apart from the socially oriented dialogue, inasmuch as the social norms set by society through the institution *school* also constitute the interrelationships and problems existing in this discourse. However, before the typically ideal idea of instruction can be realized, there appears to be an insolvable difficulty, which to a large degree influences the research problems. Instruction is confronted with the fact that a pure hermeneutic understanding between teacher and pupil is not possible because the pupil is mechanically restricted with regard to socialized acceptance. Therefore, manipulation seems to be unavoidable, even with the best intentions of the teacher in certain respects and situations. In this context a two-sided research problem presents itself; on the one hand, one might ask when and under what circumstances is the child, i.e., youth, capable of a reflective attainment with respect to the relationship structure; on the other hand, one should also enquire how the steps of a lesson can be achieved before this capability has been reached, so that socially mechanical processes are not unduly strengthened or unnecessarily prolonged. In answer to the first point of this question, the following available examinations of classification of moral consciousness can help (Kohlberg, 1974: Piaget, 1954). These examinations start with the possible types of social orientation in the development of children and youths. In the second part of this question, however, the examinations cannot start with the genesis of the individual; rules have to be reconstructed, which the pedagogical communication in its institutional context follows. In research that is concerned with such a perspective, one can rely on theories of critical personality values (Habermas, 1968; Krappmann, 1972), symbolic interactionalism (Circourel, 1964; Goffman, 1974; Laing, 1971), or on theories on linguistic development and language pragmatism (Watzlawick, 1969; Maas and Wunderlich, 1972; Searle, 1973; Landau, 1974).

Investigations that help to prevent more fully and openly the limits of the instructional context within which one can work will also present to the teacher analytical criteria that make the previously vague relationship structures quite apparent to him. This then puts him in the position of being able to introduce and to use new communicative processes in instruction with respect to those pupils who previously were unable to respond.

Communicative means that the teacher is not prescribing the social rules occurring during the lesson, but that the making of the rules is discussed with the pupils step by step, and the children involved are given more actual responsibility for these rules. Relationship research, therefore, means a test of the pupil-teacher relationship with regard to repressive manipulative tendencies, not only in the type of rules established, but also in the way in which the regulations are enforced (among the pupils and by the teacher).

With a view to *discussion ability,* the following didactical question is asked: In what way can the pupils actively contribute to such a test? To be consistent with the aim that has been set up, and which is concerned with the specific point, pupils should learn through their own experiences in instruction "to transfer unconscious motivation, and as such explainable and manipulative behavior, into conscious behavior" (Apel, 1970, p. 333).

CONSEQUENCES FOR A CONCEPT RELATED TO SPORT INSTRUCTION

It is unimaginable that the educational theoretical positions presented in this chapter and the resulting research strategies can in any way be combined. The controversial views held concerning the social functions of instruction, in other words, concepts touched upon previously to reveal in what ways the social interaction of pupils can be integrated into society, require a much more basic decision about one or the other of these approaches. To prepare for such a decision in sport pedagogy, the discussion cannot take only an isolated view of the teacher-pupil relationship. It also has to be discussed with the aims, content, and organizational problems of instruction taken into consideration.

In the following chart an attempt is made to present a final point of discussion and rationale for the problem of decision.

	Concept of Influence	Concept of Communication
Concept/aims of sport instruction	The priority of motor perfection (improvement of condition and the learning of motor patterns in sport); adaptation of the sport to activity outside of school	Communicative action in sport instruction; reflective participation in sport (ability to judge one's own motor status and to see one's level of interest in view of the range of sport activities

Continued

	Concept of Influence	Concept of Communication
		offered); the acquisition of subject and political competence to enable one to take a rational position in sport-political processes
Organization of instruction a) outward aspects	Instruction in sport, i.e., training set-up, system of specialized teachers	Possibility of meta-communicative instruction on action behavior in sport instruction, i.e., relationship structure in the sport set-up (including more than one subject)
b) inner aspects	Teacher is planning instruction, i.e., structuring and controlling the training processes; pupil is participating in the overt training process	Teacher and pupils work together in instructional planning; increasing self-organization among pupils
Research problem teacher-pupil-pupil	Improvement of the social climate; behavior training of the physical education teacher	Interactional analysis of the institutional context; what communication rules exist between teacher and pupil [and reconstruction of the rules context of sports disciplines to clarify the type of relationship that is defined by these rules].

REFERENCES

Adorno, Th. W. 1956. Soziologie und empirische Sozialforschung. (Sociology and empirical research in sociology.) In: Soziologische Exkurse. Suhrkamp Verlag KG., Frankfurt.

Apel, K.O. 1970. Wissenschaft als Emanzipation? (Science as emancipation?) In: A. Diemer et al. (Hrsg.) Zeitschrift für Allgemeine Wissenschaftstheorie, Vol. I. 2:173.

Brezinka, W. 1971. Über Erziehungsbegriffe. (Concerning terminology in education.) Z. Pädagog. 5:613.

Brezinka, W. 1972. Erziehungswissenschaft. (Science of education.) In: Ulich (ed.), Theorie und Methode in der Erziehungswissenschaft, pp. 238–239. Julius Belz OHG., Weinheim.

Brodtmann, D., and Klein-Tebbe, M. 1974. Der Lehrplan als Sozialisationsfaktor. (The curriculum as a facotor of socialization.) In: ADL (Hrsg.), Sozialisation im Sport, p. 142 ff., Karl Hofmann, Druckerei und Verlag, Schorndorf.

Cicourel, A. 1964. Methode und Messung in der Soziologie. (Method and Measurement in Sociology.) The Free Press of Glencoe.

Flanders, N.A. 1970. Analyzing Teaching Behavior. Addison-Wesley Publishing Company Inc., Reading, Mass.

Goffmann, E. 1974. Das Individuum im öffentlichen Austausch. (Relations in Public: Microstudies of Public Order. Basic Books.) Suhrkamp Verlag KG., Frankfurt.

Grössing, S. 1972. Erziehungsstil im Sportunterricht. (Style of education in physical education instruction.) In: J. Recla (Hrsg.), Beiträge zur Didaktik und Methodik der Leibesübungen, p. 14ff. Karl Hofmann, Druckerei und Verlag, Schorndorf.

Habermas, J. 1968. Technik und Wissenschaft als Ideologie. (Technique and Science as Ideology.) Suhrkamp Verlag KG., Frankfurt.

Habermas, J. 1973. Stichworte zur Theorie der Sozialisation. (Notes concerning the theory of socialization.) In: J. Habermas, Kultur und Kritik. Suhrkamp Verlag KG., Frankfurt.

Hanke, U., and Bucke, E. 1975. Microteaching in der Sportlehrerausbildung. (Microteaching in physical education teacher training.) Sportunterricht 5,152.

Hildenbrandt, E. 1973. Sprache und Bewegung. (Language and movement.) Sportwissenschaft 1:55 ff.

Ingenkamp, K., and Parey, E. 1970-71. Deutsche Bearbeitung. von Gage, N.L. (Hrsg.), Handbook of Research on Teaching. Julius Belz OHG., Weinheim.

Jackson, P.W. 1973. Die Welt des Schülers. (The world of the pupil.) In: W. Edelstein and D. Hopf (Hrsg.), Bedingungen des Bildungsprozesses, p. 13 ff. Ernst Klett OHG., Stuttgart.

Jessen, K. 1974. Erziehung und Unterricht im Sport.—Möglichkeiten eines Verhaltenstrainings für Lehrerstudenten. (Education and instruction in sport.—Possibilities of behavior training for future teachers.) In: ADL (Hrsg.), Kongressbericht "Sozialisation im Sport," p. 317 ff. Karl Hofmann, Druckerei und Verlag, Schorndorf.

Kohlberg, L. 1974. Zur Kognitiven Entwicklung des Kindes. (Stage and Sequence: The Cognitive-Developmental Approach to Socialization.) In David A. Goslin (ed.), Handbook of Socialization Theory and Research, pp. 347-380. Rand McNally & Company, Chicago. Suhrkamp Verlag KG., Frankfurt.

Krappmann, L. 1972. Neuere Rollenkonzepte als Erklärungsmöglichkeit für Sozialisationskonzepte. (Newer role concepts as possible explanation for concepts for socialization.) In: Betrifft: Erziehung, Redaktion (Hrsg.), Familienerziehung, Sozialschicht und Schulerfolg. Julius Belz OHG., Weinheim.

Laing, R.D. 1966. Interpersonnelle Wahrnehung. (Laing, R.D., Phillipson, H., and Lee, R.A. Interpersonal Perception. Tavistock Publications, London.) Suhrkamp Verlag K.G., Frankfurt.

Landau, G. 1974a. Allgemeine Konzepte der Unterrichtsforschung und ihre Relevanz für den Sportunterricht. (General concepts of instructional research and their relevance for physical education instruction.) Sportunterricht 6:184ff.

Landau, G. 1974b. Sozialisationsmechanismen im Sportunterricht. (Mechanisms of socialization in physical education instruction.) In: ADL (Hrsg.), Sozialisation im Sport, p. 161 ff. Karl Hofmann Druckerei und Verlag, Schorndorf.

Maas, U., and Wunderlich, D. 1974. Pragmatik und sprachliches Handeln. (Pragmatism and Verbal Acting.) Athenäum, Frankfurt.

Mollenhauer, K. 1972. Theorien zum Erziehungsprozess. (Theories of the Educational Process.) Juventa-Verlag GmbH., München.

Müller-Stephan, M., and Messing, M. 1974. Sportlehrer und Sportunterricht im Wunschbild von Schülern. (Physical education teacher and physical education instruction in the view of pupils.) In: ADL (Hrsg.), Sozialisation im Sport, p. 317 ff. Karl Hofmann, Druckerei und Verlag, Schorndorf.

Piaget, J. 1954. Das moralische Urteil beim Kinde. (The Moral Judgment of the Child.) Rascher & Cie, AG., Zürich.

Schmitz, J.N. 1972. Lehr-, Unterrichts- und Curriculumprobleme. (Problems of Teaching, Instruction and Curriculum.) Karl Hofmann, Druckerei und Verlag, Schorndorf.

Searle, J. 1973. Sprechakte. (Speaking Acts.) Suhrkamp Verlag KG., Frankfurt.

Silberman, M.L. (Hrsg.) 1971. The Experience of Schooling. Holt, Rinehart and Winston, New York.

Silberman, Ch.E. 1973. Die Krise der Erziehung. (The Crisis of Education.) Julius Belz OHG., Weinheim.

Skinner, B.F. 1972. Futurum Zwei. Die Vision einer aggressions-freien Gesellschaft. (Future Two. The Vision of a Society Without Aggression.) Rowohlt, Hamburg.

Smedslund, J. 1973. Eine humanistische Position in der Psychologie. (A humanistic position in psychology.) In: W. Edelstein and D. Hopf (Hrsg.), Bedingungen des Bildungsprozesses, p. 493. Ernst Klett OHG., Stuttgart.

Watzlawick, P., et al. 1969. Menschliche Kommunikation. (Pragmatics of Human Communication. A Study of Interactional Patterns, Pathologies and Paradoxes. W. Norton Company, Inc., New York.) Hans Huber GmbH., Stuttgart.

Widmer, K. 1974. Sportpädagogik. (Sport Pedagogy.) Karl Hofmann, Druckerei und Verlag, Schorndorf.

Wilson, T.P. 1973. Theorien der Interaktion und Modelle soziologischer Erklärung. (Conceptions of Interaction and Forms of Sociological Explanation. Amer. Sociol. Rev. 35:697–710.) In: Arbeitsgruppe Bielefelder Soziologen (Hrsg.), Alltagswissen, Interaktion und gesellschaftliche Wirklichkeit, p. 54 ff. Rowohlt, Hamburg.

Zinnecker, J., and Geissler, W. (Hrsg.) 1973. Der heimliche Lehrplan. (The hidden curriculum.) Betrifft: Erziehung 6:16 ff.

Research on the Teacher - Pupil Relationship in Sport Instruction

M. Pieron

This investigation deals with the interaction of teachers and pupils in a renewed pupil-centered program in sport instruction. The aim is the analysis of instruction with the observation system developed by Hough, in accordance with Flanders, which is especially concerned with the verbal behavior of teachers and pupils. It provides an objective feedback of the instructional process for the teacher with regard to pupil-centered behavior. In this explorative study this system for analysis of teacher behavior was applied to future physical education teachers in their last phase of professional training. The system consists of 16 categories in four groups:

1. indirect influences of the teacher
2. direct influences of the teacher
3. verbal behavior of the pupil
4. pause for thinking, pupil activities, behavior without intention

One phase of observation lasts twenty minutes. Every three seconds, a specific behavior within the total behavior, as well as every change of behavior, is registered. The observation is done by a trained observer. The results are presented in a histogram. The interpretation concentrates, according to percentage distribution, on the following categories:

6 = concerned with descriptions of exercises and movements (19%)
7 = the individual feedback with correcting function (15%)
8 = direct instructions for organization (16%)
13 = directed activities of pupils (48%)

Note that Category 13 is not comprised of the total behavior of the observed group but includes activities of smaller groups, too; it varies to a great extent in its intensity. Category 7 is divided into simple and important feedback groups that help the pupil to realize certain tasks. The categories that are related to the verbal and indirect behavior of pupils comprise only 4%. This indicates that the planned pupil-centered behavior remained more on the cognitive level and did not have an effect on the practical behavior. The relationship between the categories also shows that a pupil-centered relationship is seldom found.

As a conclusion, one can state that this system provides an accurate picture of the teacher - pupil relationship. The future teachers frequently assume old, traditional models of instruction, despite their knowledge of pupil-centered behavior: the feedback and the reinforcements used, although not extensive, require specific training for use as instructional skills.

Sport in the Institution Called School

The School as the Organizational and Structural Framework for Physical Education

J.E. Nixon

INTRODUCTION

This chapter is concerned with the organizational and structural framework of physical education in the schools. Because the topic is so vast, the presentation is in outline form. It proposes selected definitions, points of view, and recommendations for the consideration of the members of the Congress during the discussion periods. This chapter reflects primarily the practices and viewpoints of American educators and physical educators. Likewise, the terminology employed is of American origin.

Frame of Reference

Sport pervades most aspects of American life in one way or another. Sport, as one major component of school physical education programs, occupies a major position in American elementary, secondary, and college educational systems. In many states more students are enrolled in physical education, either on a required or elective basis, and usually for academic credit, than in any other subject in the curriculum. Also, there is extensive extracurricular participation in sport by both boys and girls, and it frequently involves more than half of the students in the school.

Theoretical Framework of Sport

The comments in this chapter are based on the theoretical structure of sport and physical education described in detail in the publication *Tones of Theory— A Tentative Perspective,* written by Celeste Ulrich and John E. Nixon, and published in 1972 by the American Association for Health, Physical Education, and Recreation, Washington, D. C. Because of the limited space available, this framework cannot be described in detail in this chapter.

Sport theory and curriculum and instruction in sport are highly interrelated. Theory gives direction and understanding to sport practices in schools. Sport curriculum and instruction provide evidence of the efficacy of the theory underlying them, and suggest subsequent revisions and clarifications of the theory. This chapter emphasizes selected practical applications of sport theory in American schools and colleges.

Definitions

The key phrase in the theme of this meeting is *Sport Pedagogy*. Brief definitions of this and other terms closely associated with it will follow from the American perspective. It is particularly difficult for the American physical educators to deal with the terms *pedagogy* and *didactics*. A perusal of selected books and magazines in American education and physical education reveals that the term *didactics* is seldom used and that the term *pedagogy,* although used a little more often, is primarily employed as a synonym for our term *teaching*. A brief discussion of selected key terms follows.

Pedagogy   According to one American dictionary of education, *pedagogy* is defined as the art, practice, or profession of teaching; the systematized learning or instruction concerning principles and methods of teaching and of student control and guidance; largely replaced today by the term *education*.

Didactics   This term simply means the art of teaching. The didactic method of teaching emphasizes rules, principles, standards of conduct, and authoritative guidelines.

Dialectic   This word means the logic of argument. Dialectic method refers to learning or teaching in which the dynamic interaction of the participants leads to a clarification of ambiguities and misunderstandings arising from the subject matter or experience under consideration.

Objectives   In the noun form, *objectives* refers to the aims or the purposes of a course of study that are anticipated as being desirable in the early phases of the activity and that then serve to regulate and direct later aspects of the learning activities.

Curriculum   Historically, and even currently, this word is generally used to designate subjects and subject matter to be taught by teachers and to be learned by students.

Instruction   Simply defined *instruction* can be considered the interaction of the teacher and the student with the subject matter as well as with the skills and behaviors that constitute the curriculum.

Teaching   *Teaching* refers to the control of the teacher or the instructor of the teaching-learning situation. It occurs whenever the teacher takes deliberate actions to try to produce *learnings* by the pupil.

Evaluation With respect to formal educational programs, *evaluation* is the process of delineating, procuring, and making available useful information for judging decision alternatives about an aspect of an educational program and about student learning. Evaluation of people typically refers to methods used to assess the extent to which the pupils have attained the objectives that were stated when the lesson or curriculum began.

THE SCHOOL AS THE ORGANIZATIONAL AND STRUCTURAL FRAMEWORK FOR PHYSICAL EDUCATION

The public school, college, and university are society's agents for transmitting major cultural values.

Physical Education Objectives

The beliefs of this author are briefly stated here as general objectives for physical education:

1. To develop a basic understanding and appreciation of human movement. This broad objective involves:
    (a) the development of an understanding and appreciation of the deeper, more significant human meanings and values acquired through idea-directed movement experiences;
    (b) an appreciation of human movement as an essential nonverbal mode of human expression;
    (c) the development of a positive self-concept and body image through appropriate movement experiences; and
    (d) the mastery of key concepts through volitional movements and closely related nonverbal learning activities.
2. To develop and maintain optimal individual muscular strength, muscular endurance, and cardiovascular endurance. It is customary to refer to this purpose as the *physical fitness* objective.
3. To develop each student's movement potentialities to the optimal level. Physical education instruction concentrates on the development of selected neuromuscular skills and on the refinement of fundamental movement patterns basic to specific skills.
4. To develop skills, knowledges, and attitudes essential to satisfying, enjoyable physical recreation experiences engaged in voluntarily throughout one's lifetime. Normal mental and emotional health is enhanced by participation in voluntary physical recreation.
5. To develop socially acceptable and personally rewarding behaviors through participation in selected movement activities. Physical educa-

tion instruction seeks to develop desirable social habits, attitudes, and personal characteristics. (Nixon and Jewett, 1974, p. 97).

The Physical Education Curriculum

There are innumerable proposals for the content of physical education curricula at various educational levels. One approach is the Curriculum Project of the Physical Education Division of the American Alliance for Health, Physical Education, and Recreation, under the Chairmanship of Dr. Ann Jewett, America's foremost curriculum theorist (see this volume, p. 213 ff.). This approach provides for the selection of curriculum experiences in terms of three key purposes or human movement goals:

1. To fulfill personal developmental potential,
2. To develop movement skills utilized in adapting to and controlling the physical education environment, and
3. To assist the individual in relating to other persons.

Seven major purpose concepts for describing the scope of the physical education curriculum have been identified:

1. *Physiological efficiency:* Man moves to develop and maintain his functional capabilities.
2. *Psychic equilibrium:* Man moves to achieve personal integration.
3. *Spatial orientation:* Man moves to relate himself in three-dimensional space.
4. *Object manipulation:* Man moves to give impetus to and to absorb the force of objects.
5. *Communication:* Man moves to share ideas and feelings with others.
6. *Group interaction:* Man moves to function in harmony with others.
7. *Cultural involvement:* Man moves to take part in movement activities that constitute an important part of his society.

These purpose concepts have been further subdivided into elements that serve as a starting point for local curriculum planners (Nixon and Jewett, 1974, p. 251).

Evaluation

The curriculum plan should include provision for several types of evaluation:

1. Student progress toward accomplishment of the objectives
2. Evaluation of the effectiveness of the curriculum
3. Evaluation of the effectiveness of the physical education instructor
4. Evaluation of the efficacy of the total evaluation plan itself

GENERAL CURRICULUM CONCEPTS

At this point, some brief comments will be introduced involving two points of view concerning the general term *curriculum*. Lately, in America, some teachers are saying that the curriculum consists of all the experiences the children have under the direction of the school, including both formal instruction in the classroom and everything else pupils do while attending school in conformation with rules and policies laid down by school authorities.

Another view sees curriculum mainly in terms of objectives. Curriculum in this sense is *anticipatory*. It refers to what children will learn (or be able to do) as a result of what they do. It is concerned with results, not with what children do after the fact. In this view much of what is currently labeled as curriculum planning is really instructional planning.

This author prefers the view that curriculum is a plan that provides sets of learning opportunities in order to achieve broad goals and related specific objectives for an identifiable population of students served by a single school center. In this view, the curriculum also is anticipated or intended. It includes objectives, design, instruction, and evaluation, all for a specific population of students. This curriculum plan is put into operation in one school.

Physical Education Curriculum Model or Conceptual Framework

There is a lack of agreement within the field of physical education curriculum concerning the rationale or models for curriculum development; therefore an attempt is made here to develop an outline of a curriculum model consisting of the following components:

1. The goals to be sought by the pupils (stated at various levels of specificity)
2. The content to be learned, the skills to be performed, and the affective outcomes to be achieved
3. A description of the rationale for this particular model, and an explication of the major assumptions underlying it (concerning learning theory, teaching theory, the nature of the subject matter to be learned, the nature of the students to be involved, the societal responsibilities of the teachers and students concerned, and the societal values that community representatives will insist be included)
4. The data sources to be employed for generating the content, the skills, and the affective domain outcomes to be learned; or, stated differently, the bases for making program decisions, (knowledge bases, value preferences, etc.)
5. An evaluation plan for
   (a) assessing the extent to which the goals have been attained after the students have been exposed to the curriculum

(b) assessing the efficacy of the curriculum itself (curriculum evaluation)
(c) assessing the completeness and the actual utility of this model as a basis for generating specific curricula
(d) assessing the effectiveness of the evaluation plan itself

Instruction and Teaching

Instruction Steven M. Corey (1970) defines instruction operationally as the "process whereby the individual is deliberately manipulated to enable him to learn to omit or engage in specified behaviors under specified conditions, or as responses to specified situations."

Instruction is regarded as a planned activity. Instruction is the deliberate manipulation of the environment in order to assist the learner to learn the specified behaviors more efficiently.

The heart of instruction is the interaction between the pupil and the teacher.

Teaching The most succinct definition of *teaching* is that it refers to the behaviors of the teacher. Teaching occurs whenever the teacher takes deliberate actions to try to produce certain *learning* by the pupil.

Some authorities distinguish between teaching and instruction in the following way. Teaching is conceived of as the acts of the teacher systematically presenting a set of planned stimuli and cues. Instruction, then, is the planning and presentation of the total surrounding environment and stimuli within which the teacher attempts to use systematic exposure to the stimuli in order to help students to emit desired responses that will result in learning.

In America, it has been estimated that approximately 700 research studies have been made to date on phenomena associated with the learning and teaching of motor skills. Nixon and Locke (1973, pp. 1210–1243) summarized the research on the teaching of motor skills in physical education involving studies that attempted to control and manipulate one or more teaching behaviors as independent variables. A diagram was presented in which curriculum events in which students engage during motor learning were paralleled with a teacher sequence involving critical decisions and interventions to facilitate psychomotor learning. In this analysis, the available research was summarized under nine categories.

INSTITUTIONS AND ORGANIZATIONS INFLUENCING SPORT PEDAGOGY IN THE SCHOOLS AND COLLEGES

It would be interesting to provide a list of the many varied institutions and organizations within the United States that exert an influence of one kind or another upon the teaching of sport and physical education in schools and colleges. An exemplary list of some of these influences in the United States follows:

Legal controls include: national or federal legislation, state legislation, county legislation, school district legislation, school administration policies, school faculty policies, and physical education department regulations. Also, court of law interpretations of law given as advisory guidance by governmental agencies at various levels are included.

Advisory influences include: national legislative offices and bureaus; state legislative offices and bureaus; county legislative offices and bureaus; school districts; individual school administration, faculty, and citizens' advisory committees; physical education chairmen; physical education faculty; student advisory committees; physical education and sport professional organizations (international, national, state, county, school district, and city,); and physical education supervisors and administrators.

Professional influences include: professional organizations (international, national, state, county, school district, and city); noted authorities; books, articles, and other forms of audio-visual learning aids; research laboratories; workshops. Of course, this list could be extended to include many more organizations and institutions.

The degree of influence of individuals and institutions on beliefs, policies, and practices in sport pedagogy and physical education teaching, is probably significantly more extensive and complicated than most people realize.

PHYSICAL EDUCATION CURRICULUM AND INSTRUCTION INNOVATIONS

A variety of so-called *innovations,* or at least changes and revisions in physical education programs, have been attempted in the United States and other countries in recent years. Their degree of success, compared with the more traditional methods they have replaced, is little known as yet because appropriate evaluative and research techniques have not been developed, or when available, are not rigorously applied. Selected innovations, more readily evident in the United States in recent years, are listed here:

School and College Physical Education Curricula

1. Nongraded, continuous performance curriculum, with each student placed in it and moving at his/her own rate of learning, based on degree of interest and differential aptitudes for learning the various tasks set forth by the curriculum.

2. The program is basically instructional rather than recreational. It eliminates traditional lock-step, rigid grouping, by squad or by grade in school. This individualized curriculum approach is based on a periodical medical examination by the family or school physician; it is adjusted to individual physical fitness levels, to specific psychomotor skills, and to aptitudes, degree of interest, and understanding of relevant cognitive content.

3. A balanced curriculum is provided, with coverage of areas previously listed in this report, such as gymnastics, aquatics, rhythm and dance, body mechanics and posture, team sports, and lifetime sports.

4. It provides a physical education learning resources center, a physical fitness laboratory, and other equipment, supplies, and facilities required to support individualized instruction and evaluation.

Physical Education Evaluation

1. Provides formative evaluation of student achievement in small units of learning over time and provides feedback and corrective information, thus serving as a learning aid and motivator, rather than as a formal end of unit or end of course grade. Also, it involves the traditional summary evaluation used at the end of instructional units or at the end of the course, in order to assess the extent to which pupils have attained the objectives that were set forth at the beginning of the class.

2. Uses periodic sample measurements of segments of the class or small groups from time to time not only in order to assess how individual students are progressing, but also to provide diagnostic information to the teacher about the necessity to change the pace, sequence, or degree of difficulty of the curriculum during the remainder of the course or the semester.

3. Revises the marking system that reports the teacher's evaluations to the pupil and to the parents. Considers use of nongraded systems, pass/fail plan, pass/no credit plan, or other combinations, along with desirable features of the traditional letter grade system. Removes the punitive influence some grading systems exert in an effort to control undesirable pupil behaviors, which should be managed through the administrative policies of the school rather than controlled by the pupil evaluation system.

Differentiated Staff

In most schools the physical education teacher, and frequently the coach of a sports team, have more students than can be effectively instructed at one time. Therefore, one means for improving instruction is to provide teachers with differentiated forms of instructional assistance.

1. Use student peers to assist the teacher either at their own grade level or with children in lower grades. Employ teacher aides having preparation and competence to be described. Employ community sports specialists and other

community citizens who can assist either voluntarily or on a paid basis for teaching a particular activity. Contract with instructors in community activity. Contract with instructors in community business enterprises, such as bowling alleys, golf driving ranges, horseback riding academies, to instruct the physical education class under the general supervision of the physical education instructor.
2. Consider differentiating the responsibilities, and therefore the required degree of professional preparation, and the commensurate salary for teachers, so that the most experienced and capable teachers will have greater responsibility at higher levels of instruction and policy-making, and that teachers at lower levels in the organizational hierarchy will carry out lower order responsibilities for commensurately lower salaries.

Pupil Grouping in Physical Education

1. Consider grouping pupils by a combination of expressed interest and demonstrated aptitude for each activity being offered. Restructure the groupings for each activity being taught. It would be possible to have five or six combined groupings on this basis. This recommendation can be combined with the previous one about providing a continuous performance, individualized, self-paced curriculum for each pupil so that students of approximate abilities can be assigned to teams for sport instruction and competitive games held as part of the instructional and recreational aspects of the physical education class.
2. Consider also varying the curricula for the different interest-ability groups.
3. Pay more attention to teacher-pupil compatibility in setting up the grouping plan. Research indicates how important this factor is in facilitating learning. Some researchers believe that the most important help to most teachers is assigning them to a class that they are compatible with, and therefore can teach effectively.

Time Allotment

Some educators believe that time, or the rate of learning, is the real indicator of aptitude for mastering a learning task. Time is a crucial variable if we really seek to provide individualized programs of physical education. Most physical education teachers attempt to crowd into limited class time too many learning tasks for the students.

1. Modular scheduling provides a more flexible time allotment to students who require differing amounts of time in order to master particular learning tasks.
2. There is a trend now to schedule certain physical education classes, intramural sports and interscholastic sports during nonschool time, late after-

noons, evenings, Saturdays, and even during the summer months between semesters.

3. Various formulas are being used to divide up a calendar year into sections of time when students are expected to be in school alternated with vacations. The year-round school has its advocates mainly because it is more economically efficient in these times of high costs. Whether or not these variations from normal, traditional time allotments affect learning results significantly is not known from research.

Instructional Technology

Physical education teachers and coaches of sport teams are utilizing equipment and facilities available from the instructional technology industry to improve their instructional effectiveness. There are many forms of instructional technology too long to list here. Portable television cameras and monitors, a variety of audio-visual machines, loop films, high-speed motion pictures and similar photographic devices, computers, programmed instruction, and teaching machines, along with many forms of visual aids, diagrams, models, and so forth, are examples of modern instructional technology. Interested researchers are attempting to determine the extent to which the utilization of one or more of these instructional aides can contribute to more effective learning.

CONCLUSION

Within a theoretical framework of physical education and sport cited earlier in this chapter, selected areas of curriculum and instruction in sport have been identified as being major pillars in the organizational and structural framework of sport and physical education in schools and colleges. The concepts and examples described here are taken from the American cultural and educational context. Hopefully, general principles may be elicited that will have the potential for application in schools and colleges in other countries. Sport and physical education leaders from countries around the world can engage in a dialogue and debate about the efficacy of the topics presented in this chapter. In this way everyone can progress in the universal desire to develop a more comprehensive understanding of the meaning and significance of *sport pedagogy*.

REFERENCES

AAHPER. 1973. Curriculum Improvement in Secondary School Physical Education. Proceedings of the 1971 Mt. Pocono AAHPER Regional Conference for Curriculum in Secondary School Physical Education. AAHPER, Washington, D.C.

AAHPER. 1970. Essentials of a Quality Elementary School Physical Education Program. AAHPER, Washington, D.C.
AAHPER. 1970. Guide to Excellence for Physical Education in Colleges and Universities: A Position Paper. AAHPER, Washington, D.C.
AAHPER. 1970. Guidelines for Secondary School Physical Education: A Position Paper. AAHPER, Washington, D.C.
AAHPER. 1973. Knowledge and Understanding in Physical Education. Rev. Ed. AAHPER, Washington, D.C.
AAHPER. 1971. Organizational Patterns for Instruction in Physical Education. AAHPER, Washington, D.C.
California State Department of Education. 1973. Physical Education Framework for California Public Schools, Grades K-6, 12. Sacramento.
Cassidy, R., and Caldwell, S. 1974. Humanizing Physical Education, 5th Ed. W. C. Brown Company, Dubuque, Iowa.
Cooper, J. M., and Strong, C. 1973. The Physical Education Curriculum (A National Program), 8th Ed. Lucas Brothers Publishers, Los Angeles.
Corcy, St. M. 1970. The Nature of Instruction. In: D. Merrill (ed.), Instructional Design Readings, pp. 5–17. Prentice-Hall, Inc., Englewood Cliffs, N.J.
Cowell, Ch. C., Schwehn, H. M., Walker, J., and Miller, A. G. 1973. Modern Methods in Secondary School Physical Education, 3rd. Ed. Allyn and Bacon, Inc., Boston.
Daughtrey, G. 1973. Effective Teaching in Physical Education for Secondary Schools, 2nd Ed. W. B. Saunders Co., Philadelphia.
Frost, R. 1975. Physical Education: Foundations - Practices - Principles, Addison-Wesley Publishing Co. Inc., Reading, Mass.
Gage, N. L. 1972. Teacher Effectiveness and Teacher Education. Pacific Books, Publishers, Palo Alto, California.
Jewett, A. E. (ed.) 1974. Curriculum Design: Purposes and Processes of Physical Education Teaching-Learning. AAHPER, Washington, D.C.
Jewett, A. E. 1971. Would-You-Believe Public Schools, 1975. J. Health Phys. Ed. Recreat. 42:41–44.
Mosston, M. 1966. Teaching Physical Education: From Command to Discovery. C. E. Merrill Books, Columbus, Ohio.
National Society for the Study of Education. (ed.) 1971. The Curriculum: Retrospect and Prospect, Part I. The Seventieth Yearbook of the National Society for the Study of Education. University of Chicago Press, Chicago.
National Society for the Study of Education. (ed.) 1975. Teacher Education, Part II. The Seventy-fourth Yearbook of the National Society for the Study of Education. University of Chicago Press, Chicago.
Nixon, J. E., and Locke, L. 1973. Research on Teaching Physical Education. In: R. M. W. Travers (ed.), Second Handbook of Research on Teaching, Chapter 38, pp. 1210–1242. Rand McNally & Company, Skokie.
Nixon, J. E., and Jewett, A. 1974. An Introduction to Physical Education, 8th Ed., W.B. Saunders Company, Philadelphia.
Siedentop, D., Rife, F. and Dodds, P. 1974. Introduction to Applied Behavior Analysis. The Ohio State University, School of Health, Physical Education and Recreation, Columbus, Ohio.
Smith, B. O. 1971. Research in Teacher Education: A Symposium. Prentice-Hall, Inc., Englewood Cliffs, N.J.
Taylor, P.H., and Johnson, M. 1974. Curriculum Development, A Comparative Study. Humanities Press, Inc., New York City.
Travers, R.M.W. (ed.) 1973. Second Handbook of Research on Teaching. Rand McNally & Company, Chicago.

Ulrich, C., and Nixon, J. E. 1972. Tones of Theory—A Tentative Perspective. AAHPER, Washington, D.C.

Vannier, M. 1973. Teaching Physical Education in Elementary Schools, 5th Ed. W. B. Saunders Company, Philadelphia.

Vannier, M., and Fait, H. F. 1975. Teaching Physical Education in Secondary Schools, 4th Ed. W. B. Saunders Company, Philadelphia.

Sport in School—
Physical Education in the School

Z. Zukowska

INTRODUCTION

School physical education, according to its exact definition, follows two distinct paths. First, it is an integral part of the whole educational process, and therefore is affected by general trends in the educational system. Second, it is an important way of preserving good health, and therefore is subject to changes within its area of teaching. The term *sport* can be interpreted in two ways:

1) Alone, it can be considered an independent social institution that is controlled by its own rules and that strives toward a clear central aim of specific physical attainment.

2) It can also be viewed as instrumental to the process of physical education, which also has a high regard for physical attainment.

There are many different opinions about the idea of evaluating the various approaches to sport in school: for example, Demel and Sklad (1974) adhere to the first interpretation. They regard this interpretation to be more correct and more close to reality. The second concept is, in the view of the above-mentioned authors, clearly a result of an overlap in two areas of competence. This may lead to a conflict between the main aims of the two institutions.

In a project dealing with basic principles concerning the introduction of the problem of health and body culture, Jaworski (1974) deals with sport in an instrumental way. However, he places sport in an exposed role from the standpoint of modern schools, where the growing role of sport in the life of modern youth must not be overlooked.

In a summary of investigations concerning the part played by the school in the development of the pupil's motor activity, Zuchora (1974a) states, among other things, that ".... the physical skills are a specific and specialized form of the educational function of the school in the area of physical education. . . ." and, further, ". . . .the level of the skills in sport is the clearest indicator of the process of school physical education." This forms the basis for development of the motor abilities of youngsters in recreational time, and favors the birth and growth of interest in sport.

Such a formulation can be accepted for physical education in school, in which the framework, sport, treated instrumentally, does not present any tendencies in the direction of autonomy. Under the term physical education in school, one can immediately imagine the active participation of the complete person in sport as a whole, whether it be organized within the framework of the instruction or outside of it. One often finds in the literature such terminology as *physical education and sport in the school,* or, *the physical education lesson,* or, also, *sport in the established system;* however, all are concerned with one and the same kind of problems.

In connection with a published report on work done in Poland on the position of school education in the People's Republic of Poland, a further report was prepared by the committee experts on physical education in the Polish school (Demel, 1973). This critical analysis of views that were held at that time on the position of physical education in schools contained:

1) a revision of the inner coherence of the system of physical education, but especially the conflicts of the accepted basic functions relating to reality;
2) an analysis of the whole physical education program in view of the attitude of the present and future elements as well as close aims and more future-oriented aims;
3) examination of the degree of integration of physical education in the fields of education, training, and health.

In view of the position of physical education in schools, Demel (1973) concludes:". . . in everyday language one finds the tendencies to accept body culture and physical education as merely movement exercises, or quite simply to identify them with sport." The discussion has taken a false turn. Instead of searching for an ambitious and modern ideology in body culture and instead of advancing the field of vision, it has remained with the debatable word *sport* in areas of usage, and thereby it unnecessarily sharpens the conflict between *sport, professional sports,* and *activity participation in sport* by society in general. Physical education and rehabilitation are, as a result, put in a position or situation of being competitive with sport, which is completely superfluous. The problem must not be allowed to be examined within the boundaries of these categories.

SUGGESTIONS

As an introductory condition to these examples (suggestions) the following points have to be considered:

1. The main conditions for criticism of the present situation.
2. Uniformity of the educational process. The reason for physical education, in view of its functions. Definition of its role and the concepts of physical education in the school.
3. The modern outlook and concepts of physical education with respect to the developing trends in the educational system.
4. The criteria controlling the ideal example of physical education in schools.

Role of Physical Education

Physical education is one of the elements of the general educational process, but for the purpose of investigation it is treated in a specialized way. This classification is a theoretical construction. In reality, the process of education remains an indivisable whole that is governed by the singularity of its aims and its main conditions. Out of these theories, which have already been sufficiently recorded along with other scientific disciplines, it has been clearly proven "that physical education must be regarded as product of advanced specialization and divided labor of people, who professionally deal with either the practice or theory of education itself" (Demel and Sklad, 1974).

After this statement, one can proceed to a generalization of the proposed ideas and ask questions concerning the function of physical education in school. The main functions of physical education in the school are: the motivational function, the stimulating function, the function of adjustment, the function of compensation, and the corrective function. None of these functions appears in isolation, and their individual effects and boundaries are still fairly unclear (Demel and Sklad, 1974; Kalinowski and Zukowska, 1975).

Analysis of these functions reveals the empirical foundation for the formulation of aims, which possess the character of normative judgments. In presenting the aims, a certain hierarchy must be observed. The starting point is a statement of the general overall aims, which one can find in educational literature and in official educational programs of the respective countries. For example, in Poland one speaks of the ideal presented in socialistic education.

In the professional literature the concern is sometimes expressed that physical education is not regarded as an educational method and therefore suffers from lack of importance, whereas in reality physical education represents an independent element of the educational process. Le Boulch (1966), for example, regards physical education as *education through movement*. According to Gilewicz (1964), this does not mean that one should under any circumstances overlook the general educational aims. On the contrary, one has to keep them clearly in view, and realize them in all possible situations. However, one must not mix them up with the sport-specific aims. A similar opinion is currently held by many physical education theorists from all over the world, as for example by Duncan who points out that declarations that overstress the position of general educational aims weaken the position of physical education, rob it of a real contribution to education as a whole, and hinder concentration on the sport-specific aims. The modern classification by Gilewicz (1964) encompasses three main categories of objectives for physical education, which can be grouped as follows: sport-specific aims, aims of general character, and aims of merely general nature. Demel and Sklad (1974) also suggest a similar threefold hierarchy of the principal aims of physical education, which they put forward in the following way: The primary aim of physical education is the actualization of all somatic possibilities, which are comparable to the set of given circumstances from Gilewicz (1964), with an adaptation to the society norm. This aim is realized through the fundamental aims of physical education. One can divide this general aim into four different parts, which still possess a high degree of generality:

1. A certain knowledge of one's own organism.
2. Abilities, i.e., skills, which convey success chances and confirm one's value.
3. Habits, which only guarantee a consistent practice if they are acquired in conjunction with a motivation.
4. Attitudes, that is, the emotional and intellectual relationship to physical education and sport. This attitude must be of a positive kind, and come from an active interest in sport, so that participation in sports is not an unpleasant necessity, but rather gives satisfaction to the demands and aspirations of the young people.

Demel also lists the specific aims of physical education. These are called *tasks* by some authors. Thus, Zukowska, for example, differentiates between direct and indirect exercises within the realm of physical education in school (Zukowska, 1973; Kalinowski and Zukowska, 1975).

The realization of these aims should enable one, in the opinion of Demel, to be introduced to the world of physical culture. Physical education should mean an introductory course, adapted to the various stages of development, to sex and to a future profession. "It is an all too common mistake to put physical education next to real components of established physical culture, such as sport, tourism, and recreation. Physical education is not simply a part of such physical culture, but rather it is its foundation. This foundation encompasses physical culture of the young generation as a whole, and also sport, tourism, and recreation" (Demel, 1973).

Concepts of Physical Education

Modern civilization is, according to Suchodolski (1974), characterized by a dynamic development of science and technology as well as by a variety of forms. It demands from people that they always strive to adapt themselves to new targets. This confirms the point of view that a person is educable for his entire life. Because of this capability of man to understand and to accept changes to a great extent and therefore to change himself, it is possible, in our way of life, to make further advancement. In view of this, educational results are to be understood as a permanent willingness and ability to undergo educational processes.

The young person can, during his various stages of development, be influenced very easily. His organism demands the satisfaction of the natural needs of his age group; his own psyche or personality is collecting innumerable impressions, which are responsible for his education. The intellect needs knowledge, which at present is changing in a very dynamic way.

The content of modern school physical education should be in agreement with the developing trends of the present-day school system. The main tendencies are the following: permanent training, an education directed towards the future, autodidactic methods (self-learning), autocreation, autosocialization, development of the intellect, humanization, and individualization, as well as schools for continuing education and so-called *milieu* schools. All of these tendencies in the system of education through sport are accompanied by the individual's own initiative, which, within the boundaries of modern education, plays an ever-increasing role. In addition to biological preconditions, the influence of class and background environment, and the proposed educational measures, the personal initiative of the individual is a factor that determines the development of the person, not only with regard to the direction of development, but also with regard to its result.

Sport is that form of human activity that, on the one hand, satisfies the needs of the young person and activates and intensifies his development, and, on the other hand, represents his own interests and relates to moments of pleasurable experiences and achievements. This is an experience that is desirable in the life of a young person; namely, the experience that is offered to him is pleasant, and may sometimes become a passion for his entire life, and not just for a passing moment (Zuchora, 1974b; Zukowska, 1973a; Zukowska, 1974; Widmer, 1974; Zukowska, 1975a).

Basic Criteria

The following may be accepted as basic criteria of the given model of physical education in school: completeness, complexity, openness to new educational methods, and a feeling of equality (Demel, 1973).

Characteristics of the Proposed Model

Before looking at the characteristics of the model of physical education in schools, we have to consider the following:

Content of physical education
Methods in physical education
Organizational structures
Professional profile of the physical education teacher

Content of Physical Education

One finds that in all criticisms of physical education in school and in all attempts for modification, the emphasis has been for the most part squarely placed on the teaching program. Whether this be right or wrong, it has for a long time been recognized and therefore has been given a special significance, since it forms the basis for, and affects, all aims, tendencies, and concrete contents of physical education in schools.

> The content of physical education says Demel, "should link actual elements, immediate aims, general perspectives and a function of *hedonic* recreativeness; actual active pleasure or entertainment and recreation should balance out, to everyone's own satisfaction, with the systematic and serious work involved. This last point can only be taken into account if one can go out from, and rest upon, the preconditions, which are based on many motivations (intellectual and emotional) and thereby acknowledge the basic foundation of the individual and group competition (Demel, 1973, p. 41).

In Poland, in connection with the planned school reform and the introduction of the 10-year general educational program for high school, a discussion is taking place concerning the concepts of the new program. One of the most interesting and at the same time most discussed projects is that of the introduction of health problems and physical culture presented by Jaworski (1974). He has assumed that the content of the aims and attitudes presented in a socialistic education of the younger generation have to be fair and equated with the needs of the future society, inasmuch as encouragement is given to activity and everyone of the pupils is given the opportunity to achieve personal satisfaction. He reaches the conclusion that a new concept has to be strived for that builds up the person as an integral whole, and that consequently must be realized. Whereby it follows that it should proceed in a clear and precise manner. Under no circumstances should the relationship between the traditional methods and the apparently new modern image be presented in a way that makes it a mockery or a caricature.

Jaworski has completed comparative research on the systems of physical education in various countries of the world (over 20 such systems were examined). The research included a thorough study of the history of physical education in the People's Republic of Poland during the last 30 years, and a generalized examination of different specialized scientific fields. The results of this research, together with practical experience, have led this author to the concept of a new face for the treatment of content of different, yet related and complementary, didactic and educational branches of activity in the educational system. This concept, which has appeared in a specialized form in the educational system previously, and which has not been developed in relation to the others, is after all the best. Under this concept we find, among others, several fields of participation, which have to some extent been summarized under the following headings: physical education, introduction to health education and its allied problems, general hygiene, personal hygiene, problems of nutrition, work and relaxation, recreational hygiene, sport and tourism (Jaworski, 1974). Jaworski suggests an integration of these fields and advocates their realization in the teaching program, within the framework of one complete didactic and educational teaching subject, under the name *An Introduction to Health Problems and Bodily Culture*. Within the program structure of the new concept of physical education in the school, one can differentiate between two basic areas of content for these compulsory subjects.

1. As a central content for all schools, the following areas should be planned and carried out in the same way on a national level: man and his environment, morphophysiology of man, general motor activity and personal hygiene, hygiene and the foundations of dietetics, work and relaxation hygiene, safety and first aid, sexual knowledge, and family affairs.

2. Teaching content, at the request of the teachers who are responsible for the various divisions of the program, should be confirmed by their headmasters or directors. This pertains to certain areas of sport, active recreation, and sport tourism, which satisfy practical needs and interests and lie within the possibilities and under the concrete working conditions of certain schools. This content should also be determined to some extent by the surrounding environment or countryside. The choice of a program for this area could be confined to the boundaries of a set discipline, which would be decided upon by the main official body of the school authority, with an active participation by pupils, parents, and a consultative body of non-school persons also taking part. With respect to both areas, Jaworski presents projects and how they might be tackled. These projects have been under open discussion. Among others, pupils of the upper classes of secondary schools were consulted, as well as students of physical education colleges, physical education teachers, and school directors. The results of the questionnaires will be taken into consideration in completing the final form of the 10-year program for compulsory schooling.

Methods in Physical Education

The corresponding new proposals with regard to the teaching content demand an improvement and modification of working methods, for which the following areas should be emphasized:

1. Subjectivity (autodidactic, autocreation, autosocialization)
2. Intellectualization
3. Intensification
4. Activation
5. Many-sidedness and attractiveness
6. Interest and motivation

One should encourage and use all these different aspects and initiatives, which strive to realize previously mentioned goals. This pertains especially to all attempts to integrate theoretical elements into physical education, i.e., the introduction of self-control and self-analysis in addition to the control and analysis given by the teacher, the humanization of the process of physical education, the omitting of *dresseur*-like exercises, the introduction of a genuine attitude towards physical education—while at the same time using all values of sport, recreation, and tourism—the introduction of schoolbooks in physical education and of homework in this subject, the development of self-discipline in youngsters, and the cooperation of the physical education teacher with other members of the staff, the parents, the school doctor, etc.

Above all the work of the physical education teacher in the school demands a creative relationship of the teacher to his work with youth. This attitude requires the application of diagnostic and prognostic methods with regard to the pupil. Also, methods of evaluating progress that allow for measuring both quality and quantity accurately have to be used, thereby allowing an objective and just foundation and judgment of both the pupils' work and the teacher's.

Organizational Structures

The further suggestions presented here are intended to have an effect on the organizational structure applicable to content and method:

1. According to the suggestions of Jaworski, all previous forms and contents of physical education, prophylactic health education, hygiene, sport, tourism, and recreation have to be taken together in one problem block. The function of coordination is in all instances left up to the specialized teacher.
2. It is necessary to develop three parallel paths in physical education, namely:
   a. For healthy, movement-talented, sport-interested and oriented pupils—the sport instruction
   b. For the average gifted pupil—a general program of physical development
   c. For the weaker, late developers, and uncoordinated pupils—a corrective and adjustment program

3. It is better for the school to do away with its monopolizing and universal role and accept a distributive one. This means that one has to accept the concept of the *open school,* which cooperates with out-of-school sport organizations and institutions for rehabilitation and recreation. This cooperation must have a dual character, so that:
   a. the pupils can make use of the external sport institutions
   b. the school maintains its relationship to its surroundings and stands to serve the surrounding environment in various ways.

Professional Profile of the Physical Education Teacher (Zukowska, 1964a, 1964b, 1964c, 1975a; Widmer, 1974)

One consequence of the new concepts about physical education in schools is change in the teacher training programs. How these new concepts will actually be realized and what the results of their realization will be have yet to be decided. The four-year study system presently followed in Poland guarantees in general that the specialized teacher for physical education is, in most cases, capable of carrying out the many duties of his job. In accordance with the future role of physical education teachers, the natural sciences and intellectual sciences are developed. Scientific studies concerning the new concept and the realization of the working methods of the physical education teacher in school are carried out. Work on the first set of textbooks for pupils is currently in progress. Because of the trend toward a more intellectual approach to the study of physical education on the one hand, and because of the need for a practical preparation in sport on the other hand, the training of teachers for physical education in higher education needs to be changed to some degree. Higher education should guarantee the physical education teacher a many-sided and thorough preparation for his work in the school department in the fields of physical education, various sports, recreation, tourism and school hygiene, as well as in the field of health education. Moreover, the great differences in the various stages of development, the state of health, the motor capabilities, and the interests of children and youth have to be considered, as well as the definite class surroundings and the working conditions of the school.

In accord with this concept, the graduate of such a training program should have sufficient knowledge to teach and to be a referee in the basic sport disciplines found within the programs of the schools, and should also have sufficient knowledge to instruct in recreation and health.

The question of specialization of the physical education teacher, which is similar to the qualification of a coach, is still open. There are many who are in favor of introducing this specialization into the study program. However, opponents of this idea point out that the possibility exists for individual specialization in further studies, which can be done after the general study program that leads to a diploma. This last viewpoint is based on the points that the place, the working conditions, and the needs of the surroundings are the deciding factors about what specialization in sport actually should be, so that the teacher will be fully utilized in the school and the milieu.

Changes and modification are also demanded in the work environment of the physical education teacher. Under this term more is understood than merely facilities, equipment, and other requisites. The modern working tools of the teacher are composed of at least four elements:

1. Diagnostic and control apparatus
2. Specialized material for counseling purposes and for better recognition of individual and group profiles
3. Teaching aids
4. Sport equipment and instruments, with special consideration of newer aspects with respect to design, care, storage, and use

For optimal realization of each concept of physical education, a good physical education teacher who has been well prepared for this task is important. The surroundings, the working conditions, the position of the school directors on physical education, the facilities, equipment, and sports materials, and the general attitude toward sport play an indirect role. They either make the teacher's work easier or more difficult, but they are never the deciding factors in the actual result of the work. A good teacher of physical education, who regards his work with a certain amount of dedication and inspiration, never remains without influence on the model and the final position of the previously mentioned factors. Neither a traditionalist nor somebody who likes to improvise, but rather a physical education teacher, who is an inventor, is in the position to develop within the school practice a modern model of physical education. Excellent education can only be the result of an excellent educator.

REFERENCES

Boulch, J., 1966. L' education par le mouvement. (Education through movement.) Les Editions Sociales Francaises, Paris.
Demel, M. 1973. Raport dla Komitetu Ekspertów: Wychowanie fizyczne w szkole polskiej. Szkice krytyczne o kulturze fizycznej. (Report for the expert committee: physical education in the Polish school. Critical issues on physical culture.) Volksverlag, Warszawa.
Demel, M., and Sklad, A. 1974. Teoria wychowania fizycznego. (Theory of Physical Education.) Volksverlag, Warszawa.
Gilewicz, Z. 1964. Teoria wychowania fizycznego. (Theory of Physical Education.) Volksverlag, Warzawa.
Jaworski, Z. 1974. Projekt za ozen programu propedeutyki zdrowia: kultury fizycznej. (Projects on the fundamentals of the program for introduction to health.) Nowa Szkoia, Nr. 12.

Kalinowski, A., and Zukowska, Z. 1975. Metodyka wychowania fizycz nego w szkole. (Methods of School Physical Education.) 2nd. Ed. Volksverlag, Warszawa.
Suchodolski, B. 1974. Problemy wychowania w cywilizacji nowoczesnej. (Problems of education in modern civilization.) Volksverlag, Warszawa.
Widmer, K. 1974. Sportpädagogik. (Sport Pedagogy.) Karl Hofmann, Druckerei und Verlag, Schorndorf.
Zuchora, K. 1974 a. Rola szkoly w ksztalowaniu aktywnosci ruchówej uczniow. (The role of school in movement education of pupils.) In: Roczniki Naukowe AWF w Warszawie, Band XIX.
Zuchora, K. 1974 b. Wychowanie fizyczne naszych dni. (Physical Education in Our Time.) Volksverlag, Warszawa.
Zukowska, Z. 1964 a. Wspolczesny nauczyciel wychowania fizycznego w Polsce, proba typologii. (The modern physical education teacher in Poland. Trial of a typology.) Wychowanie Fizyczne i Higiena Szkolna. 3.
Zukowska, Z. 1964 b. Inspitivanja o licnosti nastawnika fizickog vaspitanja u poljskoj. (Original in Serbian language.) Fizicka Kultura, 9–10. Belgrad.
Zukowska, Z. 1964 c. Les traits de personalité de l' éducateur physique. (Personality traits of the physical education teacher.) Education Physique et Sport, 72.
Zukowska, Z. 1973 a. Rola dydaktyki w nowoczesnym procesie treningu sportowego. (The role of didactics in the modern training.) Sport Wyczynowy, 5.
Zukowska, Z. 1973 b. Effects of sport on the Personality of the Young. In: O. Grupe (Hrsg.), Sport in the Modern World—Changes and Problems. Springer, Berlin.
Zukowska, Z. 1974. Sport in the Life of Contemporary Youth. Wychowanie Fizyczne i Sport 1.
Zukowska, Z. 1975 a. Wychowanie przez sport i dla sportu. (Education through and for sports.) Lekko-atletyka 5.
Zukowska, Z. 1975 b. Cultural and social activity of teachers of physical education) Int. Rev. Sport Sociol. 1.

Models for School Sport in Austria

H. Ertl

Sport has great importance in our present society, but it is not recognized in the primary and secondary school, which provide only two or three hours of physical education a week. The situation in the *Gymnasium*, which provides four hours of physical education per week, is slightly better, as is the preparation of the teachers. In the school reform that occurred during the Sixties (which was realized not just in Austria) the tendencies for intensification, differentiation, and diversification of instruction were quite important, as was the institutionalization of sport promoted in so-called experimental schools.

The situation in Austria is described here, using an international comparison with regard to the differences in aims and objectives and organization of sport instruction. The procedures and models for developing school sport and athletics are divided into three larger fields.

The first model comprises the improvement of the educational aspects of sports, which means the introduction of interest groups, which is realized by the traditional school sport disciplines in compulsory and voluntary schools, as well as by the diversification of sport instruction in experimental schools, where lifetime sports have been especially included. The realization of so-called sport weeks is an example of this trend. An important area for measurement of improvement, realized under educational aspects, are all experiments with general sport aims and objectives in different types of schools. In Ober-Österreich, there are sport primary schools in addition to sport classes in normal schools. In all other states, there are *sport secondary schools* and seven sport *Gymnasia,* in which the aim is the integration of sport and general education, not the production of top-level athletes. However, these sport schools have an elite character and require entrance examinations. The *sport Gymnasium,* especially, aims at systematically developing top performance in all sports. The graduates of these schools are advised to enter professional schools dealing with sport.

Until recently, the sport schools had an experimental character. Today, they are categorized as special types of the different school forms. In order to justify their emphasis on sport it may be pointed out that the results of the daily sport lessons, which involve lessons on different effective cognitive and motor behavior patterns, are basically positive. Further developments include the recognition of school sport and athletics as being mutually enhancing. The *Sport-Hauptschulen* concentrate on special interests that have a specific aim in sport, as for example the *Ski-Hauptschulen*. The instruction is strongly geared towards ski racing; the requirements of the school as a whole are met by instruction at different times, according to the time of year. This instruction is differentiated by performance, and is often accompanied by scientific investigations. There are training camps that serve several schools together, in connection with the ski associations. After finishing the *Hauptschule,* a student can attend trade school or a branch of the school of physical education in Vienna and become a physical education teacher or coach. In order to meet the requirements of advanced education, there exists a *Ski-Gymnasium* in Stams that forms the upper level of this school.

Another experimental implementation of athletics in the *Gymnasium* is a boarding school for swimming in *Wiener Neustadt*.

In general, the efficiency of these schools is obvious; however, the problem of a performance ideology oriented in nationalism is also clearly seen. But, the existence of sport schools is justified by the following argument: they perform an educational task while producing top-level athletes.

Aims and Objectives of Physical Education

The Aims of Sport Instruction

C. Menze

Whether scientific conclusions concerning aims of instruction are possible is as much a point of dispute today as it was at the beginning of the century. Are aims legitimate indicators of norms of character or are they merely statements that are available? Weber has pursued the argument of this question from the radical, narrow boundaries of scientifically recognizable possibility into scientific publicity (Weber, 1956, pp. 186-262). This question in fact has the appearance of a continuous discussion that has occurred in Germany throughout the 1960s (Adorno et al., 1969). It has polarized the various viewpoints rather than bringing them together; individuals have taken sides in the argument. The results of these differences extend into the attempts to define instructional aims and also lead to irreparable opposing positions. The various basic positions include discussions about values and normative statements. As a result of these discussions, over a long period of time, the question of the legitimacy of statements of aims has overshadowed all other deliberations on aims. Thus, other possible stands, such as changes that would offer a limited but reasonable discussion of aims, were almost impossible.

A change first came about in the beginning of the 1960s, when the empirical-analytical direction became popular in the German-speaking countries. By developing the procedures, one also began to analyze the aim dimension of acting. In the wake of this reception, research workers could, with the help of the analytical procedures, realize their aspirations and enrich their sport lessons as a result of their research work. Up to this point their work had been marked by the traditional didactic and methodological methods and had not been affected by the scientific approach. This substantially altered attitude had meaning and influence in every pedagogical sector, thus affecting the combined attitude toward a physical education lesson. Therefore, in the discussion concerning physical education lessons, statements developed that were not only contrary to the question of the legitimacy of its aims but also separate from other legitimate demands. Also, discussions about what is actually to be strived for and what actually can be achieved in a physical education lesson have been carried out. The movement away from only verbal requests and controls with the inclusion of scientifically worked-out knowledge and experience was very apparent. This more technical direction also forced those supporting basic positions to be consciously aware of the basis of experience, but without casting aside their principal considerations. It is impossible to consolidate within this framework the total meaning of these statements concerning aims. One has to deal with many nuances and differences as well as with an overview of the research methods used today to evaluate aims. Klauer (1974) has drawn these together and analyzed them critically. His explanations can be broken down into three aspects, as follows:

1. To provide a general statement about the aims under consideration within the given limitations.
2. To analyze and judge those aims presented in a certain place in the historical development of physical education and sport lessons.
3. To consider various aspects of the controversial field, that is, to imagine and enlarge upon the aims that should pertain to present-day physical education lessons.

Although these assumptions have to be very general, they still have limitations.

1. The term *physical education lessons* means solely physical education for the young person in the school. Sport or physical education in clubs, teaching courses in the community, and similar situations have not been taken into consideration.
2. *Aims of physical education lessons* mean those statements that surpass the single purposes of the various levels of the school and the schools themselves. Therefore, it does not concern itself with ordering of concrete aims for the various levels because concrete aims change in the same way that maturity and preconditions change. Everything that is motor-influenced or influenced within its definition is directed toward certain aims; without this, learning becomes very difficult. In most cases, a complete mastering of a certain technique then becomes impossible.
3. A timely continuum of aims has not been proposed. The hope that the *right* aims are gained through possible natural constancy has been strongly refuted from the beginning. Therefore, there are basic statements discussed that in no way can be suspended. Moreover, it is proposed that they often reappear in either a direct or indirect way.

THREE BASIC WAYS TO DEFINE AIMS

With all the many-sided concrete conclusions to questions in the area of aims and the problems presented thereby, one can still differentiate three main streams of thought, which, despite all their differences of appearance, can be presented in the following way:

1. The empirical-analytical direction
2. The normative-deductive direction
3. The counseling community, which strives for sense and norms in their respective situations due to the belief in collective rationalism.

Empirical-Analytical Direction

The empirical-analytical direction argues the possibility of scientific legitimacy of aims. However, it is possible to determine if the requirements of the aim can be realized, even though nothing can be said about the validity of the aim itself. Moreover, it is assumed that the accepted aim is taken as a factor in its solely hypothetical form. It can only be proven in the technical, critical form, as has been mentioned by Weber (1956, p. 187). No construction on the empirical-analytical level, as well as the construction of bridge principles (Ebert, 1968, p. 76), leads away from this point of view. It is true that the normalcy of norms and the validity of values are not open to scientific discussion. Scientific statements can only be made about material that has been presented or that is available. Values and norms, however, do not rely on presented material; rather, they are the result of subjective attitudes or intentions about what is available. Aims are not concerned with a quality applicable to the presented qualities, but rather to the result of a point of view; otherwise, they are not comprehensible. In the area of lesson aims, this means that stating definite lesson aims is principally optional. A statement to the effect that they should or should not be strived for is scientifically impossible. In any case, a nonscientific institution must decide what should be the outcomes.

Normative-Deductive Direction

The normative-deductive direction appears to be the most broadly accepted, even though it has been criticized rather severely during the last few years. From the most valid and highest norms, aims are derived in a secure and impregnable deductive system that are also normative for concrete actions. The two weak points of this system have received much attention. First, what is the explanation of the absolute certainty of top norms? Second, can one achieve concrete material aims out of the necessary highest abstract norms without the introduction of circumstantial conditions? For the validity of aims in a lesson this means that the acceptance of instructional aims can be derived from the legitimacy of the highest aims, and also that the looked-for, desired, and required safety must be included.

It seems that with these two basic directions and their respective variations, all possible statements of aims and objectives have been covered. The two basic positions described really cannot be combined. The mutual critic on these positions seems to explain, however, that both premises are valid but neither can hope for scientific explanation nor for emphatic acclamation of the other point of view. With regard to the empirical-analytical direction, which proceeds according to principles of absolute clearness and uniqueness in terminology, the following can be said. It will have to overcome many difficulties, even with such a start, because a certain basic attitude guides the investigation of the phenomenon with an intent to explain it. Thus, the aspect of making the factual reality an absolute one is quite true. The argument, therefore, is a kind of metaphysical one known under the term positivism. Even if one maintains a distant stand from such a metaphysical point of view in a very precise way, the statement that everything is uncertain and therefore may possibly be revised is true in itself and cannot be revised. If the contrary were true, this whole direction would lack a fundamental precondition for its existence. Generally critics of this position try to do the following:

1. To explain questions concerning its justification, and to explain values in moral sentences that necessarily have to be kept open.
2. To give solemn answers to such questions as are found in the arguments.
3. To identify and to show that such a subreption is necessary since the stated premises can no longer be legitimized on the basis of such thinking.

In regard to such a proposal, very often strong counterstatements are formulated on the basis of very clear disjunctions. The disjunction itself implies what still has to be explained. Such a discussion should be left to the philosophers and it should not appear again in the discussion of aims and objectives for instruction, for education in general, or for certain instructional disciplines. When such discussions are related to the field of education they take on a very pragmatic relevance.

On the other side, the critics of the normative-deductive position and its consequences are also quite numerous. The amount of criticism even appears to be more concentrated. The critical point on the precondition is that there is one fixed cosmos of values that is valid for all people in the same way. The critics, furthermore, show that it is not possible to derive by deduction aims and objectives in the concrete instructional situation from the very general aims and objectives that are given. Finally, a point should be made on the type of science that should provide theories, hints, and programs for the concrete realization of aims and objectives sanctioned by science. If one overlooks the historical change with regard to the aims and objectives guiding human action, one disregards the great change of values even in our time. At the same time, one is not disregarding new questions of a new time and their respective answers.

From a scientific point of view, the following aspects cannot be tolerated: a) norms resulting from closed systems, b) philosophical dogmatism, c) ideology of aims and objectives, d) neglecting experience, and e) methods that analyze situations and do not work in deductive ways with the requirement of general validity (however, they still may show some deficiencies). The use of evidence, ethics, and ideas on natural right cannot convince. Clear deficiencies of the empirical-analytical approach do not justify the recognition of the opposite point of view.

This leads to the following questions: Which possibilities for argument with regard to aims and objectives are available in view of these mutual critics? Is it not at least true that there is one point of view accepted even if there are certain variations, modifications, restrictions, and questions? Is there not available within all these positions an aspect of practical positivism, so that finally subjective preferences and voluntary decisions are valid, and so that the things that should happen are under the jurisdiction of the person who is deciding, while this cannot be separated from the one who possesses the knowledge?

Counseling-Community for Norms

In recognition of all these problems, a third direction is constituted of all the contradictory arguments that have been given and apparently covers all possible arguments as well as the other two basic viewpoints. This position will not harmonize, but, recognizing the other two positions and the opposition to them, it will attempt to find a way out of the dilemma (Fink, 1970). This increasingly accepted approach can, in summary, be characterized as follows:

An analysis of the present situation shows that tradition and culture have until now paid dearly for their equally important role in setting the norms for life's happenings. Their specific traits, inasmuch as they haven't been artificially preserved or dissolved in a mixture with other cultural systems, are abused by mutual exchange, and there is a tendency for unification, which is not derived from new norms, but from real and determined pressures of technical-scientific civilization. These pressures are the bases of the links between all cultures, in the form of aims and objectives yet to be realized. This technical and scientific age presents us with examples of development and with rules for the realization of a given status whose fixation and interpretation would release continuous argument on the ideological level. The loss of a sense of life that is valid for everyone shows that a normative preliminary definition of education is no longer possible. Hereby, the educational aims of anticipated ethics, even the traditional attitudes and ideals of truth, have displaced themselves. The result is a deep change in the fundamental question of pedagogy. This has resulted in a change beyond the fundamental pedagogical terms presented that has been held impossible until recently. This change has occurred in the categorical structure of pedagogical thinking and has influenced pedagogical problems and tasks. Out of the ruins of the outlived meanings, it has now become impossible to put together a new and complete norm as uppermost in normative absoluteness. The consequence is a reduction of education on a technical problem that eliminates the request for the reason and proof of aims. Such educational acts, however, are not possible without meanings and aims. Therefore, they cannot be merely taken away. The educator needs these, although one cannot come to terms with aims and meanings in this way, so that in the consciousness of the correctness of his judgement and action, one can hold an opinion towards others in a normative way. One can, therefore, from a position of apparent knowledge, no longer give hints of orders to the young person who stands opposite him. He needs advice that he can get from no one. In this situation of genuine helplessness, should the helpless look for help within themselves and continuously revise the attempts for common actions? This means that the radical upheaval of traditional understandings of education and the way in which this was carried out have created change in the corresponding educational institutions. For educational and lesson aims it means loss of the right to set general norms. They are theoretically no longer legitimate; now they only possess the quality of being situatively valid. In the general action of the subjects a theory arises, which, for a moment, may offer the acting person certainty, yet at the same time provides no security about one's own practice of the collective and practical understanding that develops within the step-by-step process of self-communication.

Critics of such a theory point out that, although the legitimization for educational action by adults towards children is suspended, in all normative processes, the theoretical basis of equality of all educators and young people omits all outward influence. This influence, however, becomes all the more felt. The professional educator cannot without any further thought get rid of his own experiences (even if he appears to be rid of them). The helplessness of the young person is of a different nature than that of the educator, because above all he first must learn to understand his own helplessness and to draw conclusions about it. In any case, the aims, given by a so called collective/practical understanding, are rid of their dogmatic value. In practice, however, they are norms for young people for a longer term, because without them these norms have to be justified by the educator. The insight of the educator into his helplessness leads to a structure that has no constructive meaning for the whole job of educating, but that has, for his own method of action, an exculpatory function. Being helpless among helpless people, he gives up his function as educator in the hope of creating productive independence. He strives for theoretical wishes, envisioning reality as dangerous to the young people as a dogmatic assumption under apparent legitimate forces. In spite of his holding back from direct normative interventions. he leads with his advice, giving the young person one direction or another. The elimination of the traditional pedagogic thinking does not lead to a new pedagogy, but rather to a loss of constitutive elements of education in general. The question about the role of given norms in the self-development of norms remains unsolved.

THE PROBLEM OF TRADITIONAL AIMS

It might appear that statements of traditional aims and objectives of physical education lessons have little meaning, because the practical relevance of such never-ending theoretical discussions apparently counts very little. The theoretical ending of such thought makes quite clear the difficulties that are opposed to a legitimization of the aims that should be realized by young people. Consequently, mentioning the aims of practical sport comes more through the confession of knowledge rather than through scientific necessity. On the other hand, it should not be overlooked that the discussion of aims and objectives that has taken place for such a long time has led to positive results, independent of the represented scientific theoretical viewpoints. The attitude towards prescribed aims has become more critical. Rationalism, no matter how it is interpreted and evaluated, is the demand to which all assumptions have to be subjected. Also, the realization of possible aims belongs to the necessary conditions of meaningful discussions about aims.

This theoretical statement is plausible. It is evidenced by looking at the history of aims in physical education and in sport. Just as in pedagogy in general, in physical education and sport pompous aims were preferred to clearly tangible conditions for many decades. Desirable and worthwhile results of actions were strived for, and were eventually reached, or at least were given out as attainments to be strived for. Their realization was accomplished whenever it was said that the aim for which one was striving had been reached. Necessarily, such discussions included only general aims, which, however, still provided one much to think about, without which a good result could hardly be attained.

There are a large number of examples that document such incidents. I have restricted myself to two: A look back at *Die Deutsche Turnkunst,* by Jahn, and a look at a 1967 publication that proves the continuity of this point. Jahn endorsed aspects of war exercises in the framework of gymnastics:

> War exercises, even without guns, build manly traits, awake and revitalize the feeling of order, train one to obedience and to observation, teach the single individual to feel being a part of a whole.... Every gymnast should mature into a military man without being drilled (Jahn and Eiselen, 1816, XVII).

Dance as a physical activity is said to develop *good attitudes and good posture,* but under the present practices it shows itself as "a danger to health, [a] ruiner of morals and [a] leader into sin." About horseback riding in one's childhood and early youth it has been said that this is "damaging for youth, health and moral behavior." A horse for a young person "damages him and profanes him"—"puts the proudness of adulthood and big ideas into his head, leads him towards extravagance and proud lusts, and moods" (Jahn and Eiselen, 1816, XVI).

In an article by Wischmann (1967) concerning "values, meaning, and task of high achievement drive in sport" it was stated

> sportive striving for achievement requires willpower, hardness, concentration, endurance, nerves, courage. . . . On his [the top sports performer's] hard way of trial and work he will become acquainted with the knowledge that every big achievement in life needs the use of iron willpower and strength and takes a lot of hard work, . . . that not only the winning in sport, but also the high achievements and attitudes of mind draw pride, attention and respect . . . , that in no other field of our life, character and attitude are as much weighed in the judgment of an achievement as in sport (Wischmann, 1967, p. 12).

Physical education lessons lead, therefore, to a willingness to perform above that of a readiness to participate in sport. It is very noticeable that both pieces of evidence speak of a far-reaching impression of sport to the physical, psychical, moral, and cognitive behavior of a person.

While in the first document cited negative actions resulting from sport participation are seen, even if these are on the same level as the final effort for seeking values, and their negativeness can be understood outside of the historical situations. In the second piece of evidence, not even one point is made regarding the negative effects of sport participation. This is not solely due to the large generality in which both pieces of evidence fall. It can also be assumed that within such statements the main interests are concerned with values outside of the sport system. It might be said that this should detract from scientific insight and hold a position principally characterized by property and psychological values, including the present attitude towards transfer. This has been shown already in the psychological concepts of Herbart and Beneke. The unconscious idea of presenting such aims belongs to a special type of personality, which is characterized by some very general indicators and their negative correlates, and which allows numerable amounts of variance for the individual. Because these markers have not been dealt with more closely, they leave a gap for interpretation. and as a result exclude nothing. The accepted abstractness turns itself into a vague definition to which again actions can be attached to heterogeneous aims. The deficiency lies therefore in the lack of precise aim formulation. The result is that one cannot determine exactly what is to be gained from a certain concrete action. Again, this results in some actions that are no longer carried out, because out of their necessary combination with certain aims they produce undesirable results. Such categorizations, the definite reality of undesirable aims derived from riding in youth and the sought-after aims attained through swimming, are hard to make clear.

Such global aims can nowadays hardly be termed representative. Sport activities are associated with aims that they do not at all intend and that they can never realize, at least not in their abreviated form. However, this does not exclude that, on a general level of sport and physical education,

> education in a meaningful form, physical education, leads not only to a healthy way of life, through bodily enjoyment in dance, games. and sport but also to bodily capability in those fields of man's life, as for example, work, competition, preservation of mankind, festive occasions, which are in memory of the dead and to the glory of the Gods. Physical education does not only include an academic substructure of man, the care and cultivation of natural ways of life, it is a part of the whole man (Fink, 1970, p. 59).

One should distinguish between such basic statements and immediate combinations of general and normally positive aims of the sport actions in which these aims are realized almost automatically.

Nowadays contradictions to such interference of traditional aims are widespread. It is no longer difficult to prove that such lists of aims cannot be realized. However, it still has to be pointed out, because critics generally overlook the fact that, in such aims, particular wishes and expressions come about through a certain sport activity. An activity should strive for something very important, and in a given time something really worthwhile should come to fruition. A history of changing aims in this regard could clarify this fact for everyone. The scientific self-awareness of the physical education teacher and of the sport theorist (like that of educationists) has not always been very strongly represented. Physical education and sport were activities in which one engages, but not as a field of reality worthwhile for scientific investigations. Certainly, some physical education teachers have had different ideas on this. A concordance of their ideas, however, could not be hoped for; therefore, they decided for themselves what their supported aims were and stressed the benefits gained through their work.

That this approach overestimated the pragmatically attainable results is merely a reflection of their far-reaching refusal. In their alliance with their contemporaries, they were able to build up a position for themselves that with their refusal at the same time refuted those general necessities of attainable aims. They could only succeed if the incongruence of their actions with desirable aims could have been proven clearly. Such a proof would have even provided the critics with difficulties, at least because this would be a form of immunization against the premises of their own positions.

In general, such an attitude is in no way an example that restricts itself to physical education and sport. The dispute over the position of reality in high school in the 19th Century presents a similar picture. In this very lively and great spirited debate, the transfer of knowledge of physics and chemistry into industry and society is not mentioned (which might have been expected). The formal meaning of such subjects is stressed for the formal education under the demand of a vague humanity which is realized traditionally by languages and mathematics. In this respect the discussion of the aims of physical education and sport reflect that which in specific historical situations was regarded as valid. The given aims reflect the wants, wishes, and also the fears of certain important people. The stated relationship between attitudes and effects of a physical education lesson were valid then as long as the contrary could not be explicitly proven and the general aims, in the eyes of the watching public, were smoothly integrated. To rely on disregarded utility due to a misinterpretation of general education would have made it impossible to discuss this in the "gymnasium."

In the framework of a drill, or spontaneous pedagogy, of a political or humanistic education, the aims of the physical education lesson can be fixed in many different ways. Although the actual components, such as playing, running, jumping, throwing, gymnastics, swimming, and dance, are in themselves hardly changed, one looks at them apart from the "side effects of the lesson," which on the other hand has changed a great deal from the nineteenth to the twentieth century. It would, however, still be a mistaken assumption of the present day to assume that the period of fixed aim proclamations has been overcome. That this was not always the case has been shown, and this also applies to other subjects. A physical education lesson is forced to prove itself in competition with other subjects in the curriculum. An example of this is, for understandable and good reasons, the successful claim of sport as a performance subject in the framework of the reform for the senior classes of the high school. The justification for placing sport in this category leaves many schools with the possibility of reactivating the moralistic approach, as if sport were the universal therapy for all misdemeanors of our time. Whatever might be the reasons for such backward steps, be it inferior higher education, animosity towards science, verbal embarrassment in the reaction to a certain situation, or religious and atheoretical enthusiasm, which withdraws itself from reflection in order to keep its own values, these demand an investigation of their own. They provide endurance that a scientifically recognized fact needs time in order to come to the consciousness of the acting people. Theoretical insight and reality are often held far apart for too long.

CONCEPTUALIZATION OF AIMS FOR SPORT INSTRUCTION

Conceptualizing aims in sport could offer the opportunity for observing the discussion in light of scientific theory and the various differences of opinion about used-up aims with a certain amount of placidness. In itself, however, it is not necessary to disturb one's own theories, but rather to continue in unreflected consent of the present day attitudes to carry out one's aims. Instructional research, and with it the determination of aims, no longer allows for fixed contributions or even fixed positions to arise. The consequences of this demonstrated lack of validity of traditional aims makes it impossible to match sport activities that one likes with those aims that have been regarded as praiseworthy. There is no longer place for such options in a time when instruction has become more and more a matter of science. Just as in other subjects the aims of sport instruction are governed by scientific control. However, this does not prevent as before a scientific debate on the determination of aims and objectives. The proof does not exist, but is a process that has to be considered in very strict general terms, and that could force the agreement of everyone. The choice of a certain aim finally cannot be separated from the pedagogical responsibility of the educator. The task of science in this regard is therefore more critical than constructive. It does not prove, rather it has the task of looking for, legitimizing, or rejecting it. The consequence for science is to consider aims and objectives and to limit itself to hypothetically stated aims. Out of the structure of a field of action, aims are not the automatic result, as in the area of sport instruction, where condition is the result of engaging in sport. Such an altogether praiseworthy and possible relationship does not necessarily result. The reduction to merely hypothetically given aims does not immunize the area of aims from science, but rather opens it. It pushes aside the long all-inclusive overshadowing question of proving aims out of the focal point of speculation and turns instead to aims that are already being used. Out of this arises a great number of problems that have to be considered in this area. Already those questions related to the definition of aims, like the degree of generality of aims, their hierarchy, classification, and taxonomy, analysis, and possibility of demands in aims lead to very questionable points. The relationship between the valid general aims and the subsumed specialized aims, the sequence and the structure of certain aims and similar, apparently only "special," questions, remain controversial. However, it is also proven that these questions are closely related to the content and behavior patterns.

All such considerations always require a definition of aims of one kind or the other. Therefore, the question of which lessons demand aims is not primary, inasmuch as they are lesson aims that have to be met, but what these aims really are, so that they can, for the case of instruction, become subject to a desirable technical preparation. Although in this direction one treads an uncertain path, because a valid theory of finding aims does not exist, some considerations for sport instruction have to be made. Like all pedagogical aims, these aims can be brought into order in different ways. Certain personality types, personality traits, demands about content conditions for the teacher, psychic circumstances, and physical aptitudes are all often, in a colorful way, related to understandable considerations initially. However, which aims should sport instruction follow?

At this point a small reflection will help our understanding. Sport instruction is part of school instruction. Just as other school subjects are required to, as part of a certain type of school sport, it too must cover certain given aims and work towards specified contributions. This alone is the reason why it represents school sport. The specific contribution of sport instruction can be recognized as education of motor abilities. This does not mean that it has to limit itself to these specifications and thus out of necessity neglect parallel results. Still this task does not provide the basis for sport instruction. However, such a statement has proven to be still much too vague to be really meaningful in this unstructured way. Education and use of motor abilities, for example, cover the major part of engaging in sport. As a result, a rule has to be given that allows at the same time both for a limit to be set and for structuring to take place. This rule can be seen as follows: In school sport instruction, the only activities that should be taught are those that the young person in his future life will be able to utilize without having to be a specialized sportsman of any kind. This general rule has to be explained in order to prevent misunderstanding right away. It says that sport instruction should not be a direct preparation for professional sport, just as mathematics or a language lesson in one's mother tongue does not always prepare one to be a mathematician or an expert in language. That is why usage does not mean utility in its strictest form; rather it encompasses a feeling of well-being, luck, and opportunity of participation in one's life. Also the orientation to such an understandable future use of sport instruction should not relegate it to a future aim, but also try to accomodate the wishes and needs of young people in their immediate present situation. Also, it can be considered as an element for sport instruction, and should agree overall with other subjects and their approaches and thus be a specific introduction to the world around the youngster. It should be able to make possible specific areas of experience, to increase them, and to make the child sensitive to heterogeneous wishes. For the concrete aims of sport instruction one can then apply the following general rule for defining specific performance:

Life-long Sport Activity

Through sport instruction young people should become qualified to carry on with sport beyond the limits of school, and this not necessarily because of the many arguments put forward concerning health, about which especially young people care little, or similar aims, but rather to practice sport from the essential point of making contacts and learning to socialize with other people. It is, therefore, the task of sport instruction to teach various types of sport known in our society, and to utilize the general avid interest that youngsters show in sport. It is, therefore, possible to pick out preferably the following sports, without demeaning the others: swimming, games (above all volleyball and soccer), skiing, and dancing. Such conditions are basically open and are variable according to the environmental conditions of every school (Schmitz-Scherzer, 1974, p. 148; Artus, 1974, p. 59, p. 120). Types of sport like tennis, diving, and riding are at the moment, very popular in many places. Others, such as boxing or gymnastics, seem to be disappearing into the realm of the club. Sport instruction should not be afraid in the light of such conditions to shy away from the accusation that it always stays with the traditional way. It is also said to have made itself to be a less critical function of a diffuse time understanding and of following fashions. Only in its orientation to far-reaching sport activities will it be possible for it to maintain the interest of those who want to do sport after school and not to join a club. The criteria for choice, lead to the decision about such sports are their frequency and general acceptance.

General Physical Conditioning

Next to the orientation to such varied types of sport, whose mastery in regard to knowledge and movement is rich in meaning for this world, sport instruction should train movement abilities, which allow the young person to find for himself new kinds of sport. This means that a large part of the aim of sport instruction is the conditioning of the body. Strength, endurance, speed, flexibility, and dexterity have to be practised. Through these, the young person puts himself in a better position to engage in other types of sport if he so wishes, for example, sports that he may not have had the opportunity to learn in school, such as canoeing or long distance running. Therefore, sport instruction should not lead into the world of sport by patterning this world in a traditional way; rather it must equip the young person to find for himself his own way in the world of sport, so that he can go in for that kind of sport or sporting field that he would like to try out for himself or that he would himself like to follow more intensively, to specialize in for his specific needs. A much-asserted final aim is to decide something for oneself, to come to grips with this, and to use the results in a meaningful way. That moment of outward determination as in education cannot be altogether eliminated even in a sport activity which has stemmed or been instigated by instruction. That in this case, there is a connecting, directing, leading and advice-giving necessity, there certainly needs to be no further explanation.

Creativeness in Movement

Sport instruction should bring about the conditions for self-participation in sport. It should qualify a young person to combine movement patterns so that under observation of a situation which he finds satisfying and practical in the way of movement, behavior can take place. In other words, to engage in a sport action without any view to norms of others, which he can find and achieve for himself, and which appears to him to be a successful kind of sport participation. Among playing children it is often observed that they allow themselves very imaginative types of movement patterns and games, representing variations of well-known games or sometimes representing new creations. Such creativity should quite consciously be maintained and definitely be encouraged.

Knowledge of Sport Theory

Sport instruction seems to differ from other subjects in that its aims lie less in the acquisition of theoretical knowledge as in mastering of a practical form as well as in skills and in the practical use of these. A simple reduction of sport instruction to these practical aspects should be avoided. Much more should be included in an explanation of the practice (experience). Why something is carried out in sport and something else is overlooked or left out, what in sport acts actually accompanies sport participation, can possibly be explained to the pupils too. These explanations, just as in other subjects that are also taught, need not be pedagogical or even political. The explanation about the respective sport practice leads to questions of sport science, which the teacher has to explain on the corresponding age level. This means that in sport instruction not only practical sport is necessary but also the study or knowledge of sport. This should in all cases accompany sport instruction. This does not mean that special lessons for sport knowledge should be introduced in the primary school; but it does mean that even in the primary school not merely practical sport should be carried on, but that information about sport should also be taught. If and when specific lessons for sport knowledge are introduced, if it is at all a good idea, and to start first in the framework of the performance subject, sport, can certainly be discussed controversially. But in the framework of sport instruction at all school levels, sport should be explained, and there should be a great deal of agreement.

This last point could possibly lead to protest, since in addition to these aims, the actual results of sport instruction might be considered too narrow. That is, a combination of adjustment to the present and organic training are to a great extent represented for their own sake. At the same time it could be assumed that with such a listing one would be left with an uncoordinated togetherness of a so-called material and formal training. The necessary grouping in sport instruction, just as in any other subject, would under these extreme heterogenous aims be destroyed (disciplines of sport, basic abilities, spontaneity, creativeness, and sport theory). Against this one must point out that these aims should not or cannot under any account be separated from each other in their application. They are related much more to one another, stand in unalterable changeability to one another, and lastly indicate the specific main points, under which special sport activities are categorized and directed towards special aims. It is, therefore, not a case of a time sequence as in the case of reproduction, variation, creation, and reflection, but rather the consideration of all aspects with the specific emphasis of one aspect containing the primary aim. One does not attempt to prevent the *side effects*. For example, swimming lessons also develop fundamental abilities. Certainly the striving involved in reaching for such an aim presents a link in the broadest sense with that which is known as personality development. If the form of instruction considers such non-primary side effects in sport instruction, sport instruction is achieving aims that in other subjects are not possible to cover in a systematic teaching program. However, this does not mean that it necessarily simply adds something to the other subjects. Its achievements lie in the framework of the total instruction with tasks and aims, which also can be attained in specialized ways in other subjects, but at the same time go beyond the attainment of specific results for a subject. In the same way, within sport instruction not merely subject specific performances are valid, but also effects that occur in conjunction with sport instruction and that extend beyond the subject-specific aspects and enter into the realm of personality development, whether it be intended or not.

Such effects that occur beyond the boundaries of the subject are still part of subject attainment, because the contribution of sport instruction does not appear in a general sense but it is supposed to be looked for. At this point statements about the aims of sport instruction run into difficulties. There are insufficiently reliable pieces of research that have looked into the relationships between certain defined forms of sport instruction and the disciplines of sport, which are taught in the lesson, and thus also of the developing personality (Singer and Haase, 1975). The assumed effects do not have to be more abstract than those subject-specific effects, which also have certain predefined aims, which in no way allow themselves to be limited only to the field of motor behavior. The now touched-upon aims are not of the kind that they can be realized alone from the subject. They span distances and reach from one strived-for personality trait right up to such norms as emancipation or solidarity. Here one can categorize the various aims according to various criteria. They can be sorted somewhat according to their degree of generality or even possibly according to the part of sport specific action played in their realization.

It is noticeable for all these aims that they are not a direct product of action, but first arise out of a *reverse effect* of action on the acting person, and lead to a change in the personality type; therefore, they change also the disposition towards an observable behavior. This means that the international structures themselves are changed or built up in a different way. What is meant here shall be made clear by an example. One valid teaching aim for all subjects could be the diminishing of fear. Without instituting this context there is no lack of arguments for such a conclusion as the reduction of fear or even the overcoming of fear as a possible aim. One can indicate how such a really general and complex pedagogical aim can be made attainable under an educational situation. Concrete tasks allow themselves to be described whose solution presents an overcoming of certain aspects of fear. These tasks can be sorted into certain task categories. Then it can be determined which method, which problem, and which class, under the present conditions, could best reach a far-reaching diminution of fear. Certainly such a procedure of classification and determination is mixed with decisions. However, these cannot come about in any optional way, but are a matter of judgment, which in its own definition does not follow any rule developed through experience. As a result of this method, even sport instruction could be used for the realization of such an aim. So it could thematize a sport-specific class of problems, whose overcoming belongs to the attainment of such an aim. It does, however, still leave us with the question whether a reduction of fear in such sectors leads to an eventual reduction of fear in general. Other types of fear cannot be overcome with such specific sport activities. Although it can be seen that in the field of sport, one can reduce the state of fear through various specific actions, the exercise of behavior patterns in which are found basic forms of fear could lead to an overall lowering of the feeling of fear. The difference between statements made now and those beliefs that were previously held lies in the fact that now one does not attach to the use of a certain kind of sport participation a "deus ex machina" consequence; it is true, rather, that, primarily by aimed use of sport actions, certain elements of aims are realized and checked for their validity. The difference between that which happens and that which is being aimed for is not unattainable and therefore it is controllable. For instruction this means that it can be planned better in regard to the development of such an aim. This also makes the pupil feel more independent, because he can learn better about a concrete objective. The effectiveness of instruction increases because one can check the results.

However, such a procedure is often criticized. The criticisms relate to the neglect of the individual within the process of learning, and to the reduction of general aims into concrete classes for tasks with the justification that the solving of the tasks does not occur simultaneously with the reaching of the general aim. Furthermore, political attitudes are criticized, which nowadays seem to appear frequently when complex procedures are related to the determination of technical aspects. A few such elements of critical intervention should not be swept aside immediately. Fruitful alternatives, however, seem to be lacking. Therefore, it can only be pointed out that there is in this field no perfect technical solution, that some momentary clarity, that the teacher has to know of the boundaries of his working area and of the acting space left to him, and that there is no theory that is at the same time practiced and that could clearly and always set norms for the concrete structures of practice.

At any rate there appears, even in this area of aims, an extensive and meaningful field for research on sport instruction. This research would in this connection meet with many problems, which also present themselves from the viewpoint of other subjects. Thus, the example explains that fear cannot be merely contained and reduced through sport instruction alone. Contrarily, it must be asked if a reduction of fear is at all possible without taking into consideration sport participation. After this roughly sketched procedure it is also possible to reach other worthwhile aims, such as social independence . . .

However, there are also other aims, such as emancipation, self-realization, and freedom, which cannot be tackled in this way, in that they can be simply filed under different categories of tasks. This does not eliminate, considering the non-operational nature of such expectations, for often statements can be made, which actually can make the direct approach to such aims easier. It is not without fascination that one can observe in such suggestions a definite oscillation between concrete actions and final general decisions with regard to norms. Even if such connections cannot easily be clearly seen or made available technically, yet it should be attempted to bring together such statements of aims with sport instruction. However, not so much high-blown eloquence is needed to this end, but rather concrete empirical research. In general, the rule should be that aims are to be formulated so that they contain concrete indications of how they can be reached. This leads back to the platitude that empirical research on teaching aims is also to be encouraged and further developed. Certainly some results can be taken from other areas. Still, in this type of research the specific components of sport should be stressed especially.

SUMMARY AND CONCLUSIONS

In conclusion, one can say that a specific contribution of sport instruction has to be found that realizes the aims of instruction. If the attainments can be brought about through other disciplines as well, there is no necessity to insist upon it. At the same time these specific forms of attainments should also be related to generally stated aims, for the realization of these aims sport activities are also useful, and without them the aims themselves are attainable only by these actions. Finally, such aims are also to be integrated into general pedagogical relationships. Such a distinction is under no circumstances compulsory. The one does not automatically lead to the other, or lead out from it. Rather, the various groupings themselves have to be decided upon, in such a way that they result in a certain degree of plausibility and not through excessiveness or over-emphasis of one or the other, which may lead to undesirable effects. Everyone knows that active sport participation under certain circumstances is beneficial to one's health, that it also increases the feeling of well-being, and that it leaves one with a feeling of luck. But it is just as true

Schmitz-Scherzer, R. 1974. Sozialpsychologie der Freizeit. (Social-Psychology of Recreation.) Kolhammer, Stuttgart.

Weber, M. 1956. Soziologie. Weltgeschichtliche Analysen. Politik. (Sociology. Analysis of World History. Politics.) Kröner, Stuttgart.

Wischmann, B. 1967. Wert, Bedeutung und Auftrag sportlichen Hochleistungsstrebens. (Meaning and Task of Sportive Striving for Top Performance.) Südwestdeutsche Verlagsdruckerei. Hornberg, Waldfischbach.

Aims and Objectives of Physical Education: Subject Matter and Research Methods of Sport Pedagogy as a Behavioral Science

A. E. Jewett

Each of the three topics of this Symposium is exceedingly broad in scope. This paper was prepared on aims and objectives of physical education, but also includes aspects of the subject matter, methods of research, and the position of sport science within the realm of human and natural sciences. In order to deal with this assignment, it was necessary to make some difficult choices. First, I chose to speak from a particular philosophical position rather than to attempt to present each of the major views concerning the derivation of aims and objectives. Second, I elected to share certain theoretical propositions, curriculum concepts, and research findings that have not yet been widely disseminated through American educational literature, in preference to those for which my most widely read American colleagues are best known. And, third, I decided to place my emphasis on subject matter and research methods, although it would be possible for me to elaborate on conclusions concerning sport pedagogy as a behavioral science if the opportunity is presented. This paper is not organized in outline form, or with thoughtful capsulized headings. The sequence of the remarks moves from the identification and analysis of general objectives of physical education curricula to the development and classification of instructional objectives. Selected studies utilizing a variety of research tools and techniques are reported.

Macdonald and Clark (1973) have stated that the derivation of objectives is the most fundamental problem in curriculum. They have pointed out that there is little or no research or theory to aid us in solving this problem. The 1973 summary of research on teaching physical education by Nixon and Locke (1973), which is clearly the most authoritative work done in the United States on this topic, offers a *learning framework for teaching and research*. This framework has outstanding potential both for analyzing available data and for identifying important research gaps. However, a learning framework does not deal with the actual derivation of curricular objectives. The resolution of value problems basic to curriculum focus remains critical and continues to be one of my major concerns.

Voluntary movement is a significant function of man. Thus, the education essential to each individual person includes learning concerned with how human movement functions in his experience and in achieving common human goals. Physical education has long been recognized as the school subject using games, sports, dance, exercise, and other movement activities as media for learning. More recently, physical education has been viewed as the series of school programs concerned with the development and utilization of the individual's movement potential. Currently, physical educators attempting to realize the full potential of this area of human experience are seeking to extend concepts of physical education to help meet the needs of learners of all ages in both school and noninstitutional contexts. Physical education is increasingly viewed as personalized, self-directed learning, using selected movement learning media to achieve individual human goals. A physical education program is now defined as a sequence of experiences through which an individual learns to move as he moves to learn.

THE PURPOSE-PROCESS CURRICULUM FRAMEWORK

The purposes of physical education have been stated at many levels of sophistication. Its overall aims are individual development, environmental coping, and social interaction. Human beings of all ages have the same fundamental purposes for moving. The child needs movement learnings that will function meaningfully in his real world; the youth needs physical education that will aid him in becoming a fully functioning adult; the adult needs movement activities that will permit continuing self-actualization and more nearly complete individual-environment integration. The same key purposes can be used to design programs of movement opportunities for all persons. Identification and statement of these purposes is achieved through study of the pedagogical literature and logical analysis of human experience and educational practice. A conceptual framework of human movement purposes may serve as the basis for defining the scope or content of physical education. One such framework, developed through group study and partially supported by the American Alliance for Health, Physical Education and Recreation (Jewett and Mullan, 1977), includes 22 purpose elements for identifying the content of physical education experiences. The Purpose-Process Curriculum Framework is postulated on the premise that each individual person may seek personal meaning through any combination of the following movement goals.

Man, Master of Himself:
Man Moves to Fulfill his Human Developmental Potential

A. Physiological Efficiency: Man moves to improve or maintain his functional capabilities.
   1. *Circulo-Respiratory Efficiency.* Man moves to develop and maintain circulatory and respiratory functioning.
   2. *Mechanical Efficiency.* Man moves to develop and maintain range and effectiveness of motion.
   3. *Neuromuscular Efficiency.* Man moves to develop and maintain motor functioning.
B. Psychic Equilibrium: Man moves to achieve personal integration.
   4. *Joy of Movement.* Man moves to derive pleasure from movement experience.
   5. *Self-Knowledge.* Man moves to gain self-understanding and appreciation.
   6. *Catharsis.* Man moves to release tension and frustration.
   7. *Challenge.* Man moves to test his prowess and courage.

Man in Space:
Man Moves to Adapt to and Control his Physical Environment

C. Spatial Orientation: Man moves to relate himself in three-dimensional space.
   8. *Awareness.* Man moves to clarify his conception of his body and his position in space.
   9. *Relocation.* Man moves in a variety of ways to propel or project himself.
   10. *Relationships.* Man moves to regulate his body position in relation to the objects or persons in his environment.
D. Object Manipulation: Man moves to give impetus to, and to absorb the force of, objects.
   11. *Maneuvering Weight.* Man moves to support, resist, or transport mass.
   12. *Object Projection.* Man moves to impart momentum and direction to a variety of objects.
   13. *Object Reception.* Man moves to intercept a variety of objects by reducing or arresting their momentum.

Man in a Social World: Man Moves to Relate to Others

E. Communication: Man moves to share ideas and feelings with others.
   14. *Expression.* Man moves to convey his ideas and feelings.

15. *Clarification.* Man moves to enhance the meaning of other communication forms.
16. *Simulation.* Man moves to create an advantageous image or situation.

F. Group Interaction: Man moves to function in harmony with others.
17. *Teamwork.* Man moves to cooperate in pursuit of common goals.
18. *Competition.* Man moves to vie for individual or group goals.
19. *Leadership.* Man moves to motivate and influence group members to achieve common goals.

G. Cultural Involvement: Man moves to take part in movement activities that constitute an important part of his society.
20. *Participation.* Man moves to develop his capabilities for taking part in movement activities of his society.
21. *Movement Appreciation.* Man moves to become knowledgeable and appreciative of sports and expressive movement forms.
22. *Cultural Understanding.* Man moves to understand, respect, and strengthen the cultural heritage.

Such aims or goals may be expected to hold personalized meaning for students participating in thoughtfully selected movement experiences. Although the meanings internalized by student participants cannot be studied by completely objective techniques, research methods for evaluating the content validity of a particular set of purposes are not limited to the typical questionnaire or survey of opinion. The Delphi technique has proved to be a useful research tool for seeking consensus judgments. LaPlante (1973) used a modified Delphi technique to evaluate the set of purposes for physical education defined by the Purpose-Process Curriculum Framework. A panel of approximately 200 judges was selected in order to secure judgments from five groups: curriculum theorists, human movement researchers, state directors of physical education, city and county supervisors of physical education, and teachers of physical education.

Questionnaires were sent to the panel of judges three times. Each questionnaire asked the respondents to rate the importance of the selected purpose statements of student learning outcomes and to rank them in order of importance from 1 to 22 for both present educational development and future educational development. The respondents were given an opportunity to make changes in the purpose statements, delete unnecessary purposes, or add new purposes, but were asked to provide a brief statement of the rationale for taking any of these actions. The data from the questionnaires were compiled, and with each succeeding questionnaire, respondents were given the mean ratings and rankings and a summary of comments. In light of this feedback, the respondents were asked to repeat the original two tasks.

To determine the validity of the purpose statements, the degree of consensus of both agreement and disagreement and the suggested changes, additions, and deletions were analyzed. A split plot factorial analysis was used to test the hypotheses of no difference among the five groups, no difference in present and future ratings, and no change from round one to round three. From the LaPlante study it was possible to conclude that this set of 22 purposes identified all those viewed as important by the panel of judges. Since no significant differences were found among the five groups of judges, it was concluded that these physical educators viewed the purposes for physical education in unique ways not necessarily dependent upon their roles in curriculum development and implementation.

A significant difference did appear between ratings of the purposes for physical education for present curriculum development and implementation in contrast to future curriculum development and implementation. The judges rated self-knowledge, awareness, and expression as more important for students in the future than for present students; they also rated competition and object projection as less important in the future. LaPlante's findings suggested that physical educators do identify a difference in the education of young people to live and play in today's world and the education suitable to enable them to cope with a changing and unstable future. The Delphi technique appears to be an appropriate methodological tool for the study of physical education aims and objectives.

Another research methodology that has been applied to such study is the semantic differential. The semantic differential was developed by Osgood, Suci, and Tannenbaum (1971) for the purpose of defining the meaning of a concept as its location in semantic space. It consists of a set of bipolar terms separated by a seven-point scale on which subjects indicate the direction and intensity of the meaning associated with the concept. The semantic differential has been used in a number of physical education attitude studies. Kenyon (1968) developed a Physical Activity Inventory based on semantic differential scales; he and others have published considerable research on attitudes toward physical activity.

Using a semantic differential instrument, Chapman (1974) evaluated the affective responses of students to the 22 purposes for human movement identified in the Purpose-Process Curriculum Framework. A total of 420 subjects were randomly selected from a large midwestern school district. Seventy males and seventy females from each of the three grade levels (seventh, ninth, and eleventh grades) participated in the study. Chapman designed an instrument to evaluate student attitudes in two dimensions toward each of these 22 purposes. Each purpose statement was followed by eight bipolar semantic differential scales, four representing each dimension. The instrument yielded two scores for each purpose statement, a likeability score and a utility score. Results were analyzed using an analysis of variance statistical procedure.

Chapman found significant differences, both in the dimensions of likeability and utilty in the responses of students in the three selected grade levels. Analysis of student responses demonstrated the following:

1. Students preferred (or "liked" better) moving for purposes of team work, relocation, joy of movement, neuromuscular efficiency, circulo-respiratory efficiency, and mechanical efficiency to moving for purposes of leadership, maneuvering weight, cultural understanding, and simulation.

2. Students perceived as more "useful" movement purposes of circulo-respiratory efficiency, neuromuscular efficiency, relocation, mechanical efficiency, teamwork, and relationships, in contrast to purposes of awareness, competition, leadership, clarification, cultural understanding, and simulation.

3. Ratings on the utility factor were slightly higher than those of the likeability factor. Even though some purposes were not extremely well liked, they were perceived as very useful.

4. Grades seven and eleven were more positive in their affective responses to the purposes for moving than was grade nine. Students in grade eleven were more discriminating in their responses than those in either grade seven or nine.

Physical educators tend to assume that students share their views about what is important in their education. In most cases, such an assumption is clearly unwarranted. An interesting comparison between the rankings of purposes of movement upon which professionals base their stated educational objectives and those of students can be made using selected data from the LaPlante and Chapman studies. Although circulo-respiratory efficiency, mechanical efficiency, and neuromuscular efficiency appear high in both physical educators' and students' rankings, and although simulation, clarification, and cultural understanding appear low in both lists, relocation and relationships are viewed as highly useful by students, but are considered as relatively less important by professional physical educators. In contrast, competition and leadership are ranked above the median by physical educators, but are among the least useful purposes as perceived by the students.

As indicated earlier, broad goals or general objectives of physical education can be identified through the study of pedagogical literature and processes of logical analysis. However, sound curriculum planning depends upon the validation of theoretical constructs, which provide the basis for translating generalizations into curriculum content. The methodology of construct validation is illustrated by Jones' (1972) in a definitive study of the construct of body awareness.

Body awareness was defined as an element associated with the major purpose concept of spatial orientation. Jones postulated two major components of dynamic body awareness in space. The first was defined as body shapes focusing primarily on how the body can move. Included were knowledge of body parts, how these parts move, and the ability to position body parts in specific ways. The second major component was defined as spatial coordinates focusing on where the body can move. Included were knowledge and ability to move in various spatial coordinates: directions, levels, and pathways. Jones designed instruments to measure the ability to discriminate and to move in these spatial coordinates. The tests were administered to first- and third-grade children.

Data were treated statistically in order to determine the adequacy of test items, the interrelationship among the tests, and the differences between performances according to age, sex, and motor vs. cognitive ability. The results of the analysis of variance computations indicated that there was no significant difference in performance between males and females. There were, however, statistically significant differences between six-year-olds and eight-year-olds and between performances on the motor and cognitive subtests. The interrelationship among tests was determined through correlation techniques. The findings suggested that each test measured a discrete constituent of the body awareness construct, thus supporting the theoretical construct of body awareness as postulated by Jones.

TAXONOMY OF EDUCATIONAL OBJECTIVES

Thus far, curriculum concepts and research methodology have been discussed in relation to purposes, aims, or relatively general objectives in physical education. Specific objectives that guide decision making at the instructional level should emphasize movement processes. Bloom (1956) Krathwohl (1964), and their associates have popularized the use of taxonomies of educational objectives. Writers of educational taxonomies are concerned with identifying process skills and classifying the intended behavior of students as contrasted with classifications of the usual subject matter content.

Bloom and his associates described three domains: cognitive, affective, and psychomotor. Physical educators have been particularly interested in the study of educational objectives in the psychomotor or motor domains. It is readily recognized that each person responds as a whole thinking-feeling-acting being. Attempts to abstract and to classify behaviors into three domains represent an emphasis and bias accepted so that we may organize curricular content and guide instructional processes more efficiently. In physical education it seems most desirable to plan learning activities in terms of our bias toward movement and our emphasis on desired educational outcomes in the motor domain.

Mager, Popham, Baker, and others have given much attention to the use of taxonomies in the statement of behavioral objectives. I have assumed that others will deal with this topic during this Symposium. I view the statement of objectives as an important problem, but secondary to the actual derivation of objectives. My efforts in this area have been primarily directed to the development of a process-oriented taxonomy.

Successful utilization of any taxonomy of educational objectives requires the identification of conceptual referents in addition to the selection of the appropriate process skill category. I am convinced that the key to selecting, stating, and achieving the most meaningful and humanizing of physical education objectives is an effective combination of purpose and process concepts related to human movement. Learning movement processes can be combined with the learning of purpose concepts if the teacher uses these categories as the basis for writing instructional objectives in the motor domain. The Purpose-Process Curriculum Framework (Jewett and Mullan, 1977) offers a taxonomy for educational objectives in the motor domain that classifies movement processes into three major types of movement operations and seven movement process categories.

Generic Movement

Generic movements are those movement operations or processes that facilitate the development of characteristic and effective motor patterns. They are typically exploratory operations in which the learner receives or takes in data as he or she moves.

1. *Perceiving:* Awareness of total body relationships and self in motion. These awarenesses may be evidenced by body positions or motoric acts; they may be sensory, in that the mover feels the equilibrium of body weight and the movement of limbs; the limbs are manipulated; or they may be evidenced cognitively through identification, recognition, or differentiation.

2. *Patterning:* Arrangement and use of body parts in successive and harmonious ways to achieve a movement pattern or skill. This process is dependent on recall and performance of a movement previously demonstrated or experienced.

Ordinative Movement

Ordinative movement includes the processes of organizing, refining, and performing skillful movement. The processes involved are directed toward the organization of perceptual-motor abilities with a view to solving particular movement tasks or requirements.

3. *Adapting:* Modification of a patterned movement to meet externally imposed task demands. This would include modification of a particular movement to perform it under different conditions.

4. *Refining:* Acquisition of smooth, efficient control in performing a movement pattern or skill by mastery of spatial and temporal relations. This process deals with the achievement of precision in motor performance and habituation of performance under more complex conditions.

Creative Movement

Creative movement encompasses those motor performances that include the processes of inventing or creating movement that will serve the personal and individual purposes of the learner. The processes employed are directed toward discovery, integration, abstraction, idealization, emotional objectification and composition.

5. *Varying:* Invention or construction of personally unique options in motor performance. These options are limited to different ways of performing specific movement; they are of an immediate situational nature and lack any predetermination externally imposed on the mover.

6. *Improvising:* Extemporaneous origination or initiation of personally novel movement or combination of movement. The processes involved may be stimulated by a situation externally structured, although conscious planning on the part of the performer is not usually required.

7. *Composing:* Combination of learned movement into personally unique motor designs or the invention of movement patterns new to the performer. The performer creates a personal motor response in terms of an interpretation of the movement situation.

Although there is a considerable body of research dealing with the processes of motor skill acquisition, research designed to further the development of educational objectives based on movement process categories has been extremely limited. One study that makes a contribution in this area is a study of feedback diversity by Harrington (1974). Harrington designed an instrument for systematic descriptive analysis of teacher feedback using the three elements of intent, form, and content to reflect purposes, modes of teacher feedback, and movement processes indicated. The categories of intent and form were based on the work of Fishman and Anderson (1971). The category of intent included teacher verbal behavior, which indicated the purpose of the feedback in response to student motor performance (evaluative, descriptive, comparative, explicative, prescriptive, and affective). The category of form identified the mode of teacher feedback (auditory, tactile, and visual). The category of content was based upon the motor taxonomy described above and included teacher verbal behavior, which indicated the processes of student motor performance (perceiving, patterning, adapting, refining, varying, improvising, and composing). Four physical education specialists were trained in the use of this classification system. They observed ten teachers as they taught physical education in grades six through nine. Data were analyzed through descriptive statistics and analysis of variance.

Harrington's findings demonstrated that students were most often viewed by the teachers as patterning or refining movement. Most of the feedback (82.5%) was auditory in form. The predominant intent of the teachers in providing feedback was to prescribe for successive movements. Concurrent examination of intent and content showed that the intent when indicating processes of patterning and refining was usually prescriptive or affective. Analysis of content, intent, and form for concurrent occurrences showed that the predominant mode of verbal feedback was usually prescriptive in nature, while the processes indicated were most often patterning or refining. Analysis of variance techniques supported the generalizability of the classification system, with reliability and inter-observer objectivity coefficients ranging from 0.83 to 0.99. Descriptive analytic research tends to support the discrete nature of the movement process categories and their usefulness for stating physical education performance objectives as well as for analysis of certain aspects of teacher and student behavior.

Scholarly analysis of the aims and objectives of physical education has recently entered another area of concern. Awareness of previously unstudied aspects of the process of schooling is increasing. The term *hidden curriculum* appears frequently in the literature, sometimes defined as the unintended outcomes of schooling (Nixon and Locke, 1973), by others defined as attitudes and values inclusively represented in the education environment (Apple, 1971). Isolation and measurement of the effects of the hidden curriculum on students has been difficult. At least one study of the hidden curriculum in physical education is worthy of mention, however.

Bain (1974) conducted an investigation to describe values implicit in secondary school physical education classes and tested hypotheses concerning differences between male and female classes and between urban and suburban classes. The Bain Implicit Values Instrument for Physical Education consisted of three subsections: observation of teacher verbal behavior, observation of class organization, and a questionnaire concerning procedural regulations. Items were scored on six value dimensions according to the logical relationship of the behaviors to the dimensions. The value dimensions, selected and defined on the basis of a review of the hidden curriculum literature, were achievement, autonomy, orderliness, privacy, specificity, and universality. The sample consisted of six male and six female physical education teachers in four city secondary schools and a comparable group in four suburban secondary schools. Two-way analysis of variance was employed to examine value differences.

Female classes scored higher than male classes on the privacy dimension, the difference being greater in urban schools than in suburban schools.

Female classes also tended to score higher on specificity, and female teachers made a larger number of verbal comments (total frequency 2,894 for female teachers, 1,844 for male teachers). Bain's findings failed to verify sex differences in orderliness predicted as parallel to the hidden curriculum reported in other curricular areas. Although this study was perceived as an initial effort, it did provide a theoretical network for analyzing the hidden curriculum in physical education, procedures recommended for construct validation of the theoretical network, and a useful instrument for further study of certain aspects of the hidden curriculum in other physical education situations.

Aims and objectives of physical education have evidenced much consistency through the years of development into a profession with a recognized discipline and acknowledged role in education. Human beings have always aimed toward self-fulfillment, more complete control of the natural environment, and greater satisfaction in interpersonal relationships, although the emphases have varied in different societies according to changing philosophies and social expectations. Current analysis of physical education objectives discloses that they have guided us toward greater understanding of human movement phenomena and expansion of pedagogical subject matter. Objectives are now stated with greater specificity and precision. At the same time, process goals and objectives have received attention once reserved entirely for desired product outcomes.

Scholars of physical education have clarified the theoretical bases of the field of knowledge and conceptualized frameworks for educational practice. Since 1972 American physical educators have been able to base continuing development of theory on a significant AAHPER publication, *Tones of Theory,* edited by Ulrich and Nixon (see p. 45). Methods of research have increased in number and in degree of sophistication. The Delphi technique is being used to focus expert opinion and seek consensus judgments. The semantic differential provides a tool for researching attitudes toward aims and objectives as well as toward particular subject matter content and pedagogical practices. The application of contrast validation processes has permitted the refinement of curriculum and instructional theory and stimulated the generation of new theories. Systematic descriptive analysis affords an approach for identifying teacher intent and focus of attention as well as for analyzing teacher-student interaction and the values implicit in the education environment. Physical educators have clarified aims and expanded subject matter. We have analyzed our objectives and learned to state them more accurately. We are asking new research questions about aims and objectives and utilizing new research tools to seek solutions to pedagogical problems.

Sport pedagogy has become a behavioral science. It uses knowledge developed through experimental studies in the biological and physical sciences, but its research methodologies are primarily those of the social sciences. The key concepts of physical education relate to empirical, aesthetic, and ethical meanings. Insights from many disciplines must guide the philosophical development, research analysis, and educational impact of physical education aims and objectives.

REFERENCES

American Association for Health, Physical Education and Recreation (Co-investigators, C. Ulrich and J.E. Nixon). 1972. Tones of Theory. AAHPER, Washington.

Apple, M. 1971. The hidden curriculum and the nature of conflict. Interchange 2(4):27-43.

Bain, L.L. 1974. Description and analysis of the hidden curriculum in physical education. Unpublished doctoral dissertation, University of Wisconsin, Madison.

Bloom, B.S., et al. 1956. Taxonomy of Educational Objectives, Handbook I: Cognitive Domain. New York: David McKay Company.

Chapman, P.A. 1974. Evaluation of affective responses of students to a selected list of purposes for human movement. Unpublished doctoral dissertation, University of Wisconsin, Madison.

Fishman, S.E., and Anderson, W.G. 1971. Developing a system for describing teaching. Quest XV:7-16, January.

Harrington, W.M. 1974. Feedback diversity in teaching physical education. Unpublished doctoral dissertation, University of Wisconsin, Madison.

Jewett, A.E., and Mullan, M.R. 1977. Curriculum Design: Purposes and Processes in Physical Education Teaching - Learning. Washington: American Alliance for Health, Physical Education and Recreation.

Jones, L.S. 1972. The construct of body awareness in space as reflected through children's ability to discriminate directions, levels, and pathways in movement. Unpublished doctoral dissertation, University of Wisconsin, Madison.

Kenyon, G.S. 1968. Six scales for assessing attitude toward physical activity. Research Quarterly, 39:566-574.

Krathwohl, D.R., et al. 1964. Taxonomy of Educational Objectives, Handbook II: Affective Domain. New York: David McKay Company Inc.

LaPlante, M. 1973. Evaluation of a selected list of purposes for physical education utilizing the Delphi technique. Unpublished doctoral dissertation, University of Wisconsin, Madison.

MacDonald, J., and Clark, D.F. 1973. Critical value questions and the analysis of objectives and curricula. In: R.M.W. Trawers (ed.), Second Handbook of Research on Teaching, pp. 405-412. Rand McNally & Company, Chicago.

Nixon, J.E., and Locke, L.F. 1973. Research on teaching physical education. In: R.M.W. Travers (ed.), Second Handbook of Research on Teaching, pp. 1210-1242. Chicago: Rand McNally & Company.

Osgood, C.E., Suci, G.J., and Tannenbaum, P.H. 1971. The Measurement of Meaning, Revised ed. Urbana: University of Illinois Press.

Aims and Objectives of Sport Instruction

D. Brodtmann and A.H. Trebels

After a short description of the basic position of Menze, this chapter gives a critique of the aims and objectives of sport instruction. This chapter offers an alternative concept of sport instruction as a field for social action that is defined by sport and instruction, and that has as its aim securing the active competence of the pupil in the field of sport. The limitations of Menze's concept are presented through contrast with this concept.

The main aspects of Menze's concept are as follows: the aims and objectives of instruction cannot be legitimized through science. Science has a critical function—it refuses dogmatic absolute requests as unscientific, and examines the aims and objectives of instruction in order to determine whether or not, and under what conditions, they can be realized.

The available aims and objectives of sport instruction are not in line with the criteria of scientific rationale; the phase of postulating general aims and objectives is not yet over. If the scientific definition of aims and objectives is the analysis of these, a precondition is the setting of aims bound by the educational responsibility of the people engaged in the field of education.

The aims and objectives of instruction have to be justified from an educational point of view. They are divided into two categories: aims and objectives that can only be realized in sport instruction, and aims and objectives that can only be realized in cooperation with other subjects. In the first case, the specific task of sport instruction is the development of motor skills; however, the aim should not be to specialize, but rather to enable young people to realize well-being, happiness, and creativity in their lives.

These aims and objectives should be realized on four levels:

1. Teaching of well-known sport disciplines.
2. Development of physical condition.
3. Qualification of the pupil to combine movement patterns.
4. Information and knowledge of sport ("Sportkunde").

The author criticizes the structure of sport disciplines, in that, according to the present popularity of sport, it has only limited possibilities for the "contact and communication" intended by Menze.

The development and improvement of physical condition seems to be too complex an aim. Because of limited organizational possibilities, there is a conflict between this aim and the aim to provide education for self-responsibility (social competency).

In self-activity, mentioned as the third aim, one has to consider that the possibilities to move in a free way are limited by the movement patterns learned in the sport disciplines. Performing movement patterns with others is not mentioned as an aim. Preserving the creativity of young children is criticized because the content of their creativity will change as they become adults.

The criticism of the fourth aim is that it is not enough to just transmit information, especially if educational and political aspects are excluded.

An alternative concept, based on action theory, is to judge sport instruction as an intersection of two action fields by analyzing the following preconditions: a) to make the normative decisions apparent in instruction and b) to structure the action field sport according to intentions and patterns for action.

Normative decisions influence the task and function of learning in school, which is geared to develop the self-responsibility of adults. Learning is structured three ways: it is oriented toward science, it clarifies the relationship of theory to practice, and it contributes to social competency.

The action field sport has two structural divisions: the intentions of action and the intentions of respective action patterns. We can distinguish four aspects:

1. *Competition* and *success* as they are attained through improvement and achievements.
2. *Health,* as it is attained in connection with the *Trimm* movement, calisthenics, etc., and as it is derived from physical fitness.
3. *Aesthetics,* as achieved as they are served by dance and rhythmical calisthenics.
4. *Communicative action.*

The central aims and objectives of sport instruction can be identified as aspects of action competency. The main points are:

1. social orientation of adults toward sport;
2. structuring and defining different intentions and patterns of action in sport;
3. social competency, called self-responsibility.

In conclusion, Menze's concept is seen by these authors as being traditional, while they suggest changing sport practice by developing alternatives, especially stressing alternatives aims and objectives that have an orientation toward criteria such as processes and problems.

Appendix

Scientific Terminology for Sport Pedagogy

The Development of a "Thesaurus" for the Scientific Terminology of Sport Pedagogy as Part of Sport Science

H. Haag and W. Weichert

In order to develop a "thesaurus" for sport pedagogy, the basic structure of the field has to be defined. The following presentation states the aims and objectives of this investigation. Furthermore, it presents some information on the methods used in this research project.

The results of this research project are available both as an alphabetical list of terms and as a structured and systematic model for the terminology in sport pedagogy. Finally, we present a critical review of the development of a "thesaurus" in relation to the clarification of the nature of sport pedagogy as part of sport science.

STATEMENT OF THE FOCUS OF THE INVESTIGATION

In sport pedagogy and sport science, one constantly has to work with literature basic to the teaching and research processes. The selection of this literature very often is accidental, incomplete, unsystematic, and subjective. These aspects are not at all characteristic of scientific procedures.

Recently the information and literature have become so extensive that it is necessary to develop a structured system of documentation and information with regard to sport pedagogy as one aspect of sport science.

These problems and deficiencies were a starting point for the development of a research design for this investigation, for which the following steps seemed necessary:

a. To develop a list of descriptors that could be used to systematically organize and store literature.

b. To develop an instrument that would serve as a retrieval system for literature and information.
c. To control the terminology and definitions of scientific terms that represent a so-called "system-speech," in order to structure the theoretical field of sport pedagogy.
d. To develop a scientific theory by which it will be possible to give a clear and structured content description of this aspect of sport science.
e. To make available an aid for organizing reflections in this theoretical field in a more conscious and objective way, and, by doing this, get rid of unnecessary information and concentrate on the essential aspects.
f. To develop further the concept of sport pedagogy as one aspect of sport science by having a clear, logical, and structured basis for the scientific terminology.

Therefore, with the assistance of a "thesaurus" (which in old Greece meant a treasure house to store gifts) it is possible to repeat, in a controlled and open-ended maneuver, a structuring process which otherwise is often carried out in a coincidental and uncontrolled manner.

RESEARCH METHODS, TECHNIQUES OF DATA COLLECTION, AND DATA TREATMENT IN THIS INVESTIGATION

Basically, the research method we employed was descriptive, since the actual terms relevant to sport pedagogy were collected by using available sources and systematically selecting and organizing the material. As a basis for applying the techniques of data collections, the following served as resources: (a) the index of the sport science dictionary; (b) indices of different dictionairies and handbooks for sport science and education; (c) the sport thesaurus of the Federal Institute of Sport Science (BISp); (d) an alphabetical list of the decimal classification system (DK 1974); (e) an alphabetical list of a literature retrieval system of the Department of Sport Pedagogy; and (f) material from lectures and research studies.

The techniques for data treatment involved the use of a so-called *Wortfeldkarte* (word-field-card) (see Figure 1 for a facsimile); with this system for analysis of terminology every term was analyzed with respect to the following relationships: (a) logical and/or ontological categories for oversetting or undersetting; (b) setting side-by-side; (c) relationship and associations; and (d) synonyms, homonyms, differences in quality, and definitions.

In a second part of the project, these *Wortfeldkarten* (word-field-cards) were analyzed by a specific computer program. The result was a complex system of relationships composed of the information of all *Wortfeldkarten*. This was called a *generierter Thesaurus*, which means a large volume with

Development of a "Thesaurus" 233

WORTFELDKARTE WGLS. Wien: "SPORTTHESAURUS"

DESKRIPTOR: Eishockey FACETTE: _____ Sportpädagogik

SYNONYMA = UF (USED FOR): OBERBEGRIFFE = BT (BROADER TERM): GESAMTBEGRIFFE = TT (TOTAL TERM):
　Wintersport
　Sportspiele

HOMONYMA: SYNONYMA BT: SYNONYMA TT:

EINSCHRÄNKENDES MERKMAL = DT UNTERBEGRIFFE = NT (NARROWER TERM): TEILBEGRIFFE = PT (PART TERM):
(DETERMINANT TERM) Regeln
a) Eis b) Hockey Puck
ASSOZIATON = A Schläger u.a.

NATATION DER DR: VERWANDTE BEGRIFFE = RT (RELATED T.): NACHBEGRIFFE = CT (CONTIGUOUS TERM):
　Eissport
　Eisschnellauf
DEFINITION Eiskunstlauf u.a.

BEARBEITER Wei
ORT U' DATUM: 25.3.75

Figure 1. Facsimile of a *Wortfeldkarte*.

many terms in alphabetical order; the computer printed the surrounding terms for each term, that have a logical and/or ontological relationship to each other.

The procedure can be summarized in the following three steps:

1. Extensive search for the relevant terms
2. Development of a theoretical model to bring the terms into a systematic relationship
3. Summation of the terms discovered through indexing of the sport science literature

This research project was characterized by simultaneous collection of data, e.g., the terms of the theoretical field sport pedagogy were collected at the same time that the theoretical concept that became the basis for the structure of the "thesaurus" was being defined and developed.

DEVELOPMENT OF A THEORETICAL MODEL FOR SPORT PEDAGOGY AS A BASIC STRUCTURE FOR A THESAURUS OF SPORT PEDAGOGY

The aim of this research project was to develop an alphabetical and structured thesaurus. Even if a structured thesaurus had not been planned, one would need a theoretical model from which to derive criteria for the decisions that have to be made regarding including or not including certain terms.

Sport pedagogy, as one theoretical field of sport science, deals with possibilities and boundaries for education through sport. This concerns a broad range of factors that are important for the teaching-learning process in sport.

In order to explain sport pedagogy by using a structured pattern, there are many models for didactics available that could serve as the theoretical framework. The basis for this research project was the so-called *lerntheoretisches Didaktikmodell* developed by Heimann/Otto/Schultz, a research group from Berlin. This model seems to be very comprehensive and includes many factors that are relevant to the teaching-learning processes in sport, which in turn compose the main content of sport pedagogy.

According to this model, two factors of condition and four factors of decision are relevant to explaining the teaching-learning process. These six factors are interdependent.

Factors of Condition

1. *Anthropological determination of instruction*
   (Includes both teacher and pupil, with their personality structures, and especially aspects of teacher and pupil behavior with respect to aspects of learning, and child development psychology.)

2. *Socio-cultural determination of instruction*
   Four types of situations have to be regarded in this aspect:
   2.1. Individual situation of the pupil (home, etc.)
   2.2. Situation of the class (cooperation in class)
   2.3. Situation and position of the school (all day school, vertical or horizontal school organization, etc.)
   2.4. Situation of the society (all socio-cultural factors of a certain period)

Factors of Decision

3. *Aims and objectives*
   In the teaching - learning process, the bases are intentional processes (i.e., educational intentions)
4. *Content of instruction*
   It is necessary to analyze exactly the themes, objects, and contents of the teaching-learning process and to define their structures.
5. *Methods of teaching*
   The following aspects are important: distinction of the instructional process according to phases, group and space organization, specific teaching procedures, models for methods, and educational principles.
6. *Media/audio-visual aids*
   It is important to consider the representation of content through certain media—speech, books, pictures, diagrams, tapes, film, etc.

These six factors served as criteria for the further analysis of the teaching-learning process. Figure 2 explains this model and shows the mutual interdependence of these factors.

Basically, there are six questions to be answered in order to analyze a teaching-learning process:

1. *Who/whom:* Question of the behavior of teachers and learners in physical education instruction and of the factors that are responsible for this behavior.
2. *Where/when:* Questions of the space-time conditions of physical education instruction and of the factors that are responsible for these conditions.

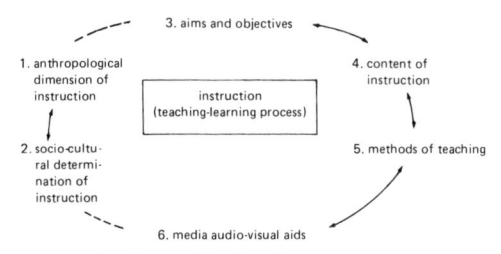

Figure 2. Factors that comprise the teaching-learning process.

```
                    Theory field of sport science
                   (part of general education science)
                              │
                         sport pedagogy
                      (theory of physical education)
                              │
                    scientific theory/methodology
                              │
                           research
              ┌──────────────┼──────────────┐
           methods        content    methodological aids
                              │
                              │
(historical dimension) ──── contents of sport pedagogy ──── (comparative dimension)
                              │
                        (socialization)
                              │
                         (education)
                              │
              school ──── instruction ──── outside of school
                         (sport didactics)
                              │
                   ┌──────────┴──────────┐
              curriculum theory    instructional theory
                   │                     │
            ┌──────┴──────┐       ┌──────┴──────┐
       problem of    problem    theory of    theory of
       decision      of aim     teaching     learning

┌─────────────────────────────────────────────────────────────────────┐
│              social-cultural  anthropological              media    │
│ aims/objec-  content of  determination  determination  methods  audio-visual│
│ tives        instruction of instruction of instruction of teaching  aids │
└─────────────────────────────────────────────────────────────────────┘
```

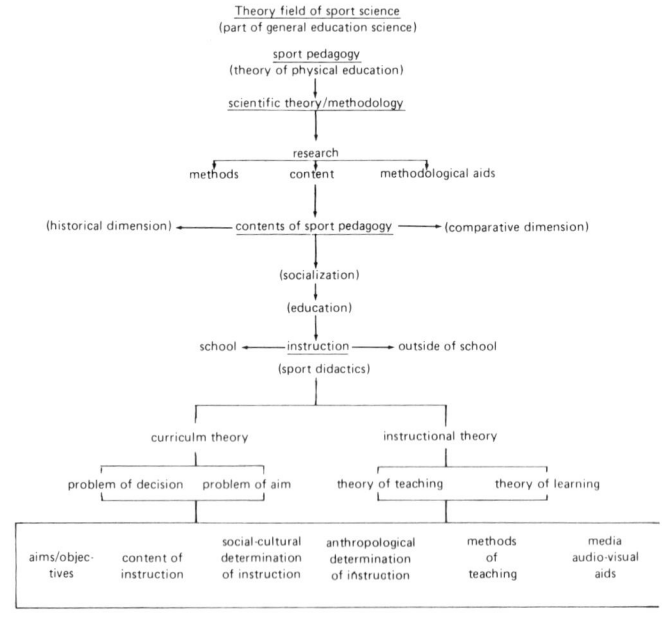

Figure 3. Theoretical framework of sport pedagogy.

3. *Why:* Question of the educational outcome of physical education instruction and its justification.
4. *What:* Question of the content of physical education instruction.
5. *How:* Question of the right and suitable methods for instruction in physical education.
6. *By what:* Question of the media applicable to instruction in physical education.

These factors are in turn a central part of the two basic aspects of sport pedagogy, namely, 1.) curriculum theory (problem of decision—problem of aim), and 2.) instructional theory (theory of teaching—theory of learning).

The theoretical field of sport pedagogy, however, cannot be analyzed without the basic aspects of scientific theory/methodology and of foundations for research. These aspects are especially important for a field of science that is just developing, in the same way that it is very important to develop a thesaurus for such a "young" scientific discipline.

In addition to the systematic approach to the analysis of the content of sport pedagogy, it is also necessary to consider the historical and comparative dimensions in order to develop a comprehensive pattern for a theoretical framework of sport pedagogy as basis for developing an alphabetical and systematic thesaurus.

This theoretical framework is explained in summary by Figure 3.

PROBLEMS IN DEVELOPING A MONO- OR MULTILINGUAL SYMBOLIC LANGUAGE FOR SPORT SCIENCE (THESAURUS)

The problems arising in developing a thesaurus involve different levels of complexity:

Problems on the Linguistic Level

One word can have different meanings depending upon the viewpoint of the observer or of the content. In contrast to this, several words can have the same meaning. Furthermore, there are various relations according to the complexity of the terms. There are, for example, logical, causal, and ontological relations.

Problems on the Philosophical Level

Due to different positions in regard to scientific theory, distinguishing categories for structuring are applied especially with the social and behavioral sciences.

Problems of Political and Ideological Influences

Many terms used in Western countries are seen differently in the Eastern countries; some terms are even completely unknown. The same problem also exists in reverse.

Problems on the Multilingual-International Level

There exist several logical structures, according to the language patterns, that are used in certain parts of the world. Accordingly, there are diverse ways applied in building word families.

CONCLUDING COMMENTS

This chapter attempted first of all to provide a statement of the aim and problem of this investigation. Furthermore, the research methods, techniques of data collection, and data treatment utilized were explained. The main part of this research project consisted of constructing a theoretical framework that served as a basis for selection of terms and for arranging these terms in a systematic order. Finally, it seemed necessary to indicate the major problems connected with this procedure for developing a thesaurus, especially on the multilingual level.

With the help of the following example, we should attempt once more to give an answer to the basic question: What is the practical use of a thesaurus for sport pedagogy? The example is: "Success and acknowledgement as learning conditions for swimming with small children." In this case, a thesaurus would indicate immediately the terms that are closely related to the given topic. One would find, for example, the term *motivation,* including the words frustration, merit, punishment, etc. Therefore, not only is it possible to store and recall literature with the help of descriptors found in a thesaurus, but also it is possible to improve the perception of a certain topic within sport pedagogy by using a structured *thesaurus.*

It is very important, especially for a young science, that an exact terminology is available in order to improve the quality of teaching and research in this science. Therefore, the different attempts to develop a *thesaurus* for certain aspects of sport science can be regarded as excellent models for laying the necessary foundations in any scientific field. Sport science is characterized by many closely related established sciences; therefore, the variety of terms used in sport science is very broad. Furthermore, one has to decide how many of the terms of the so-called "mother sciences" (for example, education) are necessary to develop a clear understanding of a certain theoretical field (for example, sport pedagogy).

In comparison with other sciences, and in relation to the relatively short time in which sport science has been in existence, this project, developing a thesaurus for sport pedagogy, indicates that sport science has reached a stage where it is possible to follow up an actual trend within the scientific world. This development, therefore, will further clarify the nature of sport pedagogy and by this the nature of sport science, also. Furthermore, it could be that a multilingual thesaurus will improve international understanding between people engaged in sport science. This in turn will improve the quality of sport science by making possible an international exchange of ideas and a mutual understanding.

REFERENCES

Haag, H. 1970. Der Auftrag der Sportwissenschaften an die Information und Dokumentation. (The task of the sport sciences for information and documentation.) In: J. Recla (Hrsg.), Sportdokumentation im Durchbruch, pp. 149–157. Osang Verlag Bad Honnef.

Haag, H. 1976. Die Bedeutung der Sportinformatik für die Sportwissenschaft. (The importance of sport information for sport science.) In: J. Recla and R. Timmer (Red.), Kreative Sportinformatik, pp. 56–63. Karl Hofmann, Druckerei und Verlag, Schorndorf.

Heimann, P., G. Otto and W. Schulz. 1965. Unterricht - Analyse und Planung. (Instruction - analysis and planning). Schroedel, Hannover.

Hirsch, S. 1967. Thesaurus als Grundlage der Recherchensprache. ("Thesaurus" as a foundation for the retrieval language.) In: J. Recla (Hrsg.), Moderne Sportdokumentation. Graz, pp. 156-162.

Hirsch, S. 1970. Der Fachthesaurus Körperkultur und Sport. (The subject matter "thesaurus" physical culture and sport.) In: J. Recla (Hrsg.), Sportdokumentation im Durchbruch, pp. 195-217. Osang Verlag, Bad Honnef.

IASI, (Hrsg.) 1975. Dynamic development in todays sports information. Haarlem.

Lang, Fr. 1970. Ein automatisiertes Literatur-, Organisations- und Informationssystem zur kombinierten Herstellung von Katalogen, Auswertung von Texten, Ausarbeitung von Thesauren und Durchführung individueller Suchaufträge. (An automatic literature, organization, and information system for the combined production of catalogues, evaluation of tests, development of "Thesauren" and realization of individual retrieval requests.) In: J. Recla (Hrsg.), Sportdokumentation im Durchbruch, pp. 90-109. Osang Verlag, Bad Honnef.

Recla, J. (Hrsg.) 1967. Moderne Sportdokumentation. Von der Bibliographie, Klassifikation, Information und Dokumentation zur automatischen Dokumentation. (Modern sport documentation. From bibliography, classification, information and documentation to automatic documentation.) Graz.

Recla, J. (Hrsg.) 1970. Sportdokumentation im Durchbruch. (Sport documentation in development.) Osang Verlag, Bad Honnef.

Recla, J., and Ringli, K. (Red.) 1973. Sportinformatik. (Sport information.) Magglingen.

Recla, J., and Timmer, R. (Red.) 1976. Kreative Sportinformatik. (Creative sport information.) Karl Hofmann, Druckerei und Verlag, Schorndorf.

Schindler, G. 1970. Der Thesaurus-Sorgenkind odor wichtiges Hilfsmittel der modernen Dokumentation. (The Thesaurus—trouble-maker or important aid of modern documentation.) In: J. Recla (Hrsg.), Sportdokumentation im Durchbruch, pp. 217-221. Osang Verlag, Bad Honnef.

Tscherne, Fr., et al. 1967. Grundlagen der Terminologie der Leibesübungen und des Sports. (Foundations of terminology of physical exercises and sport.) In: J. Recla (Hrsg.), Moderne Sportdokumentation, pp. 104-117. Graz.

Tscherne, Fr. 1970. Ein automatischer Thesaurus—Sport—im Werden. (An automatic thesaurus—sport—is developed.) In: J. Recla (Hrsg.), Sportdokumentation im Durchbruch, pp. 217-221. Osang Verlag, Bad Honnef.

Tscherne, Fr. 1976. Tätigkeitsbericht 1974/75 der IASI - Kommission thesaurus. (Activity report 1974/75 of the IASI commission thesaurus.) In: J. Recla and R. Timmer (Red.), Kreative Sportinformatik, pp. 131-132. Karl Hofmann, Druckerei und Verlag, Schorndorf.

Structure of the Terminology for Sport Pedagogy

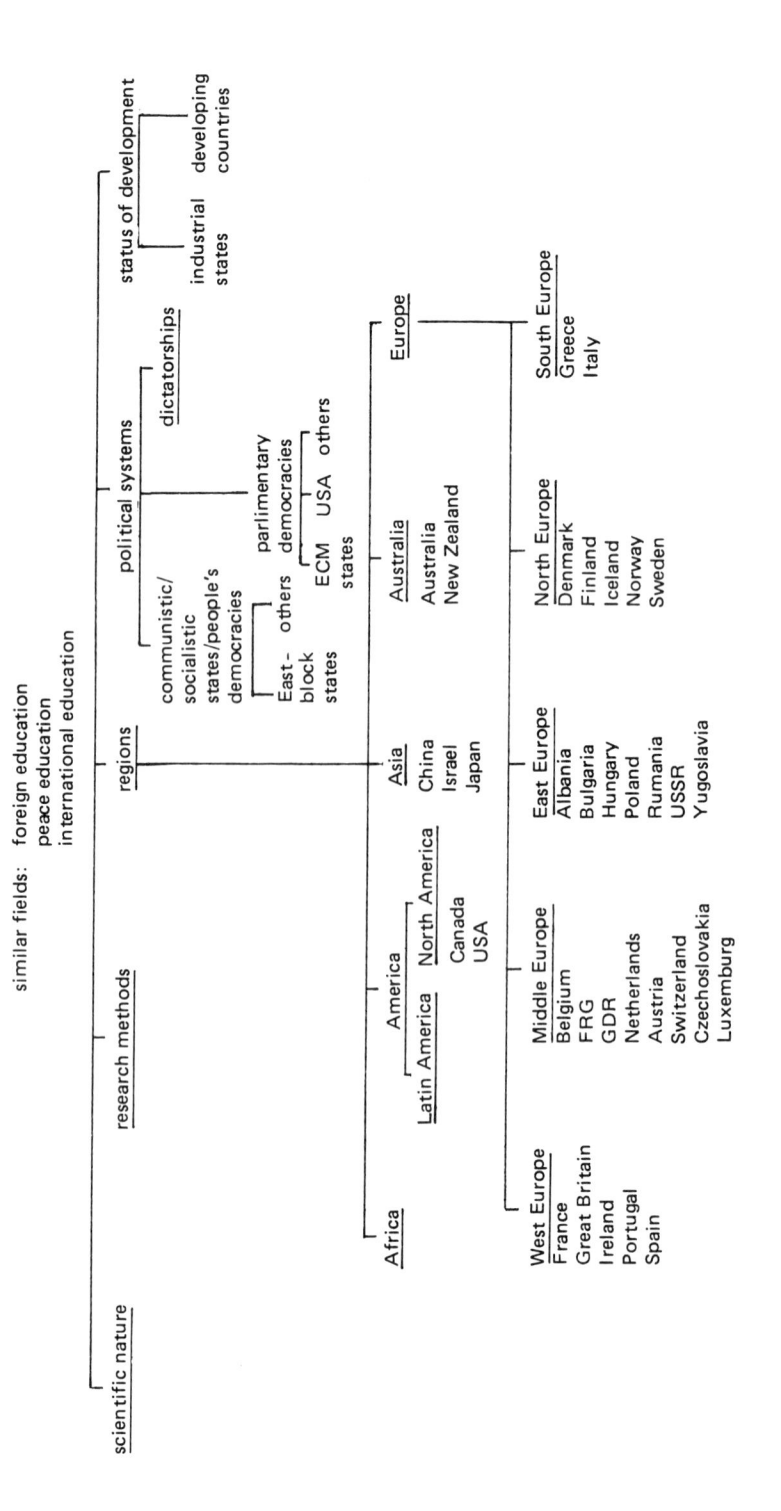

aspects of comparative education
aspects of sport pedagogy
sport pedagogy (comparative)

similar fields: foreign education
peace education
international education

B

scientific nature | research methods | regions | political systems | status of development

status of development
- industrial states
- developing countries

political systems
- communistic/socialistic states/people's democracies
  - East-block states
  - others
- parliamentary democracies
  - ECM states
  - USA
  - others
- dictatorships

regions

Africa

America
- Latin America
- North America
  - Canada
  - USA

Asia
- China
- Israel
- Japan

Australia
- Australia
- New Zealand

Europe

West Europe
- France
- Great Britain
- Ireland
- Portugal
- Spain

Middle Europe
- Belgium
- FRG
- GDR
- Netherlands
- Austria
- Switzerland
- Czechoslovakia
- Luxemburg

East Europe
- Albania
- Bulgaria
- Hungary
- Poland
- Rumania
- USSR
- Yugoslavia

North Europe
- Denmark
- Finland
- Iceland
- Norway
- Sweden

South Europe
- Greece
- Italy

244

C

aspects of curriculum theory
aspects of instructional theory
aspects of conditions (system of conditions)
anthropological conditions

social psychology	educational psychology	learning psychology	developmental psychology
pupil/student (learning system)		teacher (teaching system)	

pupil (student)

social group
- student — pupil — others
  - physical education student
  - beginner
  - good pupil
  - advanced
  - weak pupil (outsider)
  - pupil behavior
  - behavior disturbed
  - pupil (special education)

age (level of age)
- children
- youth
- adults
- old people

sex
- boys
- girls
- man
- woman
- sexuality

anthropological dimensions

affective conditions
- aggression
- fear
- need
- attitude
- interest
- performance dispositon
- performance motive
- motivation

cognitive conditions
- intelligence
- knowledge

psychomotor conditions

constitutional conditions
- weakness of posture
- posture
- motor abilities
- weakness of muscles
- weakness of organs

condition for performance
- aptitude
- abilities
- skills
- individual situation
- talent

skills

development
- acceleration
- development (cognitive)
- development (emotional)
- development of performance
- puberty stage
- step
- retardation
- status of performance

teacher

professional training situation
- institution of higher learning (University)
- teacher training college
- college of sport and physical education
- school for sport and calisthenics
- sport science institutes
- college for introduction to teaching

professional preparation
- training
- in-service training
- study
- continuing education
- didactics for higher education
- hospitation
- micro-teaching
- training of teacher-behavior

professional (teaching) qualification
- physical education teacher with diploma
- subject matter teacher
- sport teacher
- sport teacher with second field
- coach
- teaching assistant

teacher behavior
- style of leadership and teaching
- authoritarian
- democratic
- "laissez-faire"

professional rule
model

aspects of curriculum theory
aspects of instructional theory
aspects of conditions (system of conditions)
<u>soci-cultural conditions</u>
society (aspects of classification)

D1

normative/concerning
standards
equality of chances
standard

social/
material
social class
laborer
middle class
higher middle class
lower class
class

spatial

Federal Republic
of Germany

states
Baden Wurttemberg,
Bayern, Berlin,
Bremen, Hamburg,
Hessen, Niedersachesen,
Nordthein – Westfahlen,
Rheinland – Rfalz, Saarlancl,
Schleswig – Holstein

temporal
present time
past
future

parts of society

politics
educational politics,
educational planning,
education, guidelines (curricula)
legislation, sport politics

economy
consumption

culture

sports   school

media   labor   leisure   family

sport (social)

military

addressees
sport for older people
family sport
woman's sport
children's sport
mass sport
man's sport
people's sport

noninstitutionalized sports

leisure
vacation
weekend sport

sport in clubs
sport for all
sport federation,
performance sport,
training center, higher
performance sport
professional sport,
factory sport, disabled
person's sport,
prison sport

physical
education
in school
school sports club
<u>school and club</u>

institutionalization

institutionalized sports

university
extension
sport

college
sport

federations (school/university)
ADL, ADH, DSLV

interaction
group
team
championship
sport event
competition

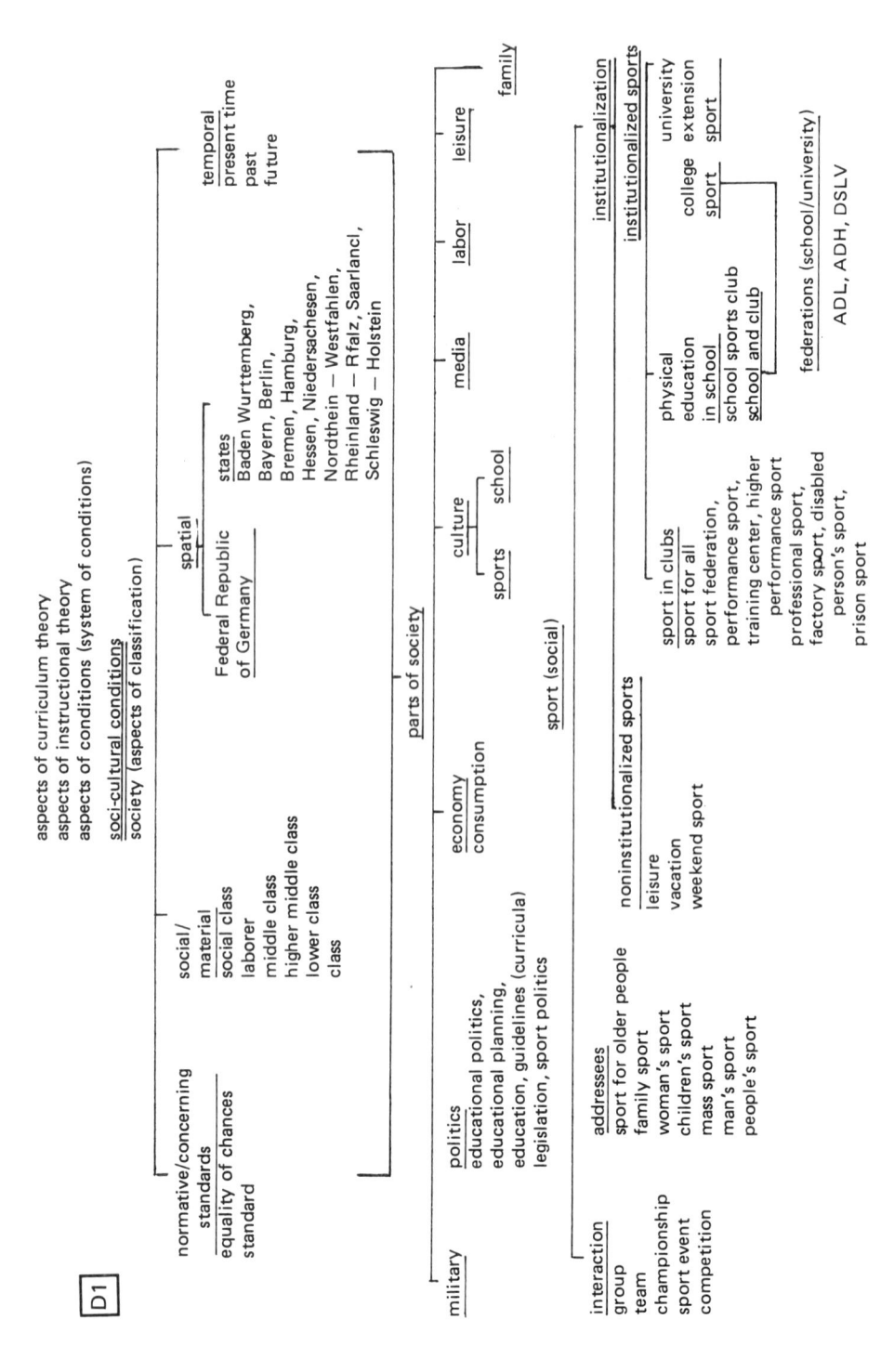

246

D2

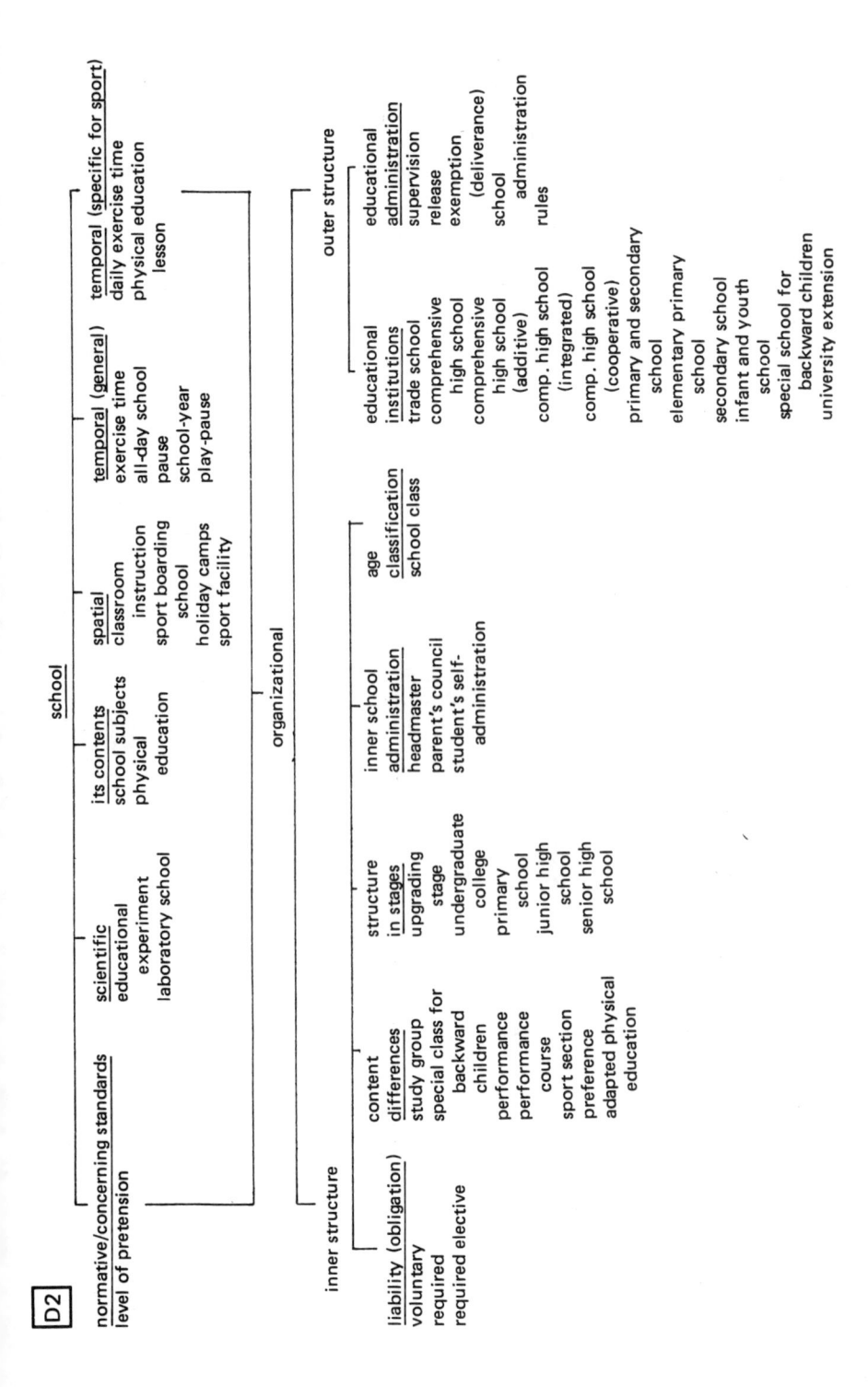

school

- **normative/concerning standards**
  - level of pretension
- **scientific**
  - educational experiment
  - laboratory school
- **its contents**
  - school subjects
  - physical education
- **spatial**
  - classroom
  - sport boarding school
  - instruction
  - holiday camps
  - sport facility
- **temporal (general)**
  - exercise time
  - all-day school
  - pause
  - school-year
  - play-pause
- **temporal (specific for sport)**
  - daily exercise time
  - physical education lesson

organizational

- **inner structure**
  - **liability (obligation)**
    - voluntary
    - required
    - required elective
  - **content differences**
    - study group
    - special class for backward children
    - performance
    - performance course
    - sport section
    - preference
    - adapted physical education
  - **structure in stages**
    - upgrading stage
    - undergraduate college
    - primary school
    - junior high school
    - senior high school
  - **inner school administration**
    - headmaster
    - parent's council
    - student's self-administration
  - **age classification**
    - school class

- **outer structure**
  - **educational institutions**
    - trade school
    - comprehensive high school
    - comprehensive high school (additive)
    - comp. high school (integrated)
    - comp. high school (cooperative)
    - primary and secondary school
    - elementary primary school
    - secondary school
    - infant and youth school
    - special school for backward children
    - university extension
  - **educational administration**
    - supervision
    - release
    - exemption (deliverance)
    - school administration
    - rules

objects of curriculum theory
aspects of instructional theory
aspects of decisions

<u>aims and objectives</u>
(educational objective, learning objective, qualification)

<u>categories for aims and objectives</u>
(taxonomy of learning)

cognition	leisure	joy/pleasure	adventure	health	body and	personality	social	pre-military
ability to	education	and pastime	and primary	fitness	movement	education	education	training
review	consumer	joy and pleasure	experience	health	education	emancipation	fairness	
intellectual	education		esthetic	education	endurance	individualization	sociability	
ability	life-time		fashioning	posture	agility	ability to	coeducation	
			creativity	education	motor skills	review	communication	
			musical and	rehabilitation	flexibility	cognitive	cooperation	
			rhythmical		skillfullness	education	resocialization	
			education		versatility	creativity		
			rhythm		basic education	spontaneity		
			play education		coordination			
					strength			
					ability to perform			
					balance			
					reaction			
					speed			

<u>realization of aims and objectives</u>
operationalization
transfer

<u>evaluation of aims and objectives</u>
test (fitness)
test (skills)
test (knowledge)
test (concomitant learning)

E

F

aspects of curriculum theory
aspects of instructional theory
aspects of decisions

contents

(learning contents/elements of curriculum)

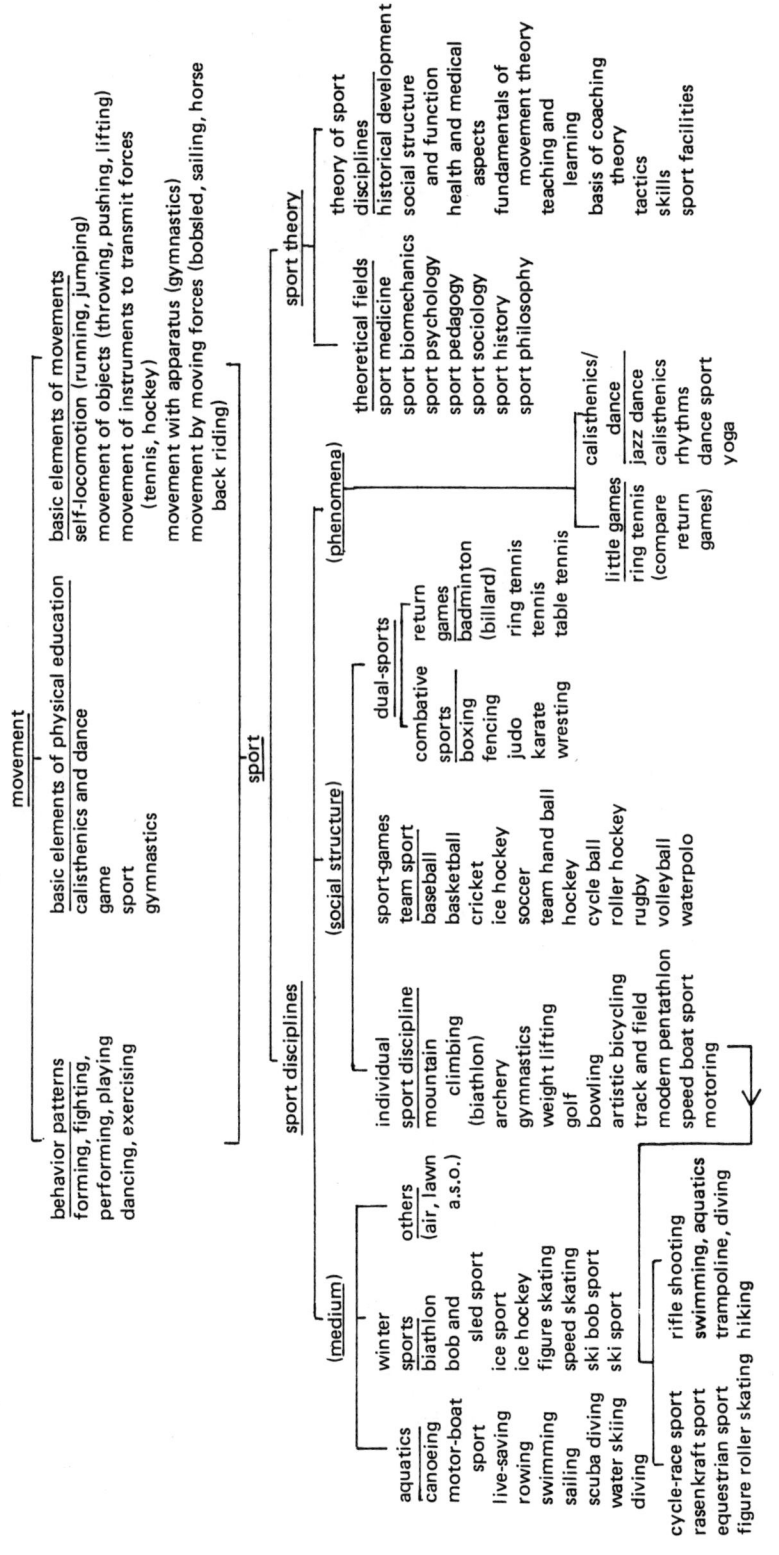

movement

basic elements of physical education
- calisthenics and dance
- game
- sport
- gymnastics

behavior patterns
forming, fighting, performing, playing, dancing, exercising

basic elements of movements
- self-locomotion (running, jumping)
- movement of objects (throwing, pushing, lifting)
- movement of instruments to transmit forces (tennis, hockey)
- movement with apparatus (gymnastics)
- movement by moving forces (bobsled, sailing, horse back riding)

sport

sport disciplines

(medium)

aquatics
- canoeing
- motor-boat sport
- live-saving
- rowing
- swimming
- sailing
- scuba diving
- water skiing
- diving

winter sports
- biathlon
- bob and sled sport
- ice sport
- ice hockey
- figure skating
- speed skating
- ski bob sport
- ski sport

others (air, lawn a.s.o.)
- rifle shooting
- swimming, aquatics
- trampoline, diving
- hiking
- cycle-race sport
- rasenkraft sport
- equestrian sport
- figure roller skating

individual sport discipline
- mountain climbing
- (biathlon)
- archery
- gymnastics
- weight lifting
- golf
- bowling
- artistic bicycling
- track and field
- modern pentathlon
- speed boat sport
- motoring

(social structure)

sport-games / team sport
- baseball
- basketball
- cricket
- ice hockey
- soccer
- team hand ball
- hockey
- cycle ball
- roller hockey
- rugby
- volleyball
- waterpolo

dual-sports

combative sports
- boxing
- fencing
- judo
- karate
- wresting

return games
- badminton
- (billard)
- ring tennis
- tennis
- table tennis

(phenomena)

little games
- ring tennis
- (compare return games)

calisthenics/dance
- jazz dance
- calisthenics
- rhythms
- dance sport
- yoga

sport theory

theoretical fields
- sport medicine
- sport biomechanics
- sport psychology
- sport pedagogy
- sport sociology
- sport history
- sport philosophy

theory of sport disciplines
- historical development
- social structure and function
- health and medical aspects
- fundamentals of movement theory
- teaching and learning
- basis of coaching theory
- tactics
- skills
- sport facilities

249

aspects of instructional theory/aspects of decisions

methods
(methods of teaching)
theory of methods
general theory of methods

G

- teaching arrangement
- teaching organization
- discipline
- coeducation
- micro teaching
- forms of organization
- frame of organization
- project work
- team teaching
- thematic instruction
- performance testing

form of instruction
- frontal instruction
- group instruction
- circle instruction
- section instruction
- station instruction

planning
- annual planning
- structure of lesson
- pattern of a lesson
- lesson-design
- lesson planning
- period of instruction
- weekly planning

methodical approaches
- analytical
- synthetic
- deductive
- inductive
- natural methods

performance levels
- optimizing
- training
- coaching
- exercising
- loading
- fatigue
- interval
- recreation

methodical aids
- movement analysis
- movement accompaniment
- movement explication
- demonstration
- help and secure
- methodical aids
- apparatus
- support
- punishment
- -reward
- rythmical sequence
- game sequence
- exercise sequence

learning steps
- accentuation
- differentiation
- basic instruction
- orientation
- specialization
- graded curriculum
- form of play
- form of exercise
- form of performance
- form of competition

programmed learning

mental training

total approach
- theme for moving
- story for moving

task-oriented method
- movement task
- self-control
- spontaneity

teacher oriented method
- moving instruction
- demonstration
- object-treatment
- object-mediation

teaching
- learning program
- learning sequence
- linear programs
- branch programs

aspects of instructional theory
aspects of decisions
contents of media-didactics

media
―――――
(teaching and learning aids, learning technology)

media (mechanical)	visual	acoustic/verbal	complex
apparatus	school pictures	instructional language	audiovisual media
sport wear	book	music accompaniment	teaching program
sport facilities	slides	acoustic movement-	learning machine
	television	accompaniment	
	film/movie	record	
	school-book	tape recorder	
	black board		
	film-recording		
	of instruction		
	'videorecorder'		

Selected Publications on the Concept and Nature of Sport Pedagogy

German Language Publications

Begov, F., and Kurz, D. 1972. Sportpädagogik in westeuropäischen Ländern. (Sport pedagogy in the states of Western Europe.) In: H. Baitsch et al. (Hrsg.), Sport im Blickpunkt der Wissenschaften, pp. 141–151. Springer-Verlag OHG., Berlin.

Beyer, E., and Röthig, P. (Red.) 1976. Beiträge zur Gegenstandsbestimmung der Sportpädagogik. (Contributions to define the present status of sport pedagogy.) 1. Internationales Symposium für Sportpädagogik des ADL. 23 September–9 Oktober, 1975, in Karlsruhe. (Sport Pedagogy—Retrieval to Thinking or Guideline for Action.) Karl Hofmann, Druckerei und Verlag, Schorndorf.

Brodmann, D., et al. 1977. Sportpädagogik—Rückzug ins Denken oder Anleitung zum Handeln. Z. Sportpädagog. 1:8–37.

Größing, St. 1975. Einführung in die Sportdidaktik. Lehren und Lernen im Sportunterricht. (Introduction to Sport Didactics. Teaching and Learning in Sport Instruction.) Wilhelm Limpert-Verlag, Frankfurt.

Grupe, O. 1968. Studien zur pädagogischen Theorie der Leibeserziehung. (Studies Concerning the Pedagogical Theory of Physical Education.) 2nd Ed. Karl Hofmann, Druckerei und Verlag, Schorndorf.

Grupe, O. 1969. Grundlagen der Sportpädagogik. (Foundations of Sport Pedagogy.) Johann Ambrosius Barth, München.

Grupe, O. 1971. Revision des Sportcurriculum. (Revision of the sport curriculum.) Sportwissenschaft 2:109–236.

Grupe, O. 1977. Einführung in die Theorie der Leibeserziehung. (Introduction to the Theory of Physical Education.) 4th Ed. Karl Hofmann, Druckerei und Verlag, Schorndorf.

Güldenpfennig, S. 1973. Grenzen bürglicher Sportpädagogik. Zum Gesellschaftsbegriff in Didaktik der Leibeserziehung und Sportcurriculum. (Limitations of Civil Sport Pedagogy. Concerning the Term Society in Didactics of Physical Education and Sport Curriculum.) Pahl-Rugenstein Verlag, Köln.

Gutsche, Kl.-J. 1973. Bemerkungen zum Problem einer Sportpädagogik als erziehungswissenschaftliche Disziplin. (Remarks concerning the problem of sport pedagogy as a discipline of educational science.) In: Kl.-J. Gutsche (Red.), Sportwissenschaft in der Entwicklung. Ansätze zu einer interdisziplinären Forschung. Pressedienst Wissenschaft 4–6, Berlin.

Gutsche, Kl.-J. 1975. Zur gegenwärtigen Problematik der Sportpädagogik. Versuch einer Standortbestimmung. (Concerning the Actual Problem of Sport Pedagogy. Experimental Definition of Its Status.) Verlag Czwalina, Ahrensburg.

Haag, H. (Hrsg.) 1972. Didaktische und curriculare Aspekte des Sports. Festschrift zum 70. Geburtstag von Prof. Dr. Ludwig Mester. (Didactic and Curricular Aspects of Sport.) Karl Hofmann, Druckerei und Verlag, Schorndorf.

Haag, H. 1972. Sportpädagogik in den Vereinigten Staaten. (Sport pedagogy in the USA.) In: H. Baitsch et al. (Hrsg.), Sport im Blickfeld der Wissenschaften, pp. 173–180. Springer-Verlag OHG., Berlin.

Jost, E. (Hrsg.) 1973. Sportcurriculum. Entwürfe—Aspekte—Argumente. (Sport Curriculum. Concepts—Aspects—Arguments.) Karl Hofmann, Druckerei und Verlag, Schorndorf.

Kurz, D. 1973. Sportpädagogik, Sportdidaktik, Theorie des Sport-curriculum. (Sport pedagogy, sport didactics, theory of sport curriculum.) In: E. Jost (Hrsg.), Sportcurriculum. Entwürfe - Aspekte - Argumente, pp. 117–125. Karl Hofmann Druckerei und Verlag, Schorndorf.

Meinberg, E. 1976. Pädagogische Anthropologie und Sportpädagogik. (Educational anthropology and sport pedagogy.) In: W. Decker and M. Lämmer (Hrsg.), Kölner Beiträge zur Sportwissenschaft, 4: 93–135. Karl Hofmann, Druckerei und Verlag, Schorndorf.

Menze, Cl. 1976. Die Herauslösung der Sportpädagogik aus der allgemeinen Pädagogik. (The differences between sport pedagogy and general pedagogy.) In: G. Hecker, A. Kirsch, and Cl. Menze (Hrsg.), Der Mensch im Sport. Festschrift zum 70. Geburtstag von Professor Liselott Diem, Hum.D., pp. 72–84. Karl Hofmann, Druckerei und Verlag, Schorndorf.

Mester, L. 1969. Grundfragen der Leibeserziehung. (Basic Questions of Physical Education.) 3rd Ed. Georg Westermann Verlag, Braunschweig.

Meusel, H. 1976. Einführung in die Sportpädagogik. (Introduction to Sport Pedagogy.) UTB-W. Fink Verlag, München.

Niedermann, E. 1976. Sportpädagogik als Grundlage der Unterrichtspraxis. (Sport pedagogy as the basis for practical instruction.) In: H. Andrecs and S. Redl (Hrsg.), Forschen—Lehren—Handeln. Sportwissenschaftliche Beiträge zum Gedenken an Univ. Prof. Dr. Hans Groll. Österreichischer Bundesverlag für Unterricht, Wissenschaft und Kunst, Wien.

Röhrs, H. 1970. Die Pädagogik der Leibeserziehung oder Sportpädagogik. (The pedagogy of physical education or sport pedagogy.) In: Allgemeine Erziehungswissenschaft, pp. 378–402. Julius Belz OHG., Weinheim.

Röhrs, H. 1972. Die Sportpädagogik als erziehunswissenschaftliche Disziplin. (Sport pedagogy as discipline of scientific education.) In: H. Rieder (Hrsg.), Bewegung—Leistung—Verhalten. Zu aktuellen Fragen der Sportforschung. Fesschrift zum 70. Geburtstag von Prof. Dr. Otto Neumann, pp. 113–126. Karl Hofmann, Druckerei und Verlag, Schorndorf.

Schmitz, J.N. 1973. Fachdidaktik und Curriculumtheorie in der Sportwissenschaft. (Special didactics and curriculum theory in sport science.) Sportwissenschaft 3, 251–276.

Schmitz, J.N. 1970 f. Studien zur Didaktik der Leibeserziehung. (Studies concerning the didactics of physical education.) Teil I, II, III, IV. Karl Hofmann Druckerei und Verlag, Schorndorf.

Schwidtmann, H. 1972. Sportpädagogik. (Sport pedagogy.) Theorie und Praxis der Körperkultur. Beiheft 3: 25–31.

Widmer, K. 1974. Sportpädagogik. Prolegemena zur theoretischen Begründung der Sportpädagogik als Wissenschaft. (Sport Pedagogy. Prologue for the Theoretical Foundation of Sport Pedagogy as Science.) Karl Hofmann, Druckerei und Verlag, Schorndorf.

Willimczik, K. 1968. Wissenschaftstheoretische Aspekte einer Sportwissenschaft. (Aspects of a Scientific Theory of a Sport Science.) Limpert-Verlag, Frankfurt.

English Language Publications

Abernathy, R., and Waltz, M. 1964. Toward a Discipline: First Steps First. Quest. Monograph II. April.

Bennett, B.L., et al. 1975. Comparative Physical Education and Sport. Lea & Febiger, Philadelphia.

Clarke, D.H., and Clarke, H.H. 1970. Research Processes in Physical Education, Recreation, and Health. (Part I.) Prentice-Hall Inc., Englewood Cliffs, New Jersey.

Henry, F.M. 1964. Physical education: An academic discipline. J. Health Phys. Ed. Recreat. 7:32–33.

Kenyon, G.S. 1970. On the conceptualization of sub-disciplines within an academic discipline dealing with human movement. In: H.S. Slusher and A.S. Lockhart (eds.), An Introduction To Physical Education. Anthology of Contemporary Readings, pp. 285–300. W.M.C. Brown Company Publishers, Dubuque, Iowa.

Kroll, W.P. 1971. Perspectives in Physical Education. Academic Press Inc., New York.

Locke, L.F. Research in Physical Education. Teachers College Bureau of Publications, Columbia University, New York.

NCPEAM and NAPECW (ed.) 1967. The Nature of a Discipline. Quest. Monograph IX.

Nixon, J.E., and Locke, L.F. 1973. Research on teaching physical education. In: R.M.W. Travers (ed.), Second Handbook of Research on Teaching, pp. 1210–1242. Rand McNally & Company, Chicago.

Rarick, G.L. 1967. The domain of physical education as a discipline. Quest. Monograph IX. December.

Simri, U. (ed.) 1974. Concepts of Physical Education and Sport Sciences. Proceedings of an International Seminar. Wingate Institute.

Singer, R.N. (ed.) 1976. Physical Education: Foundations. Holt, Rinehart, and Winston, New York.

Singer, R.N., Lamb, D.R., Loy, J.W., Jr., Malina, R.M., and Kleinman, S. 1972. Physical Education: An Interdisciplinary Approach. The Macmillan Company, New York.

General Information Related to Sport Pedagogy

Journals and Organizations

The development of sport science and its theoretical fields also created a variety of opportunities for publications and for establishment of organizations dealing with sport, sport education, and sport science. In order to work in the field of sport science it is necessary to know about these sources of information, which are already differentiated to a great extent according to the theoretical fields of sport science.

Two aspects within the general information related to sport science and to sport pedagogy specifically, will be covered in this chapter, namely, journals and organizations.

JOURNALS

Within the publications in the field of sport, scientific and nonscientific literature can be distinguished. With regard to the scientific literature, journals play an important role in addition to that of books. Various categorizations of the scientific journals can be made:

a. Journals covering aspects of various sport disciplines (e.g., *Praxis der Leibesübungen*).
b. Journals for a specific sport discipline (e.g., *Swimming World*).
c. Journals of national organizations for sport, sport education, and sport science (e.g., *JOHPER Journal*)
d. Journals dealing with sport science as a whole, covering themes of different theoretical fields (e.g., *Quest*).
e. Journals dealing with a specific theme of sport science (e.g., *Journal of Motor Behavior*).
f. Journals dealing with a specific theoretical field of sport science (e.g., *International Journal of Physical Education;* sport pedagogy).

With regard to the last group of journals, dealing with a specific theoretical field of sport science, one can observe that, at least on the international level, every theoretical field thus far has its own journal for the publication of themes and topics that are specific to the respective fields. The development of sport science as a scientific discipline has been so rapid that even on the national level this differentiation of journals according to the various fields of sport science is already beginning. (e.g., *Canadian Journal of History of Sport and Physical Education* for sport history in Canada, or *Zeitschrift für Sportpaedagogik* for sport pedagogy in the Federal Republic of Germany).

Because this text is Volume 4 of the *International Series on Sport Sciences,* and because it deals with one theoretical field of sport science, a short overview of the scientific journals dealing with the theoretical fields of sport sciences is deemed worthwhile:

1. *Sport Medicine—Journal of Sport Medicine and Physical Fitness* (Editor-in-Chief: Dr. G. La Cava Rome, Via Flaminia Nuova, 270 - 00191, Italy.)
2. *Sport Biomechanics—Journal of Biomechanics* (Editor-in-Chief: Verne L. Roberts, Head, Bioscience Division, Highway Safety Research Institute, Huron Parkway and Baxter Road, Ann Arbor, Michigan, 48105, USA, and F. Gayner Evans, Department of Anatomy, University of Michigan, Ann Arbor, Michigan 48104, USA.)
3. *Sport Psychology—International Journal of Sport Psychology* (Editor-in-Chief: Ferruccio Antonelli, Via della Camilliccia 195 - 00 135, Rome, Italy.)
4. *Sport Pedagogy—International Journal of Physical Education* (Editor-in-Chief: Herbert Haag, Institut für Sport und Sportwissenschaften, Abt. Sportpaedagogik, 23 Kiel, Olshausenstrasse 40 - 60. Federal Republic of Germany.)
5. *Sport Sociology—International Review of Sport Sociology* (Editor-in-Chief: Andrzek Wohl, Akademia Wychowania Fizycnego, Warszawa, ul. Marymoncka 34, Poland.)
6. *Sport History—Journal of Sport History* (Editor-in-Chief: A. Metcalfe, Department of History, Radford College, Radford, Virginia 24147, USA.)
7. *Sport Philosophy—Journal of the Philosophy of Sport* (Editor-in-Chief: H.J. Van der Zwaag, Department of Sport Studies, Curry Hicks Building, University of Massachusetts, Amherst, Massachusetts 01002, USA.)

This description of the journals for certain fields of sport science on the international level uses a specific model for explaining sport science that implies seven theoretical fields. It is recognized that there are other models available; however, the one given seems to sufficiently analyze and describe sport science.

From the different categories of journals dealing with aspects of sport, two examples will be described in detail in the following, namely, 1) the specific journal for sport pedagogy, the *International Journal of Physical Education,* and 2) the journal *Quest,* as an example for journals dealing with sport science as a whole. The letter is also relevant to the theoretical field of sport pedagogy.

International Journal of Physical Education

This journal has existed since 1963. Up until 1973, it was titled *Gymnasion*. From 1963 until today it has been the official magazine of the International Council on Health, Physical Education and Recreation. It is published quarterly in the spring, summer, fall, and winter.

Responsible publisher: Karl Hofmann Druckerei und Verlag in Schorndorf, Federal Republic of Germany (7060 Schorndorf, Postfach 1360).
Editor-in-Chief: Prof. Dr. Herbert Haag, M.S., University of Kiel, Federal Republic of Germany.
Editorial Committee: Prof. Dr. Jan Broekhoff, University of Oregon, USA
Prof. Dr. Shinshiro Ebashi, University of Tokyo, Hongo, Japan
Dietrich Kaiser, Bundesinstitut für Sportwissenschaft, Köln, Federal Republic of Germany
Prof. Dr. Klaas Rijsdorp, University of Utrecht, The Netherlands
Dr. Carl A. Troester, Jr., Washington, D.C., USA
Prof. Dr. Konrad Widmer, Pädagogisches Institut, Zürich, Switzerland
Prof. Dr. Earle F. Ziegler, The University of Western Ontario, London, Canada

The process of categorizing sport science(s) has created several theoretical fields as partial aspects of sport science(s). A possible structure for these subdisciplines could be: sport medicine, sport biomechanics, sport psychology, sport pedagogy, sport sociology, sport history, and sport philosophy. Everyone of these theoretical fields has its specific journal on the international level.

The *International Journal of Physical Education* claims to be a specific journal for sport pedagogy, which means for themes and topics dealing especially with the teaching - learning process as it relates to sport (physical education). This is not to say that other theoretical aspects of sport science are ignored: however, they should have an interdisciplinary value in the sense of a correlation with the problem formulation of physical education.

At present, the journal has the following structure: Foreword - Summaries (in four languages) - Main articles (in English and German) - International Sport - Reports - Literature - BISp-News - ICHPER-News - Information - Coming Events.

Some issues have a special theme and some have different themes, but the main objectives are to support international discussion within the theoretical field of sport pedagogy, to publish research and information in this regard on a world-wide basis, and, thus, to help advance the development of the scientific foundations of sport pedagogy as a theoretical field of sport science(s).

Quest

This journal is published in two issues per year, and since 1963 has had as its aim the encouragement of the types of thought and practice that underlie improvement in standards, programs, methods, and the like. It is sponsored jointly by two organizations: The National Association for Physical Education of College Women (NAPECW), and The National College Physical Education Association for Men (NCPEAM). However, the journal tries not to be dependent on an organization but rather to represent an independent forum for professional advancement.

Editor-in-Chief: Prof. Dr. Daryl Siedentop, The Ohio State University, 1760 Neil Avenue, Columbus, Ohio, 43210, USA.

Single issues mostly deal with a central theme, but the journal deals with different aspects of sport science. There are certain issues (given by volume number) that are more closely related to the theoretical field of sport pedagogy:

VII—The Physical Educator as Professor
IX—The Nature of a Discipline
X—Toward a Theory of Sport
XV—Educational Change in the Teaching of Physical Education
XVII—Learning Models and the Acquisition of Motor Skills
XVIII—Teaching Teachers
XXV—Graduate Study in Physical Education.
XXVI—Learning How to Play

Even though this is a publication on the national level in the United States, it can be said that this journal is also internationally relevant to the conceptualization and further development of sport pedagogy as part of sport science.

ORGANIZATIONS

In accord with the rapid development of sport, sport education, and sport science during the last few years, many organizations have also originated on the national and international levels. The organizations on the international level that deal mainly with questions of sport pedagogy are of specific interest and relevance here.

Prof. Dr. Klaas Rijsdorp, the former president of ICHPER, has developed an excellent scheme and structure by which the many international organizations can be categorized and explained (compare "Memo concerning the cooperation between international organizations on physical education and sports" in: *International Journal of Physical Education,* X (1973) 4:38-39.

The developed structure is described as follows, with slight changes due to continuing development in the fields of sport, sport education, and sport science.

General Organizations

General organizations cover the entire field of physical education and sport. Examples are:

1. International Federation of Physical Education (FIEP)
2. International Council of Sport and Physical Education (ICSPE)
3. International Council on Health, Physical Education and Recreation (ICHPER)

Categorical Organizations

Categorical organizations deal with specific aspects of sport, sport education, and sport science.
1. Categorical organizations function within a *specific theoretical field of sport science*. Examples are given for each of the theoretical fields of sport science:
    1.1 Sport Medicine—Fedération International de Médicine Sportive (FIMS)
    1.2 Sport Biomechanics—International Society of Biomechanics
    1.3 Sport Psychology—International Society of Sport Psychology
    1.4 Sport Pedagogy—ICHPER—Research Committee and FIEP
    1.5 Sport Sociology—Committee for Sociology of Sport—ICSPE
    1.6 Sport History—International Association for the History of Physical Education and Sport (HISPA)
    1.7 Sport Philosophy—International Philosophic Society for the Study of Sport
2. Categorical organizations function on the basis of *specific themes and groups* within the fields of sport, sport education, and sport science. Examples are:
    2.1 International Association of Physical Education and Sports for Girls and Women (IAPESGW)
    2.2 Association International des Ecoles Superieures d'Education Physique (AIESEP)
    2.3 Internationaler Arbeitskreis Sportstättenbau (IAKS)
    2.4 International Association for Sport Information (IASI)
    2.5 International Olympic Committee (IOC)

3. Categorical organizations function for *specific sport disciplines*. Examples are:
   3.1 Fedération Internationale de Ski (F.I.S.)
   3.2 Fedération Internationale de Football Association (F.I.F.A.)
   3.3 Fedération Internationale de Natation Association (FINA)

Regional Organizations

Examples of regional organizations are:

International Working Groups on Modern Physical Education (Austria, Federal Republic of Germany, Holland, Switzerland)
Panamerican Games
Asian Games

Only two organizations on the international level will be described more closely here, because they are both of immediate relevance to the theoretical field of sport pedagogy as part of sport science, which is the focus of this text.

International Council on Health, Physical Education and Recreation (ICHPER)

The *International Council on Health, Physical Education and Recreation* originated from the desire of persons in many countries to establish an organization in the fields of health, physical education, and recreation through which they could work together on an international basis.

In 1952 a distinguished international group of educators formed an association for organizations of teachers called the *World Confederation of Organizations of the Teaching Profession (WCOTP)*. Physical educators recognized the possibility of working through such a world-wide organization.

In 1958, WCOTP made it possible to bring into its membership certain specialized groups. Thus, ICHPER originated as an international group for teachers of health, physical education, and recreation. In 1959, Dorothy D. Ainsworth (USA) became the first president, and Carl A. Troester, Jr., was appointed to the position of Secretary-General.

The purpose of ICHPER is to bring together representatives of educational organizations concerned with individuals professionally engaged in health, physical education, sports, and recreation, both in and out of school, throughout the world. The basic objective of the council is to strengthen international ties, appreciation, and understanding, and to further the following purposes:

1. Encourage development of programs in health, physical education, sports, and recreation throughout the world.

2. Improve the professional preparation of teachers of health education, physical education, sports, and recreation.
3. Foster the exchange of research and professional information.
4. Encourage the exchange of both students and teachers.
5. Cooperate with other international organizations concerned with health, physical education, sports, and recreation.
6. Initiate, sponsor, and/or collaborate on international conferences and special projects related to these fields.
7. Assist WCOTP by contributing to its aims and objectives.

Since 1961 an ICHPER Bulletin has been issued regularly in order to keep the members informed of ICHPER affairs. In the spring of 1963, the first international journal in the area of physical education, sports, recreation and health education was started, under the title *Gymnasion*. In 1964 it became a quarterly, and since 1973 it has been published under the title *International Journal of Physical Education—Internationale Zeitschrift für Sportpädagogik*, in German and English, with additional summaries in French and Spanish. In 1973, several changes were made in this publication.

In addition, ICHPER sponsors several other publications, such as the *ICHPER Congress Proceedings, ICHPER Questionnaire Reports,* etc. All of these publications are professional in nature, dealing with a wide variety of topics, such as research, comparative programs, and informational topics that keep the membership appraised of some of the latest developments in these fields of education.

Various memberships in ICHPER are available, e.g., individual, institutional, national, international (for organizations), and contributing memberships. Until 1973, there was a yearly congress scheduled. At present, a world congress is organized every two years with a different location each time. The Executive Committee and the General Assembly meet on this occasion.

The ICHPER Research Council plans and coordinates a specific research section at each world congress. Furthermore, this council intends to initiate and follow up on research projects within the field of sport pedagogy (physical education) and aspects of health and recreation education.

Because every theoretical field of sport science has some kind of organizational structure on the international level, it seems appropriate that ICHPER, with its specific units, and F.I.E.P. consider themselves the organizational forums for the theoretical field of sport pedagogy.

[Additional information on ICHPER can be received from: Dr. Carl A. Troester, Jr., ICHPER-Secretariat, 1201 Sixteenth Street N. W., Washington, D. C. 20036, USA. In the preparation of this description of ICHPER, the following publication was helpful: ICHPER (ed.) 1968. ICHPER 1958–1967. A Decade of Progress. Washington, D. C.]

International Federation of Physical Education (F.I.E.P.)

The *International Federation of Physical Education (F.I.E.P.)* was founded in 1923 in Brussels. It has as its aim the development of educational, physical, and keep-fit activities in all countries, and contributions to international cooperation in this domain. Its activities are solely within the scientific, technical, pedagogical, and social fields of physical education and sport, and exclude all discussion and discrimination of a political, religious, or racial nature.

F.I.E.P. is the oldest and most well-established of the international physical education organizations. Its influence has grown steadily for more than half a century, and, at present, it has members and national delegates in 80 different countries. F.I.E.P. is constantly involved in the organization and support of various national and international activities, including committee work, commissions, courses, and congresses. F.I.E.P. also gives its patronage to, publicizes, and participates in similar activities organized by other national and international organizations concerned with physical education and sport. Particularly worthy of note have been the F.I.E.P. World Congresses, which brought together large groups of children to demonstrate physical education in schools in front of international audiences. Since 1923, F.I.E.P. conferences and meetings have been organized all over the world.

One of the principal means of action of the F.I.E.P. is the publication of an international bulletin, which has appeared regularly, in somewhat different forms, for more than 40 years. The F.I.E.P. *Bulletin* is now edited in three languages, English, French, and Spanish, each edition separately bound. Four issues are distributed to members annually, No. 1, January–March, in April: No. 2, April–June, in July: No. 3, July–September, in October; and No. 4, October–December, in January.

In addition to articles about the work of the F.I.E.P., the scientific, school, and sport-for-all sections, there are regular features giving news of F.I.E.P. activities, other world news, and notes on new books.

[Additioonal information about F.I.E.P. can be obtained from: John C. Andrews, M.Ed., Department of Physical Education, St. Paul's College, Cheltenham, Gloucestershire GL50 4AZ, England.]